Rowland Gibson Hazard

Causation and Freedom in Willing

Rowland Gibson Hazard

Causation and Freedom in Willing

ISBN/EAN: 9783337285937

Printed in Europe, USA, Canada, Australia, Japan

Cover: Foto ©Lupo / pixelio.de

More available books at **www.hansebooks.com**

CAUSATION

AND

FREEDOM IN WILLING

TOGETHER WITH

MAN A CREATIVE FIRST CAUSE, AND KINDRED PAPERS

BY

ROWLAND GIBSON HAZARD, LL. D.

EDITED BY HIS GRANDDAUGHTER

CAROLINE HAZARD

BOSTON AND NEW YORK
HOUGHTON, MIFFLIN AND COMPANY
The Riverside Press, Cambridge
1889

Entered, according to Act of Congress, in the year 1869, by
LEE AND SHEPARD,
In the Clerk's Office of the District Court of the District of Massachusetts.

Copyright, 1883,
By ROWLAND G. HAZARD.

Copyright, 1889,
By CAROLINE HAZARD.

All rights reserved.

The Riverside Press, Cambridge:
Electrotyped and Printed by H. O. Houghton & Co.

EDITOR'S PREFACE.

THE two letters to John Stuart Mill, contained in this volume, were the result of my grandfather's conversations and correspondence with that distinguished man. However they might differ in opinion, they entertained only the friendliest feelings towards each other. Mr. Mill was the most candid and generous of antagonists, giving all the praise he could, and differing in the most courteous way. The letters were published in 1869. Mr. Mill writes of them, May 18, 1870: "Your present book confirms and increases the impression I already had of your acuteness, argumentative power, and perfect fairness, both in considering the subject and in discussing it. I do not think that your side of the question has ever been better represented. The book, like your previous ones, does honor to American thought. It seems to me, however, to mark that the discussion between us has reached the point at which there is no advantage in our carrying it any further; since the region of difference between us instead of narrowing, as is the case in controversies likely to have a successful issue, is, on the contrary, very much enlarged. The exhaustive manner in which you endeavor to meet everything which is said in opposition to your conclusion, stirs up continual new ground, and raises a great number of fresh differences of opinion. Were I to attempt to answer you, I could hardly do so but by getting an interleaved copy, and writing something on every blank leaf; for there are few pages of your book in which there is not some proposition or argument which I contest, and were you thereupon to follow my example you would have to write another book as large as this; both of us would thus spend a great deal of time for no sufficient result, since no important practical consequences depend on our convincing one another. Our opinions agree as to the point of real importance in practice, viz., that the moral government of human beings, either by themselves or by their fellow creatures, must take place by acting either upon their knowledge or their wants; *i. e.*, either upon their expectation of consequences from their acts, or upon their feelings of desire and aversion towards those consequences."

Of the other papers in this volume, those upon the "Existence of Matter," and "Our Notions of Infinite Space," were published as appendices to the "Letters to Mill." The subject of Infinite Space was one which possessed great attraction for my grandfather, and was the theme of his last conversation, only a few hours before his death.

The letters to Mill, with their Appendices, were translated into German, and published by B. Westermann & Co. in 1875.

EDITOR'S PREFACE. v

The reply to Huxley on "Animals not Automata" was published in the "Popular Science Monthly," in October, 1874.

The letter on Causation to Dr. Francis Wharton was published in the latter's essay on "Proximate and Remote Cause" (The Liability of Railway Companies for Remote Fires) in 1878. The two discourses entitled "Man a Creative First Cause," were delivered at the Concord School of Philosophy, in July, 1882, and published in book form the following year.

OAKWOODS IN PEACE DALE, R. I.,
November, 1888.

CONTENTS.

	PAGE
TWO LETTERS ADDRESSED TO JOHN STUART MILL.	
LETTER ON CAUSATION	1
LETTER ON FREEDOM OF MIND IN WILLING . . .	63
APPENDIX.	
EXISTENCE OF MATTER	201
INFINITE SPACE	219
ANIMALS NOT AUTOMATA	227
LETTER ON CAUSATION TO DR. F. WHARTON	253
MAN A CREATIVE FIRST CAUSE.	
DISCOURSE I.	264
DISCOURSE II.	298
NOTES ON MAN A CREATIVE FIRST CAUSE	337
ANALYSIS OF CONTENTS	439

LETTER I.
ON CAUSATION.

MY DEAR SIR: In your letter of June 7, 1865, I understand you to agree with me that volition and choice are different; and as you do not object to my definitions of Will and of Liberty, I assume that you accept them. You further say, that "on the subject, practically considered, I am at one with you. Your view of what the mind has power to do seems to me quite just, but we differ on the question how the mind is determined to do it." You take position and argue the question thus: " But I do not find that your arguments in any way touch the doctrine of so-called Necessity, as I hold it; you allow that Volition requires the previous existence of two things, which the mind itself did not make, at least directly, nor in most cases at all — a knowledge and a want; you consider as the peculiarity of a free cause that its determinations do not depend on the past, but on a preconception of the future; but though the knowledge and the want refer to what is future, the knowledge and the want themselves are not future facts, but present, or rather past facts, for they must exist previous to the volitional act. You seem to admit, not only that the knowledge and want are conditions precedent to the Will, but that the character of the Will invariably corresponds to that of the knowledge and want, and that any variation in either of these determines, or at least is sure to be followed by, a corresponding variation in the Volition. Now, this is all that I, as a necessitarian, require. I do not believe in anything real corresponding to the phrases Necessity, Causal Force, or the like; I acknowledge no other link between cause and effect, even when both are purely material, than invariability of sequence, from which arises possibility of prediction; and this, it seems to me, on your own showing, exists equally between Volition and the mental antecedents by which you allow that they are and must be preceded."

You then refer me, for further argument, to a chapter in your "Review of Sir William Hamilton," and in this I find reference again to Chapter XI, Book V, of your work on Logic. I may have occasion to notice portions of each; but first, as to your letter of June 7, and the statement in it that you "acknowledge no other link between cause and effect, even when both are purely material, than invariability of sequence" — no "Necessity, Causal Force, or the like." We are here at the very foundation of the question, and if we here really differ, argument upon it may be of no more avail than it would be upon a question of the color of an object, when one man said, to his eyes it was red, and another that it was green, or, perhaps, rather asserted that there not only was no redness, but nothing to be either red or green.

Your expressions, just quoted, seem to imply that change may take place without the *action of any power* to produce it. This *no-cause philosophy* precludes all argument as to Cause or Causal power, and of course as to the mind in effort as such a cause or power. It denies, or at least wholly ignores, such power, and of course any exercise of it, free or unfree.

If "invariability of sequence" is the only relation between flowing or changing events, all reasoning as to how these events come into existence, or why or how conformed to this invariable order, is precluded, and philosophy is reduced to the mere observation of the flow of events and the memory of the observed succession. We have only passively to note the events that occur, and the repetition or non-repetition of the order of their occurring. In this view, Volition or effort is but such an event, and not a mode of power by which an intelligent being originates change, and controls, creates, and modifies the future.

A wise man may perceive that it is best that he should move from a consuming fire, but if there is *no* causal force, neither the perception itself, nor the perceiving being, can cause either the consequent movement or the effort to move.

Though the expression in your letter admits of such construction, I do not think you mean merely to say that you admit of no Causal Force, as *between* the exercise of the power and the effect of its exercise — no tautology of power — in which I would agree with you; for the exercise of a sufficient power does not require the addition or action of another power to bring about the effect; but I rather suppose you to mean that, between the antecedent events and the consequent events, you recognize, outside of the events themselves, no causal power of the difference or change from the former to the latter which constitutes the effect. This view, too, seems to me to be confirmed by portions of your chapter on Causality, which I have just looked into; while in your attempt to get over the obvious objection that night and day, though invariably and reciprocally antecedents and consequents, are not causes of each other, I think you really postulate efficient causes as existing in "properties of matter," and like phrases; and in the exception you make when you say, " We could predict the whole subsequent history of the universe, at least *unless some new Volition of a power* capable of controlling the universe should supervene," you appear to admit (though possibly only in deference to the opinion of those who differ from you) that Volition may, or might be, an efficient Cause.

Before proceeding further, it may be well to inquire into our notion of Cause.

But first, as to the origin of this notion to which portions of your chapter on Sir William Hamilton's theory of Causation have called my attention. In saying, " But there is another theory: . . . that we acquire both our notion of Causation, and our belief in it, from an internal consciousness of power exerted by ourselves, in our voluntary actions; that is, in the motions of our bodies, for our Will has no other direct action on the outward world," you approach most nearly to a statement of my views; but there is still a wide difference. You add, " To this doctrine Sir William Hamilton gives the following conclusive answer.

" 'This reasoning, in so far as regards the mere empirical fact of our consciousness of Causality, in the relation of our Will as moving, and of our limbs as moved, is refuted by the consideration, that between the overt act of corporeal movement of which we are cognizant, and the internal act of mental determination, of which we are also cognizant, there intervenes a numerous series of intermediate agencies, of which we have no knowledge; and consequently, that we can have no consciousness of any causal connection between the extreme links of this chain, — the volition to move, and the link moving, as this hypothesis asserts. No one is immediately conscious, for example, of moving his arm through his Volition. Previously to this ultimate movement, muscles, nerves, a multitude of solid and fluid parts, must be set in motion by the Will; but of this motion we know, from consciousness, actually nothing. A person struck with paralysis is conscious of no inability in his limb to fulfil the determination of his Will; and it is only after having willed, and finding that his limbs do not obey his Volition, that he learns by this experience, that the external movement does not follow the internal act. But as the paralytic learns after the Volition that his limbs do not obey his mind, so it is only after the Volition that the man in health learns that his limbs do obey the mandates of his Will.'

" With this reasoning, borrowed, as our author admits, from Hume, I entirely agree."[1]

Now, admitting all Sir W. Hamilton says, I do not see that it is a conclusive answer, or even an answer at all. The question here is not, what or how we cause; nor what is the action of Cause; nor on what does it *directly* act; but how we "*acquire both our notion of Causation, and our belief in it.*" Even if it could be shown, not only that there are intermediate movements which escape our observation, but that we are mistaken in the whole phenomena of muscular movement from beginning to end, it would not prove, nor

[1] *Examination of Sir William Hamilton's Philosophy*, Chap. III. Vol. II. p. 40, Am. ed.

even tend to prove, that we do not get our *notion and belief* from the deceptive appearances. It might, in such case, be plausibly argued that the notion and belief, being founded upon erroneous assumptions, would be fallacious; but even this reasoning would not be valid, there being no necessary or real dependence of the genuine notion and belief upon the correctness of the particular observation which suggested it. If I should say that I got my notion and belief of motion from the movement of the sun around the earth, it would hardly be deemed a disproof either of my assertion, or of the correctness of my notion and belief as to motion, to say, that the sun in fact did not move around the earth at all; and even if it should be proved that motion was absolutely impossible, it would not follow that we had not thus acquired our knowledge and belief of it. Some idea of motion must precede any demonstration of its nonexistence.

This argument of Sir W. Hamilton, then, does not touch the theory as you have stated it, and if it had refuted that theory as effectually as you suppose, there was still another intrenchment to be overcome before the positions I have taken in "Freedom of Mind in Willing," etc.,[1] would have been disturbed. For it might have been shown that we could not by experience get our notion and belief of Cause from a mistaken or partial, or even from a full and correct observation of the influence of our efforts in producing change; and yet this would not have proved that

[1] *Freedom of Mind in Willing; or, Every Being that Wills, a Creative First Cause.* Published in 1864. "Creative First Cause" here signifies one that of itself begins and effects change, and not one that is prior to all others, as some of the reviewers have supposed.

such notion and belief were not the result of an innate knowledge of a faculty of effort, and of its relation to muscular movement, or even from such knowledge of the two extreme links of the chain of phenomena, — the effort and the muscular movement, — which is what I assert.

In support of this view, I have there stated that we could not obtain this knowledge by observation of movement by others, either of their muscles or our own, the connection of such movement with the effort of others not being open to observation ; nor yet from reflection, no rational connection having ever yet been discovered between them ; and further, we could not have acquired such knowledge by our own experience, in moving our own muscles, because we must have had the knowledge before any case of such experience could have arisen ; we could not make the effort to move the muscles, and especially with design to move any particular muscle, till we knew that effort was the mode of doing it. The very statement of the case precludes the supposition that it could be done by accident, without such preëxisting knowledge. The making of effort, with the design to produce a specific effect, is the antithesis of accident, and wholly excludes it. This reasoning, with the observed facts in regard to the earliest actions of all active beings, indicates that this knowledge is innate. Any proof that we cannot obtain this knowledge by experience, goes to confirm my position, rather than to subvert or weaken it. Both you and Sir William Hamilton, however, assert that this knowledge of our ability to move our muscles is acquired by our experience in moving them. In the concluding sentence of the argument, as above quoted, and approved by you, he alleges this, and even asserts that it is acquired in the same way as any bystander obtains it, by outward observation (I take your statement of it). You both hold that all our knowledge of Cause is derived from experience. But, before there can be any experience of muscular movement by effort, there must be effort, — before " the man in health learns by experience that his limbs do obey the mandates of his Will," there must have been " the Volition," — the mandate, the effort, to move the limbs; and to this end there must have been prior knowledge of the mode of making the effort, and especially of directing that effort to the *particular* muscular movement designed. There must also, prior to this experience, have been that " prophetic anticipation " which can inform us, prior to experience, that the Volition will be followed by an effect; or, at least, that there is such a relation between the two, that this is sufficiently probable to justify the effort, and which " prophetic anticipation " you say you agree with Hamilton and Mansel in rejecting. I confess that upon this subject I should have expected to find whatever three such profound thinkers, looking at the subject so differently, agreed in, invulnerable on all sides; but, for the reasons already given, I am constrained to dissent even from such authority.

There either must have been self-action, — effort before we knew how to act, or there must have been knowledge of the mode of self-action, of making the effort, prior to any experience of it. Of these two alternatives it seems to me the latter must be adopted as the only one which is conceivable, and, in that case, the knowledge of the mode of making effort, and that effort is the mode of producing muscular movement, must be innate — ready for us whenever the occasion arises.

Without some such "prophetic anticipation" of the effect of effort prior to all experience, effort never would be made, and experience as to effort never could begin to be. No rational being would put forth effort without some prior expectation that a desirable effect would be produced, though it may be only by experience that he would ascertain that his expectations were well founded, and his future confidence in them confirmed.

But all the phenomena of Instinct indicate not only that this knowledge of the mode of making effort, and that it is the mode of producing muscular action, is innate, but that from this central point, in which action has its start, there diverges the innate knowledge of the plans or series of actions, and of the order of the succession in each series, by which certain ends are reached.

That complicated series of muscular movements by which the child transfers the milk from the maternal breast to its own stomach, is as well known to it at birth as after long experience. It even knows where to find this nutriment. I hold that the distinguishing characteristic of all instinctive action is, that it is made in conformity to a mode or plan which is innately known,[1] while rational actions require preliminary effort to design the plan, or the series of efforts by which the end may be reached, and that when, by frequent repetition of the same series, we come to follow it out by memory, each act in turn being suggested by that which *preceded* it, rather than by reference to the future end designed, the action becomes habitual;

[1] *Freedom of Mind in Willing*, Book I. Chap. XI.

and thus the instinctive actions, which are our first, and prior to experience, are like the habitual (which can only be after much experience) in this, that in both we act in conformity to a plan which is already in the mind, ready formed, requiring no effort to form such plan.

This similarity has found expression in the vulgar adage, " Habit is second nature."

From what I have already said, it will appear that I do not deem it essential to our rudimental notion of Causation, that we should be conscious of all the intermediate steps, from the first action of a Cause, or Power, to its ultimate effect, however necessary this may be to the completeness of our knowledge of the phenomena which result from its action. I would, however, remark that in view of the exposition I have given of Instinct and Habit, it may be possible that we do know, or may have been conscious of, the intermediate effect of effort upon the nerves and fluids by which muscular movement is reached. We know that when, by long practice, we habitually perform series of actions with little thought about the order of their succession, portions of them are immediately obliterated, leaving no trace in memory, and that this obliteration increases with the acquired facility which habit engenders. In reading we forget that we saw the particular letters, recollecting the final result of the combination of words, or more generally only the ideas, forgetting even the words by which they were conveyed to us. It would not be strange that we should, early in life, acquire the same habit in regard to the intermediate steps in a process which was perfectly known to us at birth, which at no period ever required effort or even observation to learn, and which we are constantly repeating in every moment of our conscious existence, or that, under such exaggerated conditions, these intermediate steps should wholly cease to be the subject of memory.

Having said thus much of the *origin* of our notion of Cause, we may next inquire what the notion itself is, of which we find ourselves possessed. If we should attempt to go back of this fact of the possession of a notion which is innate, we should encounter the same difficulties which attend our inquiries into the origin of matter. We have not witnessed its creation; to us it has had no beginning, and hence the circumstances of that beginning are as inscrutable as if it were an eternity ago.

This notion as it originally exists, I think, is that of ability to do something — of power to do — to change what is, and thus bring about what as yet is not. It may be originally confined to the knowledge of particular cases, or even to the one case of muscular effort by movement, which, as before shown, must be innate or intuitive in every being that Wills, and furnishes the type of the idea of Power, than which no idea is more distinct, isolated, peculiar, and fundamental. If, however, my analysis of instinct is correct, this innate or intuitive knowledge, as I have already stated, extends far beyond this genesis of action, and embraces that of series of actions to reach an end.

It is not essential to our idea of Cause or of Power, that we should know that we can by any means extend the effects of our efforts beyond our own muscles, or beyond the moment of effort. Having this genetic knowledge of effort, we may subsequently learn from experiment the modes of extending it, as, for instance, that by the use of a rod, we may extend it in space, and that by throwing a ball we may extend it in time also. We do not thus reach the *essence* of Power, or of Cause, any more than through sensation we reach the essence of matter or of its properties. But even though we never get at this knowledge of it, we may still, in the study of phenomenal effects, and of that order of their succession which is so important to us, derive advantage from finding what existences have the property of power, and under what conditions it is manifested, as we may be aided in the study of natural philosophy by investigating the phenomena of weight, and finding what substances possess it.

That this knowledge of our ability to produce change by effort, was the original type of our idea of Cause, seems to be very generally admitted. Even Comte, while ignoring all causative power, virtually admits that Cause was originally predicated only of spirit power. I am far from supposing that a notion being general, or even universal, is conclusive proof of its correctness. A large part of our progress in knowledge consists in finding that such notions require to be modified or discarded. Still they have the advantage of actual possession, and from the necessities of the case should hold till discredited, either directly, or by producing others with a better title to our credence.

Assuming these positions, we have still to inquire what Cause really is, and whether the notion of it which arises from our conscious efforts in connection with the effects anticipated, and subsequently observed, has been properly superseded.

In this discussion I might have expected to find a leader, or at least an ally, in Sir William Hamilton.

But upon the question of the origin of our idea of Cause, he is against me; and on that of the idea itself, he does not appear to have even found the battlefield. His theory is embraced in the formula, *The cause is equal to the effect*, by which his subsequent reasoning and examples show, that he means the antecedents are equal to the consequents. Had he only used the word *adequate*, which in some senses is the equivalent for *equal*, it would have been the common expression for one of the relations of cause to its effect; but this would have pointed the thought in a different direction. Grant the equality in any and every sense, and what is gained? The question is not as to the equality of antecedents and consequents, but how, or by what agency or means, the antecedents come to be converted into the consequents; and upon this their equality or inequality has no bearing whatever. Equal or unequal, the question how or by what converted, remains the same. That a cask of brandy is in any respect the equivalent of a ton of grapes, in no way enlightens us as to how or by what the grapes were converted into the equivalent — brandy. His saying, "This, then, is the mental phenomenon of Causality, — that we necessarily deny in thought, that the object which appears to begin to be, really so begins; and that we necessarily identify its present with its past existence," with his argument upon it, seems to me only to assert that, when Cause has produced or made something, we cannot conceive that it made that something out of nothing, but that there must have been something, and a sufficient something, to make it of.

I have defined Cause to be, " that which produces change."[1]

[1] *Freedom of Mind*, etc., Chap. V.

The word "produces," here, is important. Under your view, the corresponding expression would perhaps be, that which invariably precedes change.

I notice that you use the word *produce* in connection with the advent of phenomena, but I know it is difficult to conform the language to changes of thought and belief. We still speak of the sun's rising, and even of its going round the earth. In such cases much latitude must be allowed; and hence when, in reference to certain Permanent Causes, you say, " these have existed, and the effects or consequents they were fitted to *produce* have taken place," I interpret the expression as meaning that certain permanent phenomena are fitted to be the *invariable* antecedents of the consequences which have taken place; and so of some other similar statements. But as to being *fitted*, if power to produce is ignored, I cannot see why a tornado, a horse-race, or a bonfire are not each or all as well fitted to invariably precede an eclipse of the moon as anything else is. Leaving out this idea of power, all phenomena may be conceived of as happening in any assignable order of succession, or of coexistence.

The phrase I have adopted still seems to me to express the popular, perhaps I might say natural idea of Cause, and that which is nearly universal, the exceptions being in those whose reasonings have led them to other views, and other expressions, which, were they general and uniform in this class, might properly avail against the notions of the large majority who have not investigated. I see, however, no reason to change this definition, though further elucidation and extension of it are needed.

The knowledge of our ability to make effort, and

that it is the mode by which we should seek to produce muscular movement, perhaps, gives us the notion of Power, rather than of Cause ; but with this notion of Power that of Cause is very closely allied, though not identical with it.

Cause is always the correlative to effect, and effect implies a change. Power always has some change, as the object or tendency of its exercise ; but it may be insufficient to overcome the inertia, passivity, or resistance of the present subsisting conditions, and in that case does not act as Cause.

If this distinction does not obtain, I see no difference between the idea of the exercise of Power and that of Cause.

Cause, then, may be said to be power in successful action ; *i. e.*, the exercise of a sufficient power. Power then produces a change — an effect — of which its sufficient exercise is the cause.

This using *Power* as the generic term for the primitive idea, and *Cause* to designate this sufficient application or exercise of power which produces an effect, is a mere question of definition, to be settled as may be found most convenient and useful in expressing and advancing thought. The balance of advantages seems to me to be in its favor.

Adopting this distinction, I would say that our *notion* of Power, and also of Cause, is derived from our innate knowledge of effort and of the effects anticipated from it; but that we can only know our ability to be the actual cause of any specific effect by experiment — by testing the sufficiency of our power in effort.

The change sought or tended to in the exercise of power — the effect to be produced or attempted — is always in the future. In the past, what was, cannot be obliterated or made to be what it was not; and in the present instant, what is, cannot in the same instant be what it is not.

Cause, then, always implies effect, and effect implies change. This change may be within or without us, and may arise from the variation in what before existed, or in entirely new creation.

In regard to some changes within ourselves, as variations in the arrangement of our ideas, or in the portions which we make the objects of attention, we attribute them to our own direct agency. In regard to the external, we are not conscious of the possibility of creating matter out of nothing, or out of anything else, and hence attribute all changes in it to a change in that which already exists; and this again to motion of it in some form. Even change of color we come, by experience, to look upon as taking place under this necessary condition of material change.

So far then, at least so far as relates to material phenomena, the statement that for every effect there must be a cause, is equivalent to saying, that for every change there must be motion or activity, and through this expression of it the law is resolved into the truism, that for every activity there must be something capable of acting. If that which changes has in itself the faculty of activity, we do not look beyond it for the cause of the activity, but only for the reason why it put forth its self-active power; but if it does not possess this faculty of acting, but has only a susceptibility to be moved by being first acted upon, we still seek to connect it with a self-active power, or cause, which moved or put it in motion.

We know only one such Cause, and that is in intelligent being, with the faculty or power of effort; with wants, the gratification of which requires the exercise of this power; and with knowledge to direct its efforts to this end.

Such a being has every attribute essential to a *first Cause*, is obviously fitted to act as such Cause, and could do so in the absence of every and all other power; could of itself produce effects and changes, though everything else in the universe tended to be passive and changeless.

That which acts as it perceives an occasion or opportunity, acts from knowledge, and may itself exist in a passive state, till it perceives a reason or occasion for acting; till, in its own view or judgment, action is better than inaction.

The knowledge which is requisite to, or which constitutes, this judgment, may be passively received. Knowledge not only may be acquired without effort, but never is the *direct* consequence of effort.[1]

To this original notion of Power, and of Cause, derived from our innate knowledge of the mode of producing movement by effort, and thus to create or change the future, making it different from what it otherwise would be, and which notion is constantly confirmed by our observation of external events, experience leads us (properly or not) to add that of matter in motion, and to look upon it as a power which also affects the conditions of the future, and hence, as a Cause. But, although we thus naturally come to regard matter in motion as a cause, we do not look upon it as self-active, or capable of originating motion; and hence, when we have traced some effect to the action of matter in motion, we still look for the

[1] *Freedom of Mind*, etc., Book I. Chap. III.

Power, or Cause, which put it in motion, though in the case of the effort of an intelligent being, we only look for a *reason* why that being exerted itself, or put forth its power of activity.

In the case of matter in motion (as it cannot put itself in motion), we must either refer the origin of its power to the only other cause, that of intelligent being in action, or suppose it to have been in motion from all eternity — positions which I have examined in " Freedom of Mind," etc.

If matter when at rest requires power to move it, and when once in motion has a tendency to continue in motion, — has power or force in itself, — then some effect must of necessity follow from the collision of material bodies ; for in such collision both are tending to occupy the same space, and this being impossible, the tendency will be thwarted in one or the other, or in both.

If matter was first put in motion by the effort of intelligent being, it is rather an instrument by which such being extends the effect of its causative power in time or space than a causative power itself ; and in this case any uniformity in the succession of its movements is but a uniform mode of the intelligence which put it in motion, acting through and combining with such necessary effects of material forces as have just been mentioned. If the being using these forces is deficient in the knowledge of them, he may ignorantly make efforts which will be thwarted by them.

Upon the questions as to how far matter may be cause, it may perhaps aid us to consider the real difference between material and mental phenomena, as presented to us in the earlier stages of our cognitions of them. I have before pointed out that we know no

CAUSATION AND FREEDOM IN WILLING. 19

other difference between our perceptions of external reality and the incipient creations of our own, in which by effort we realize new forms of it, than that we can change the latter by a *direct* act of Will, and cannot thus change the former; and that if, from any cause, we should at any moment find that we could not thus change our own imaginings (of a landscape, for instance), that moment the imagery so fixed would become to us an external reality.[1] Is there anything in this, the only difference known to us, to warrant our assuming that the manifestations or imagery which we *cannot* directly change at will, have any more causative power than those which we *can* so change? The imagery of both kinds is really all in the mind, but we indicate the distinction arising from this observed difference by calling that which can be directly changed by Will *subjective*, and that which cannot be so changed *objective* phenomena. Among the objective are some which we can change indirectly by effort, and others which we cannot. We can, for instance, through muscular action, move a pebble, and in so doing make it a means of extending the effects of our own efforts in space and time. We make it a secondary or motor cause.[2] We cannot thus move a granite mountain, and for this reason cannot thus make it such a Cause. The facts observed in the objective phenomena, then, indicate that what is subject to our Will is most readily converted into Cause, and, so far as the analogy goes, indicate that causative power may be more properly attributed to this than to the objective. The former, subject to be changed by direct act of Will, may, as

[1] *Freedom of Mind*, Book I. Chap. IX.
[2] *Ibid.* Chap. V.

in the objective, subject to like change indirectly, be made a secondary or *quasi* cause. Of the mathematical diagram in the mind, in which we can embody new conceptions, we can make a cause of our discovering new geometrical relations; and so far as we can by effort impart this conception and imagery of our own to other minds in fixed objective manifestation, we may make them cause of increased knowledge in others.

This analogy does not, however, suggest that either the subjective imagery, which can be changed by direct act of Will, or that portion of the objective which can be thus indirectly changed, has any causative power in itself, or that it can in any proper sense be itself Cause, but that, in both cases, the images or phenomena are merely instruments which intelligent, self-active Cause may act upon and use to extend the effect of its own efforts, as already stated.

If the existence and motion of matter have been coeternal with spirit, then matter may be regarded as a distinct causative power, from the action of which certain necessary effects follow, which in virtue of this necessity will be uniform. In the action of an intelligent being there will also be a degree of uniformity growing out of its acting from its perceptions and knowledge of the best mode of reaching a desired result, and its adopting this mode, when once ascertained, to each recurrence of similar circumstances; and a further uniformity in the action of different intelligent beings, growing out of the similarity of their natural wants, and the fact that the fountain of absolute truth from which each seeks to draw his knowledge is the same for all. The combination of these particular uniformities will constitute, or tend to, a certain degree of uniformity in the succession of events generally, enabling each intelligent being, with more or less of accuracy, to anticipate the future, which it may seek by its own efforts to vary, when it perceives an object or reason for so doing, and also a means of doing it; while the wants and imperfect perceptions of beings of finite powers and capacities are sufficiently various to disturb the uniformity which would prevail if every one wanted precisely the same objects, and agreed as to the mode of obtaining them.

There are many vague expressions, indicating as vague notions of power in association with them; but we do not naturally attach the idea of power to any *known thing*, except intelligent being in effort, and matter in motion. I hold, too, that of these two and only notions of power, our knowledge of the former is much more conclusive and imperative than of the latter. The knowledge that we can make effort, and the mode of doing it, as also that by effort we can produce change, being innate, — born with us, — and acted upon every moment of our conscious existence, has, by longer and more permanent place in the mind, a stronger hold on our belief than the facts known only by subsequent experience through our sensations, which are transitory, and, coming through an additional medium, are more liable to be distorted, as an object presented directly to the eye is more likely to appear as it really is than if seen through glass or water. But, be this as it may, we subsequently come to know the power of mental effort to produce change through experience, — through actual observation of the results of repeated experiments, — and hence the fact that mind in effort is such a Power or Cause, producing such change, is at least as well attested in these modes as the phenomenal changes themselves are through sensation.

It is not by a prior exercise of power that we make effort; effort — exertion — is itself the act of power, which may or may not be adequate to the effect intended — may or may not be actual Cause. The immediate intention of one class of efforts is always to obtain knowledge of what has been, now is, or will be, including those abstract truths which have no reference to time; or to form new conceptions, new imagery — new creations — in the mind, which may or may not be actualized, or even attempted to be, in the external world. They may be the mere castle-building of the imagination. The only other class of efforts (no less mental) is always intended to move some portion of our body. It is through our bodily motions that we act upon the remoter material world; and as we need to do this in a very early stage of our existence, we may, from the necessities of the case, as well as from observed facts, infer that we, at least in some cases, innately or intuitively know that we can extend the effect of our efforts by putting matter in motion. A child or kid would starve before it could experimentally learn that complicated series of muscular movements which it instinctively performs to obtain its nutriment.

But to return to the two only modes of Causation of which we have any real conception — mind in action, and matter in motion. To these we attribute a property which we attribute to no other phenomenon or thing, and except between these and their effects we do not look for that invariable connection or sequence upon which the law of cause and effect is founded. All other events may be conceived of as happening, and all other things as existing, in any conceivable variety of coëxistence or succession; for though it might appear that events could not happen at all without such action or motion — without cause — we can conceive of their existence abstracted from their causes.

It is certainly proper that this peculiar attribute, by which these two things are contrasted with all others, should have a specific name — that what is thus distinguished in its nature as essential to the existence of all other phenomena, or to any change in what is — should be also distinguished in terms; and accordingly we designate this *ability*, which inheres in and is characteristic of this action of mind, and this motion of matter, by the word Power; and that sufficient exercise of it which produces change, by the word Cause. We recognize that without the exercise of some power to change present existences, they would continue as they are; and this exercise of power to change, we attribute only to that which is active — to matter in motion or mind in effort.

I have already suggested that our belief, that *matter in motion* is in itself Cause, is, of the two, less strongly attested. Admitting the existence of matter as a distinct entity, with the property of resisting force, and that once in motion it has a force which tends to keep it in motion, requiring counter force to resist or overcome it (of all which, however, I have been unable to find either proof or disproof), some effect, as before shown, must of necessity take place whenever the force of such moving matter comes to be exerted upon other matter. All the effects of mere matter in motion must be of this order of necessity, for matter, unintelligent, can know no difference, and can have no power of selection. Hence, though, under the broad concessions to it above made, matter in motion might cause a certain current of events, or phenomenal changes in a certain order, it would have no power to change that order; and if any power to change this order exists, it must be in the only other form of power — that of intelligent effort. Though matter once in motion may have this restricted causative power, it cannot move itself, and hence cannot begin the series of changes, for of such series its own motion is the first step.

Even if we conceive it as having a self-active faculty in itself, still, being unintelligent, it would not know when to exert it — when to begin moving — and an existing power for the exercise of which no occasion could ever arise, would of course be only latent, *i. e.*, never being exerted, would never become causal power; and if this difficulty were surmounted, it still could not know in what direction to move, and the exercise of a power to move which tends to motion in no direction is a nullity, or, if it tends equally to move in all directions, neutralizes itself, and ceases to be power. Hence the power to begin change, if any such exists, can be only in intelligent effort, and hence any beginning of motion, and any interference with the effects of such motion, must be attributed to such effort. Hence too, when we see any such effects which are not the results of our own efforts, we reasonably attribute them to the action of some other intelligent agent, and in some cases, from the apparent power required, to an intelligence with power greatly transcending our own.

The putting of matter in motion being the only means by which intelligent beings extend the effects of their own activity, not only beyond the sphere, but beyond the period of their own action, the necessity for this means might be supposed to indicate not only the existence of matter, but that, when in motion, it has the causative mechanical power usually imputed to it. But this extension and prolongation of the effects of the efforts of a finite intelligence in producing sensations in itself, and in others, after its own efforts, and in regard to others, even after its own attention is withdrawn, can as well be attributed directly to the action of an Omnipresent and Omniactive Intelligence, directly and uniformly causing these sensations, as a sequent of the efforts of finite beings; and hence no such argument in favor of the existence of matter, or of its power when in motion, is available.

Some of the foregoing results may suggest a *corresponding* solution of the question, "Is the effect simultaneous with the action of its cause?" to which you have alluded, apparently with some doubt as to the proper answer to it.

The question may be embarrassed by the use of the word cause, to signify that actual exercise of power which produces change, and also that being or thing which, as occasion or opportunity occurs, can exert or manifest such power. This potential Cause may exist for an unlimited period without producing any effect, and of course may precede its effect by any length of time. But actual, effective Cause, being the exercise of a *sufficient power*, its effect cannot be delayed; for, in that case, during the period of delay, there would be the exercise of a sufficient power to produce the effect without producing it, involving the absurdity of its being both sufficient and insufficient at the same time. The effect must wholly result from causes in action at the time it occurs. If nine men are ineffectually pressing against a rock till with the aid of a tenth they move it, the effect is that of the *immediate* efforts of the whole ten, and the *prior* efforts of the nine are no part of the cause of its movement, but the efforts of the nine which are made simultaneously with the tenth are. It is the *simultaneous* effort of the whole ten which availed, and the previous efforts of the nine added nothing, aided nothing, the combined efforts of the ten being just as effective without these prior efforts as with them.

The common idea that cause may precede its effect, however, comes very naturally to us, for in all cases of our action on matter, even in that of the movement of our own bodies, we reach the end sought through the movement of some intermediate substance, and motion of substance implies succession, or time. We move the hand by an effort which causes a flow of blood to it; of this, however, we are not naturally conscious, nor do we naturally get the idea that the movement of the hand is not simultaneous with the effort, that there is no intervening time or phenomena. Most persons are perhaps surprised to find, as a result of scientific investigation, that such is the fact, and that the intervening time is capable of being estimated, and found to vary in different individuals. But when we want to move the hand, or any portion or all of our bodily organism, we want to move it through some space — to some place more or less remote from that which it occupies — and the reaching of this place being the end or effect in view, the element of time of necessity comes in, and the repeated association of effort with the final remote effect produces an idea that this effect may not be simultaneous with the effort. The same reasoning more obviously applies to the effect of mere matter in motion. If the momentum of the body in motion is a cause, or is the exertion of a sufficient power to keep itself in motion, no time elapses between the exercise of that power and the effect or motion; otherwise the motion would not be continuous, for this motion is itself the effect, and if it stopped at all, its momentum or power would be wholly lost, and its motion be immediately and permanently arrested. It is a case in which, through association, experience misleads us as to the abstract idea, much as in the case I mentioned in a former letter, in regard to the general belief that a moving body cannot be turned directly back, without first stopping at the extreme point of advance. These fallacies of experience, as applied to the abstract idea now in hand, may perhaps be better illustrated by another case. Suppose an unelastic tube, reaching across the Atlantic, is filled to its utmost capacity with water brought to its utmost point of compression, for which the only egress is at the farther end. Now, if a drop of water is forced into the nearer end, most persons find it difficult to conceive that a drop must be simultaneously passing out at the other, and reluctantly yield their assent to the argument that otherwise the tube must at one time hold more than it possibly can hold.

As has already been intimated, the idea that Cause may or must precede the effect is also engendered by our applying the word Cause to that which as yet is not, but which may become, Cause. A moving body becomes actual cause of motion in another body at the instant it impinges or acts upon it; but for this there must be a body in motion, and which may have been in motion prior to the effect. If, at the commencement of its motion, the moving body was already in contact with that which it moves, we regard the effect as simultaneous with the initial movement — with the action of its cause. So, also, in regard to causal effort, there must be a being capable of effort, the existence of which being may precede the effort and the effect. In either case, there always is or may be a potential cause preceding the effect, and this fact, by a confused association of the ideas, leads us to regard the action of cause as necessarily prior to its effect.

The principal reason, however, for our habit of thinking of the action of cause as prior to its effect, I think, is the fact that the effects remain fixed till they are changed by the subsequent action of some cause, and hence enduring after the action of their cause, they occupy in thought a later position. We have to identify the action of the cause with the very beginning of the effect, and cannot even make it coexistent with the subsequent enduring existence of the effect, but precedent to it, and hence come to regard it as wholly prior to such existence.

The logical order of thought, too, requires that we should first think of that without which the other would not be; otherwise there is an hiatus in our thoughts.

These views indicate that our notion of Cause does not of necessity include any idea of succession, but only the immediate action of a sufficient power at the moment, and so far militate against those definitions of it which involve the idea of succession.

A difficulty may here be suggested in regard to the flow or progress of events in time, if they are all simultaneous with their causes. This difficulty can-

CAUSATION AND FREEDOM IN WILLING. 29

not arise as to intelligent effort, for, in regard to it, periods of non-action may continually intervene; but if there are series of events and material phenomena, each of which is in turn effect and cause, it may be difficult to see how any time could elapse between the first and the last of the series. This seems to concern your theory, rather than mine. You will, perhaps, say that this difficulty disproves my position as to the simultaneousness of the effect with its cause.

If, however, as I suppose, these series of events, or material changes, are always effected through the medium of motion, it need not trouble us, for there is precisely the same difficulty in regard to our conception of the motion of matter from point to point, there being no space, or length, between any two consecutive points, and yet the body in motion gets from one end of a long line to the other, and, in this case, this difficulty just neutralizes the other. It may, perhaps, be compared to our having an irreducible surd on one side of an equation, and finding the same also on the other side; or perhaps I may make my meaning more clear, thus: A workman, in laying a pavement, wants a block of a particular shape, say a *square circle;* he can neither conceive of nor describe such a figure, but he finds among his material a block which, though equally inconceivable and indescribable, exactly fills the space, and uses it accordingly. So, even if we cannot conceive how motion involves the idea of time, we may perceive that if it does so it may be a means of conveying events which depend upon it, through time also.

From this statement of my own views, let me now turn to yours, as I find them in your " Review of

Sir William Hamilton," and in Book III. Chap. I. of your " System of Logic."

In the latter I notice two expressions in the form of definitions, though not distinctly announced as such, viz., § 3. " The real Cause is the whole of these antecedents; " and again, " The Cause then, philosophically speaking, is the sum total of the conditions, positive and negative, taken together; the whole of the contingencies of every description, which being realized, the consequent invariably follows." The context shows that you use the terms " antecedents " and " conditions " as convertible terms; and hence there is no diversity in the two expressions. To these your definition in § 5, " We may define, therefore, the Cause of a phenomenon to be the antecedent, or concurrence of antecedents, upon which it is invariably and *unconditionally* consequent," only adds the "*unconditionally*," which, if I rightly apprehend your view of it, simply means, when the sum of the antecedents which the phenomenon invariably follows is not so *changed*, either by addition or subtraction, that the phenomenon does not follow; which still, as at first, only amounts to saying that the Cause is the antecedents which the phenomenon does invariably follow, and not the antecedents which it does not follow; and this seems to be your conclusion when you say, § 6, " I have no objection to define a Cause, the assemblage of phenomena which occurring, some other phenomenon invariably commences or has its origin." In this you merge the terms antecedents and conditions in the one term phenomena, confirming the idea that you use them as convertible, or at least embrace in the former all coexisting conditions. Cause, then, as you define it, is the assemblage of phenomena which some other phenomenon invariably follows; or the assemblage of phenomena which invariably precede the effect.

These formulas seem only to indicate a mode of experimentally finding what are causes, and not to explain or define, either our idea, or the nature of Cause; and the mode thus indicated seems to me fallacious; *i. e.*, would indicate as Cause what does not correspond to our idea of it. For instance, life is a necessary antecedent condition to death, and all experiment would show that death could not occur, or be a consequent, without life being one of the pre-existing conditions or antecedents. But is life, in any proper sense, the cause of death? It is true that any causes of change must always be found among the existing conditions, and in some sense among the *antecedent* conditions; but it does not follow that the converse of the proposition — that all antecedent conditions are among the causes — is also true. If this is not already obvious, I hope to make it more clear and certain that they are not before I finish this letter.

But the definitions you have given do not eliminate causes from other antecedents, which, though necessary to the effect, have no *agency* in producing the effect. They do not discriminate between those *passive* conditions, or mere states of things which have no tendency to change themselves, but are the conditions to be acted upon — and changed — and the *active* agency which acts upon and changes them. In short, they do not distinguish what *produces* from what merely *precedes* change; nor, when applied to *potential* cause, between the susceptibility or liability of a thing to be acted upon, and a faculty of acting. Putty may be moulded, it cannot mould.

In the passive but prerequisite conditions or antecedents, there may be no tendency to that change by which the consequent is distinguished from its antecedents, and which change of the conditions is the effect, or the thing caused: there is no tendency in darkness to become, lead to, or produce light; but the change from darkness to light presupposes the existence of darkness, and of an existence which is an indispensable condition or antecedent to the effect marked in the change from darkness to light, and hence, under your definition, darkness must be a cause, or at least one of the con-causes of this change.

You directly assert and argue that all the conditions are embraced in the cause. You say, " Nothing can better show the absence of any scientific ground for the distinction between the cause of a phenomenon and its conditions, than the capricious manner in which we select, from among the conditions, that which we choose to denominate the Cause." The common mode of speaking to which you here allude, I think merely indicates a loose mode of expression, growing out of an uncertainty as to what the cause in the particular case is, complicated with a vagueness in the generic idea of Cause. In a case you mention, this vagueness arises from an uncertainty as to whether the cause of the stone's falling is in the stone, or in the earth, or in both.

But from this vagueness you infer that "it will probably be admitted, without longer discussion, that no one of the conditions has more claim to that title (of Cause) than another, and that the real Cause of the phenomenon is the assemblage of all its conditions."

This is to accept in philosophy the vague terms and

crude, unreconciled notions of common discourse, and upon the ground that they are thus common. If twenty men attribute a phenomenon to twenty different agencies, it is no indication that it may be properly attributed to the whole twenty agencies combined; but, on the contrary, the diversity in their statements tends to throw doubt upon the whole. Twenty falsities do not make one aggregate truth. Conversely, to my mind, nothing can better show the absence of any scientific ground for combining all the conditions, and deeming them the Cause, than that *you* find no better reason for it than this common notion and mode of speech.

The above reasoning I think is properly applicable to the definitions I have quoted; but you subsequently seek a rectification of them to meet the difficulty which arises from such cases as that of darkness, regarded as a necessary condition or invariable antecedent to the change from darkness to light. You say, " When we define the Cause of anything (in the only sense in which the present inquiry has any concern with Causes) to be the antecedent which it invariably follows, we do not use this phrase as exactly synonymous with the antecedent, which it invariably has followed in our past experience.

" Such a mode of viewing Causation would be liable to the objection, very plausibly urged by Dr. Reid, namely, that, according to this doctrine, night must be the cause of day, and day the cause of night, since these phenomena have invariably succeeded one another from the beginning of the world. But it is necessary to our using the word Cause, that we should believe, not only that the antecedent always *has* been followed by the consequent, but that as long as the present constitution of things endures, it always *will* be so; and this would not be true of day and night. We do not believe that night will be followed by day under any imaginable circumstance, only that it will be so, provided the sun rises above the horizon."

But you have already said (and as I understand you in the same *only sense* as the above), that the only notion of a Cause is such a notion as can be gained from experience. Now, surely, the notion of what *will be*, as distinguished from what *has been*, cannot be gained from experience; and, further, we do believe that, "while the present constitution of things endures," night *will* invariably precede day, and hence this rectification of the definition does not meet the difficulty; for still, under it, as we believe that night not only always has invariably preceded, " but as long as the present constitution of things endures " always will so precede it, night is still the cause of day. In § 3, you have suggested a point which might obviate this difficulty. It may be said that experience shows that night is not of itself a sufficient antecedent to the consequent day, inasmuch as the night lasts for a greater or less period of time, and does not change to day till another antecedent is added to it — that of sunrise. But, in connection with this suggestion, you insist that this last condition (the rising of the sun in the above instance), "which completes the tale, and brings about the effect without further delay, . . . has really no closer relation to the effect than any of the other conditions has. The production of the consequent requires that they should all *exist* immediately previous, though not that they should all *begin* to exist immediately previous. The statement of the Cause is incomplete, unless, in some shape or other, we introduce all the conditions."

CAUSATION AND FREEDOM IN WILLING. 35

Undoubtedly, as prerequisite to the change, the conditions to be changed must all exist, as well as the agency which changes them; but I question the expediency, or even propriety, of thus confounding in the one word Cause the passive conditions which, by their inertia, resist the change, with the active agency which changes them. In regard to this case of change from night to day, our *experience* is, that the change of the darkness which characterizes night to a degree of light approximating indefinitely near to that of day, does invariably precede the rising of the sun, and we believe that this not only always has, but that, "as long as the present constitution of things endures," it always will so precede it; and hence, under your definition, the degree of light so approximating would be the Cause, or, at least, *a* Cause of the rising of the sun.

Is not some other element needed to make out the distinction between antecedents which are Causes of change, and those which have no tendency to produce, but which resist such change? The existence of the antecedents, as they are, always precludes the consequents, for it is only by some change in the antecedents that the consequents come into existence.

Darkness is a condition which excludes light, and requires the power of some active agency to change it to light; and the same is true of all other fixed conditions, the change of which to their consequents is the effect for which a sufficient exercise of power — a Cause — is required. This sufficient power may be either the action or effort of an intelligent being, or that of matter in motion, or both. If matter in motion is a distinct force, intelligent being may use it to accomplish its own ends. It may put it in motion, or direct its motion for this object, or it may so change the conditions to be acted upon, that matter already in motion, and directed in its motion, will accomplish the desired object. In the case of sunrise, we may suppose that the Cause producing light is always acting, but that there is some hinderance or opposing force which it cannot overcome; and in such case any power which removes the obstruction indirectly causes light to succeed darkness, though it does not itself produce the light. The change to light is the consequence of the change which power has produced.

In this view we may say that the motion of the earth is the Cause of the change from darkness to light, and it is thus referred to one of the two only sources of power of which, in my view, we have any knowledge or real conception.

As no one can see the sun before it rises, so far as direct individual experience goes, we might as logically attribute the whole phenomena to the other of these two powers — to intelligent effort, creating, or lighting up, a sun each morning, and annihilating or extinguishing it each evening; or, dispensing with the intervention of matter, regard the successive sensations of light and darkness as the direct effect of such efforts.

I believe that you have stated no case of Causation which is not referable to one or the other of these two causative powers — these only modes of activity or change.

We return now to the question, whether our notion of Cause as derived from intelligent effort has been properly superseded. The substitutes are various. First, the generalization of external phenomena, as gravitation. Second, the phenomena themselves, either fixed, as the earth, sun, moon, and matter generally; or flowing, as events and circumstances which follow each other. In this case the antecedent phenomena are deemed the Causes of those which follow. Third, the assertion either that there is no Causal power or Force, but only a uniform succession of consequents to antecedents, or that this uniformity is itself the Cause.

In regard to the first, or generalization, of which I take gravitation as the type, there seems to be much latitude of thought as to the causal power; it being sometimes assumed to be in the name, sometimes to inhere in the generic facts to which the name is applied, and sometimes attributed to a mere hypothetical unknown power, the existence of which the generic facts are supposed to indicate, or perhaps to embody.

As to the first of these divisions, we habitually use such terms as attraction, repulsion, gravitation etc., to classify phenomenal effects; and hence, loosely associating these effects with such terms, and these again with some vague notions of power which this association engenders, we come to speak of these mere words as Causes of effects which are properly referred to them only for the purpose of classification. In this there is, no doubt, often confusion of thought as well as carelessness of speech; but that there can be no causal power in the mere name, is too obvious to require argument. Such power can no more inhere in "Gravitation," "Laws of Nature," "Invariability of Sequence," than in Equinox, Jehoshaphat, or Abracadabra.

To predicate the causal power of the generalized facts would make them collectively the Cause of themselves individually, and make them act on the past, or act as Cause before they existed; for there could be no collection of facts before the existence of the individual facts of which such collection must be made up.

The last division in the first category — the hypothesis of an unknown power indicated by the generic facts — is perhaps the most natural of the three, and is in some respects analogous to that by which we attribute all the effects which are obviously beyond our own power to that of a superior intelligence.

It also has its type in the ancient mythology, and in the rude notions of our Indian tribes, who conceive a different manitou for each variety of phenomena — one for storms, another for cataracts, etc. Science has extended the rude generalizations of these children of the forest, and embraced large classes of facts under the jurisdiction of each of its manitous, or hypothetical powers.

When Sir William Hamilton says, "Fate or Necessity, without the existence of a God, might account for the phenomena of matter," he must suppose that these terms either possess or represent some imaginary power capable of creating or producing the phenomena. This is also sometimes predicated of Chance.

The notion of a purely hypothetical Cause cannot properly displace that innate knowledge we have of power by intelligent effort, which is confirmed by constant experience in its manifestations, or even that extension of this innate idea, by which we attribute all efforts to which human agency is inadequate to a greater power of the same kind — to an intelligent being, whose power is of necessity presumed to be adequate to the production of the observed phenomena; nor has such an hypothesis as strong claims to our acceptance as that notion of power which we acquire from the phenomena of matter in motion, and the consequences which we observe, or deduce from it.

It is perhaps worthy of note, as throwing light on the natural idea of Cause, that the manitou of the Indians, as well as the ancient divinities, were *spirit-causes*, while the hypothetical Causes to which Science has led some of her votaries, seem to be mainly, if not wholly, material. Have these their primitive type in Fetichism?

The next proposed substitute is that of the phenomena themselves. These, you think, are more properly deemed Cause than either the generalizations or the hypothetical powers predicated of them, which I have just considered. Touching the question, "What is the *Cause* which makes a stone fall?" you say, "The stone therefore is concerned as the patient, and the earth (or according to the common and most unphilosophical practice, some occult quality of the earth) is represented as the agent or Cause." Again, "This class of considerations leads us to a conception which we shall find of great importance in the interpretation of nature — that of a permanent Cause or original natural agent. . . . The sun, the earth, and planets, with their various constituents, — air, water, and the other distinguishable substances, whether simple or compound, of which nature is made up, — are such permanent Causes. These have existed, and the effects or consequences which they were fitted to produce have taken place (as often as the other conditions of the production met) from the very beginning of our experience."

Again, "The permanent Causes are not always objects. They are sometimes events, that is to say, periodical cycles of events, that being the only mode in which events can possess the property of permanence. Not only, for instance, is the earth itself a permanent

Cause, but the earth's rotation is so too. It is a Cause which has produced from the earliest period (by the aid of other necessary conditions) the succession of day and night, while, as we can assign no Cause for the rotation itself, it is entitled to be ranked as a primeval Cause." These quotations, I think, give your idea of permanent Causes, embracing in it the fixed material existences "of which nature is made up," and also flowing events — all the phenomena, at least all of the time being.

The flowing events are, in fact, always connected with what I have stated to be the only Causes of which we have any idea — the exercise of a sufficient power in the effort of an intelligent being; or in the movement of matter, either as put in motion by such being, or as a coexisting and coördinate activity. A case you mention — that of the rotation of the earth — is (as I believe all conceivable cases of material Causation will be found to be) embraced in one of the forms of the latter category.

As appears from a former quotation, you hold that all Causes are only phenomena, and you make no distinction between the phenomena which constitute the Cause and those which constitute the effects. The former differ from the latter, or consequents, to the extent, and only to the extent, of the change effected. The Cause is not in the consequent, for this would make it the Cause of its own existence, and imply that it acted upon the past or before itself existed, and hence the Causal Force of mere phenomena, if any, must inhere in the antecedents alone. But among those antecedents you also recognize no real distinction between the things changed and that which changes them. You say, "The distinction between

CAUSATION AND FREEDOM IN WILLING. 41

agent and patient is merely verbal. Patients are always agents . . . all the positive conditions of the phenomena are alike agents, alike active."[1] In a case you mention, it is consistent with your notions of "permanent Causes," and that all the antecedent conditions are Causes, to say that sulphur, charcoal, and nitre are the Cause of gunpowder. The only things raised by this statement are the elements, first uncombined, and then combined, leaving out of view the object of inquiry, which is to ascertain the agency or Cause of the *change* of the separate elements into gunpowder.

In these views Sir William Hamilton seems to agree with you. He says, "Water is as much the Cause of evaporation as heat. But heat and water together are the Causes of the evaporation. Nay, there is a third Cause, which we have forgotten — the atmosphere."[2] Here he has predicated Cause of change to the water which resists the change, and also, though perhaps unintentionally, to that which hinders, — to the atmosphere, — the fact being that evaporation is produced with greater facility in vacuum. I shall presently attempt to prove that nothing, after it has become a permanent or fixed existence, can possibly be a Cause of any change whatever.

As germane to these views, you say, "The Cause of the stone's falling is its being within the sphere of the earth's attraction." It would obviously be equally proper to say, the Cause of the apple's being plucked was its being *within my reach;* but it might have been within my reach for all time, and not have been plucked. The fact *that it is within reach* has no power, no tendency to pluck, but is only a condition to a suc-

[1] *Mill's Logic*, Book III. Chap. VII. 4.   [2] *Ibid.* § 40.

cessful effort to that end. In this case, we can refer the effect to a known causal power — to effort. In the case of the falling stone we cannot, and therefore content ourselves with merely classifying it, with other like cases, under the term gravitation. We refer the case of plucking the apple to Cause by effort, and attempts have been made to reduce the phenomena of gravitation to the only other activity or conceivable active power — matter in motion. To one or other of these as causal power we always seek to trace any *change.*

You have also some expressions which imply that the *whole* past must be regarded as the causal antecedent of each phenomenon as it occurs. For instance, " The whole of the present facts are the infallible results of *all past facts*, and more immediately of all the facts which existed at the moment previous.[1] The real cause is the whole of these antecedents." You seem to make some exceptions to this, *e. g.,* when you say, " If the sun ceased to rise . . . night might be eternal. On the other hand, if the sun is above the horizon, his light not extinct, and no opaque body between us and him, we believe firmly that . . . this combination of antecedents will be followed by the consequent day ; . . . and that, if the same combination had always existed, it would always have been day, quite independently of night as a previous condition. Therefore it is that we do not call night the Cause, and therefore the condition, of day." [2] It must not be forgotten that it is not the continued existence of the day, but *its beginning to be,* that

---

[1] *Mill's Logic,* Book III. Chap. VII. § 1; *Ibid.* Book III. Chap. I. § 3.

[2] *Mill's Logic,* Book III. Chap. V. § 4.

requires to be accounted for by a causal antecedent. That which already exists will continue to exist if there is *no* Cause of change. The postulate of the necessitarian argument from Cause and effect, as you state it, is this: " It is a universal truth that everything which has a beginning has a Cause." What we really seek, in this case, is the Cause of the *change* from night to day, and to this change night is a necessary antecedent or condition. Hence, in your view, and that of Sir William Hamilton also, night is a Cause of day, and the exception seems not to be well taken.

To the postulate, or to your statement of it, as just quoted, I do not know that there is any dissent; but, in your view of Cause, does it amount to anything more than an assertion of the truism, that everything the existence of which does not date so far back as something else does, *i. e.*, as far back as that which has no beginning, had something before it — had antecedents? The element of power to produce the change involved in a *beginning* is still lacking.

I have already not only admitted, but offered proof, that if there are any unintelligent Causes, their action must of necessity be uniform; and as you assert this of all Causes, we agree in this as to those which are unintelligent, and this leaves no room, as between us, to question the application to them of the rule, that the same Causes of necessity produce the same effects, which is thus involved in Causation by material or other unintelligent forces.[1]

Now, if the whole aggregate antecedents are the Cause of any effect, then, as at each instant, the whole antecedents are the same at every point of

[1] See page 253, Letter on Causation.

space, the effects should be everywhere the same. To this it may be plausibly replied, that, the conditions acted upon being different at different places, different results may follow from the action of the same Cause.

In the first place, however, it must be borne in mind that, as these various conditions must exist before they can be acted upon, they must themselves, in the view we are now considering, be a part of the antecedents which make up the Cause. You explicitly assert that all the conditions are included in the Cause. The whole past being thus combined in one Cause, acting upon a perfectly blank and void, and therefore homogeneous, future, the effect would be the same throughout the whole length and breadth of its action. Again, admitting that the same causes, acting upon different conditions, may produce different effects, it can hardly be asserted by the advocates of the rule that the same causes necessarily produce the same effects, that the action of the same cause can itself be different; for then this different action upon the same conditions would produce different effects, thus disproving the rule. Now, the whole past, being embodied in one Cause, must have one certain specific action, and that action either (being sufficient) produces an effect, or (being insufficient) produces no effect. If it produces an effect, then this effect is added to the aggregate events of the past, so far changing the aggregate Cause; and a past Cause, which has once acted, never can again act as the same Cause, for this additional effect or event must ever remain a part of the whole past; and hence there can be no practical application of the rule, that the same causes of necessity produce the same effect, and on the other hand, if the action of this one aggregate Cause (being insufficient) produces no effect, then, as there can be no change in the Cause (and none in the conditions upon which it acted), the Cause would, of course, remain the same Cause, and its action being the same, and upon the same conditions, the result must be the same, that is, *no effect*, and there would be an end of all change, and everything would remain quiescent in the state in which this insufficiency of Cause found it.

If it now be said that the failure of this cause to produce any effect by its action is such a new event or condition that it can, as a consequence of it, act in some other manner, then, there being no change external to it, and nothing to change itself except the negative fact of non-effect, which can have no influence upon anything not cognizant of it, it follows that the Cause must be intelligent, and, as such, capable of devising or selecting some new mode of action which will avoid the deficiency of that before tried, and found to be ineffective. The Cause already embracing the whole past, nothing could be added to it from what already existed; being ineffective, no new existence has been added to it; and if, under these conditions, it changes its action, it must be self-directing, accommodating its action to circumstances which must be known to itself as a prerequisite to such accommodation. It must be intelligent Cause.

The whole of the prior state never can occur again, for the present is already added to it, and if, like a circulating series of decimals, the consequent of this whole past should be to reproduce and continually repeat the same series; and even though the observation of this uniformity, in the successive order of events, should enable us to predict the whole future, still it would not prove that the producing power was in the past circumstances. It would only prove the uniformity upon which the prediction was founded, and not the *cause* of that uniformity which still might be the uniform action of some intelligent active agent, who, perceiving some reason for adhering to this order, and having the present power, continually repeated it. Much less could it prove that power not free. The mere observed order of succession, uniform or otherwise, would not include a knowledge of the power that produced this uniformity, nor the manner of its doing it. To find this we should need to compare the effects with those of some known power in action, as those of intelligent effort or of matter in motion. Nor would this supposed dependence of the present on the past be a case of the same causes producing the same effects; for at each repetition of the effect *the whole prior state*, which is assumed to be the Cause, is different, the effect of each " prior state " acting as Cause being continually added, and if there comes a time when there is no effect, then there never can be any further effect or change, for there can then be no difference in this " prior state " or Cause, and of course no variation in the consequent — no effect.

And if, as you say, " in the general uniformity . . . this collective order is made up of particular sequences obtaining invariably among the separate parts," then the foregoing positions apply to each of these separate parts or longitudinal sections of the whole.

Your position, that in this " invariable order of succession," as in " the general uniformity of the course of nature, this web is composed of separate fibres, this collective order is made up of particular sequences obtaining invariably among these separate parts," avoids some of the difficulties which arise from embracing the whole past in one Cause producing one sequent aggregate effect. In this view, however, there would still be no room for the application of the rule of uniformity in Causation; for if any one of these *causal fibres* becomes insufficient, it could, under this rule, only repeat its insufficient action until the conditions of its action were so changed by the other fibres as to give it efficiency; and then you hold that these changed conditions make a portion of the Cause, which, of course, is not then the same Cause which before acted, and with regard to those *fibres* which do produce effects, their effects being immediately added to their past Causes, they never can again act as the same Cause.

The division of the invariable order of succession into separate fibres, with the law that the same causes must produce the same effects, necessitates the hypothesis of a plurality of Causes from the origin of existence; for no difference in the *conditions* of such fibres could begin to be till there was a difference in the producing or causative agencies. Or if it be said that in the beginning there was a difference in the *conditions* of these fibres, then, under your view, the conditions being themselves Cause, a plurality of Causes must have always existed. If a theory of the universe can be worked out at all upon this plan, it seems to me it would still not only violate the law of parsimony, but in view of the unity everywhere manifested would, in point of simplicity, compare as unfavorably with that which attributes all original Causative power to one intelligent being with a want for change or variety, or for the exercise of its powers, and which can design new efforts for new objects, as that of Ptolemy or Tycho Brahe does with the Copernican system.

The fact that the Causative powers of the former plan also are unintelligent, shows a retrograde movement in ideas, carrying us farther back than the mythology of the Greeks, or the rude notions of our Indian tribes, and landing us substantially in Fetichism. Though the time is past in which mere power was deemed the proper object of worship, still, if we believed that all the beneficent and æsthetic conditions of existence were caused by material phenomena and events, we could hardly fail, as rational and emotional beings, to adore them.

By "the existences of which nature is made up," I understand you to mean those of the material nature, or universe, as you mention these, and these only. Matter is most prominently distinguished from spirit in being unintelligent; a consequence of which, as already shown, is an inability to direct its own movements; and as all movement must have some direction, it cannot move itself. It cannot itself be the moving power and yet something else give direction to the motion; and hence, as all changes in matter are through the medium of motion in it, matter in a fixed condition, *i. e.* in a state of rest, cannot of itself become Cause. It must first be put in motion, or be acted upon, by something else, either by spirit power, or by some matter already in motion. But in regard to all existences, events, and circumstances, which are unintelligent and not self-active, or any combination of them which have assumed a fixed existence, whether for a longer or shorter time, they cannot of themselves be the cause of any subsequent change.

CAUSATION AND FREEDOM IN WILLING. 49

In " Freedom of Mind," etc., I have essayed a demonstration that nothing, merely in virtue of its existence, can be a Cause, and I would now more especially urge, that if any fixed material and inactive things can be the actual Cause of change, then, as before shown, such change, or effect, must be of necessity, and must also be simultaneous with, the first *existence* of such Causative Power. For existence being its only element of Cause, it must have been Cause at the instant it began to exist. It must then have been as a sufficient power in action, and of course have immediately produced its necessary effect.

But the change to be wrought is in these very existences, or antecedents, to convert them into the consequents ; and as this change must thus be of necessity and simultaneous with the existence of these antecedents, such existence cannot become fixed for any time whatever. Having in themselves a power of self-change, with no faculty of self-control, or of selecting time or object, this power must produce its necessary effect at the moment of coming into existence, and the antecedents in which it both inheres and acts would be metamorphosed into the consequents in the very act of coming into existence, and hence phenomena with such inhering Causative power never could become fixed or permanent existence, and, conversely, there could be no such fixed or permanent Causal existence. This is very generally recognized. As soon as we find that night can for a time exist without producing day, we perceive that it cannot be the cause of day.

The Cause, then, must be something distinct from the fixed phenomena, which constitute the antecedents to be changed. It cannot, under your view, be said that this Cause is some new phenomenon, the existence of which, being added to the previous sum of the conditions, instantaneously converts them into the consequent; for any new phenomenon is itself the consequent which, in this same view, the former fixed antecedents must have caused; and, as already shown, they cannot be the cause of any new existence or phenomenon.

The fixed or stable events being excluded from Causation, what is left? Nothing in the whole range of our knowledge, but activity in one or the other of its two and only forms — mind in action, and matter in motion; the latter either as a consequence of the former, or as an independent coördinate force. Either of these may act upon and change the existing conditions as nothing else can.

Imagine ever so many fixed conditions or phenomena, — they cannot change themselves. The foundation, the brick, and the mortar may all exist in convenient proximity, but the wall will not build or be built upward, till some activity in the form of an intelligent agent, or of matter in motion, and properly directed, is brought to bear upon them.

If darkness is the only condition or antecedent, it cannot change itself to light, or so vary its own position that the sun will change it. When to this condition of darkness you add the rotation of the earth as a cause of sunrise, you bring in one of the two elements to which alone we attach the idea of power, and it is the confounding of the non-causal phenomena with the causal that I protest against, as leading to confusion and erroneous conclusions as to the nature and function of Cause.

It may, in conformity to a common idea, or rather verbal formula, be suggested, that such permanent material existences act in conformity to certain laws, in virtue of which they may be fixed and passive for a time, and then themselves start into activity.

But this government by law, in the most common use of the term, implies that the active agent conforms itself to the law, which assumes that such agent knows the law of its mode and manner of action, and the particular time to act, as also that it has the power of self-action; and all agree that such knowledge and power are not attributes of material phenomena, or of mere events and circumstances.

The term law is also sometimes used to signify a classification of phenomena, and sometimes to indicate a mere uniformity of the relation of antecedents to consequents. The former has already been considered, and the latter will be, in its place.

We come now to the third substitute, upon the first division of which — that there is no Causal power, etc. — I have already made some comments in this letter. In a former one (touching your review of Comte) I suggested that this notion of *no cause* was a result of the concentration of the thought of this age upon material science, the great object of which, and that which makes it conducive to our comfort, is to ascertain the order of succession in external phenomena. Hence the physicists have applied themselves almost exclusively to the searching out of this order, and the convenient classification of the uniform results which they discovered. They have dealt with things and their changes. Thus circumscribed, they have been led, by repeated association, to regard the relation of uniformity in succession — a mere relation in time — as a relation of cause and effect, and those things which uniformly attend and those events which uniformly precede an effect, and even the names by which the things, events, or effects are classified, as causes. Having done this, and then perceiving that there could be no power in these inactivities, and that they derived no benefit from such hypothetical assumption of power in them, they discarded them, and were left with no Causal power at all.

Attributing Causal power to the observed uniformity must be regarded as natural, for it is common to every stage of empirical knowledge. The child will tell you that a stone falls down because there is nothing to hold it up; and observing other cases of uniformity, he generalizes, and attributes them all to the *nature of things*, or, learning something of scientific classification, ascribes the falling of the stone to *gravitation* as a cause. I would now remark, that, on the hypothesis that change may take place without any Causal power, all events would spring into existence spontaneously and contingently, without any of those relations in which intelligent beings perceive order and useful adaptation of one thing to another. On this hypothesis, if such beings could design orderly or beneficial arrangement, there could be no power to conform things to such design. Even the necessity of the effect produced by matter in motion, and of course its uniformity, depends upon the existence of some power which pertains to matter in motion — some force, without which the effect would not be necessary. The chances that the rising of the sun and the light of day should uniformly happen at the same moment, when there was no Causal power in the sun to produce the light of day, and none in the light of day to produce the rising of the sun, and no anterior Causal power producing both, would be wholly inappreciable, as against the general confusion which, in the absence of such power, would be indicated by the calculation of chances, and by our ability to conceive of such events in any and every order of succession, or of coexistence. As a design of intelligent being, there could be no "preëstablished harmony" if that being had no power to conform events to his design. The courses or succession of events which are harmoniously related are very limited, while those which are not so related are infinite, and in the absence of any controlling power, the chance that at any moment, and for one time, any such harmony would occur, is as one to infinity, and the probability that it should be incessantly repeated would be diminished in a compound ratio; so that this harmony without design or power, even without the additional consideration that it occurs in a great number and variety of cases, may be deemed impossible.

There must, then, be some power producing the uniformity, the existence of which, in the flow of events, all admit. To meet this necessity of the observed facts, the last hypothesis of our category seems to have been devised. It appears to fully cover the ground intended, for it asserts that the Cause inheres not in the events themselves, but in the invariability or uniformity of their succession. This is to say, the Cause is in the very things it has produced, the existence of which is accounted for by this Causal hypothesis; in short, that the Cause is in its own consequent. Under this hypothesis, if it be asked why one certain event succeeds another certain event, it must be replied, because it always does so; *i. e.*, it does so on the particular occasion, because it does so on all other like occasions. And if in any case the cause of this uniformity be asked for, as, for instance, why the consequent B always succeeds the antecedent A, the answer must still be, because it always does so; *i. e.*, it always does so because it always does so; or shorter, it does because it does. Nor will it help the matter to say it not only always has been, but we believe it always will be so. The *generic names* of the phenomena are now superseded by the phrase *always does*, both traceable to the same observed fact of uniformity, and both really making the phenomena in a collective form the Causes of themselves individually, which again involves the idea that the collection existed before the individuals of which it is composed.

The idea of Causative power is distinct from, and must precede, that of the uniformity of its action or its effect. The power which produces the effect may be wholly independent of any uniformity in its manifestation. It is no less Cause the first time it acts, when no uniformity can have obtained, and would be no less Cause if it varied its action every time it acted. The two ideas are not only not identical, but are essentially distinct and different.

From the conclusion which I reached, that the effect is simultaneous with the action of its cause, I have already suggested the corollary that our idea of Cause is independent of, and separable from, that of succession; and if I was correct in saying that the knowledge that we can (through motion of matter or otherwise) extend the effects of any action beyond the moment of exertion, is not essential to our idea of Power, or of Cause, we may from this also infer that succession is not a necessary element in our idea of power or of Cause; and this position, if tenable, takes away the whole foundation of those definitions of Cause which rest upon the mere succession of conse-

CAUSATION AND FREEDOM IN WILLING. 55

quents to antecedents, invariable, inevitable, or otherwise.

The idea of the exercise of power is perfect and complete in itself, even though, being insufficient, there is to it no succession, no consequence. So, also, the exercise of a sufficient power is perfect and complete in itself, even though we never should add to it the knowledge of the effect or consequent; and admitting the succession, which is involved in your definition, it comes after the exertion of power, — after the Cause, — and makes no part of it. This idea of succession becomes associated with that of Cause, from the fact that it is the evidence that the exercise of power has been successful, hence, has been Cause in producing that succession. In short, the succession of consequents to antecedents does not really enter into our idea, either of Power or of Cause, but is only the evidence that Cause has existed — that there has been a sufficient exercise of power to produce the succession, which is the effect, and not the Cause which produced it; but, as such effect, it merely indicates that a sufficient power to produce it has been exerted. To make the succession in any form the Cause of itself is virtually to ignore all power in bringing it to pass. If the Cause be in the antecedents, then, if the influence of motion in extending the effects of former antecedents be excluded, the Causative antecedents must be self-active; beginning activity in, and changing themselves to, their consequents. This involves all the difficulties which necessitarians find in the self-active power of intelligent beings without having the rational grounds upon which this power is predicated of such beings. All theories of Causation, when traced to their foundation, must bring us to something which is already active, or that has in itself the ability to become so.

In my system, Spirit-Cause — intelligent being acting as First Cause — can nowhere be dispensed with; and hence in it must be deemed to have always existed — to have had no beginning. If the ideal theory of the universe — a theory which, in its simplicity, so commends itself to the intellect, and in its grandeur and beauty so appeals to our affections — is rejected, then matter must also be regarded as a distinct entity, coeternal, in some form, with spirit; and all else, being but changes in the original conditions of these two, has been subsequent to them, and, of course, had a beginning and antecedents; and thus, in this mode, we again reach the conclusion that all power must inhere, or, at least, have once inhered, in these two things. In the original constitution of things, there was, consequently, no ground for predicating Causal power of events, or of anything which had a beginning, nor is there now any necessity for such predication.

It may be thought to be idle to speculate on the primordial conditions of existence, from which we are removed by infinite time. But the element of time does not wholly shut us out from such inquiry. After we have gone back to a period from which no knowledge could in any way have been transmitted to us, it will make no difference how much farther back we go. With regard to all the previous eternity, we can only judge as to what was by what has since been. From secondary causes (or uniform modes of God's action now observable), the geologist seeks to trace the history of the formation of the rocks of our globe through the mutations of a time which it overtasks the imagination to compass; as the astronomer, with a mightier stretch of thought, reconstructs the universe, and unfolds the mysteries of creation in its various stages of development.

And if for all this we rely upon mere observation for our facts, and trust that the forces which we now detect in such minute proportions in the laboratory were then magnificently active in the great laboratory of nature, that the principles which now apply to the formation of a soap-bubble then applied to the formation of suns and satellites, may we not have as rational and as philosophic faith, that the only power which we now know that can begin change, and modify and direct the material forces in our own little sphere, was then also active throughout the realms of space — that intelligence, so limited in us, in a mightier form, sought, designed, and executed the symmetrical arrangement which so harmonizes with our own sentiment of beauty and love of order, with our aspirations for the sublimely vast, and our admiration of the minutely perfect?

If, for all this, we feel that from the mutations of time there may be some incertitude, we still know that beyond all this empiricism there are, in the serene empyrean of thought, more pervading truths which no remoteness of time or space can affect. We know that an eternity ago, not only were all the angles of a plane triangle equal to two right angles, but that power, truth, justice, goodness, in the abstract, were then the same as now; and in regard to these and other abstract ideas, the intervention of time, even if the period be infinite, need make no difference to our speculations.

If the succession of events, and their Causes, is ever so distinct, our interest in the study of this succession, as a separate object of knowledge, is not thereby diminished. Our interest in this remains nearly the same, even if we have no notion or theory of Causation whatever. As our power by effort is innately known, it most concerns us to learn on what occasions and to what ends to apply it, and our action being always to influence the future, it especially behooves us to know what that future will be, both if we do not and if we do put forth our efforts to modify it, that we may judge between making the effort and not making it. That by observation we have found that certain events uniformly succeed certain other events, is, then, a fact of great practical importance, enabling us to predict or conjecture with more or less of certainty the future course of events by which we are liable to be affected. But it is thus important only for the reason that we have power in ourselves to act upon the future, and make it different from what, without our efforts, this uniformity in the flow of events indicates that it would be. If we had no such Causal power, then this knowledge of the uniformity of the succession of certain consequents to certain antecedents would be of no practical importance, and inductive science would rank among those which merely furnish a playground for the intellect, or gratify an idle curiosity. It may be said that we only add our efforts to the other antecedents; but if we really do this, and thus change the subsequent events, or the order of them, we act as Cause, modifying the effects of all Causes extrinsic to us, though the relation of consequents to the antecedents, which embrace these efforts, is not less uniform than in other cases. Except in regard to instinctive actions, it is because of the uniformity in the effects of effort that we can know how to influence the future. This uniformity may arise from an occult connection, making it a necessity; but this does not affect the question of our freedom in making the effort.

These questions of Causation, which seem to me to underlie those of Freedom, have taken so much more time and space than I expected, that I must, at least for the present, omit what, when I began to write, I intended to say upon the problems of the Will, and the differences in our views upon them. I hope, however, to resume that subject a few months hence, and then to be able to condense my thoughts better than, in the haste of a preparation for an unexpected journey, I have been able to do in this epistle. But that you say, in a recent letter, you are about to prepare a third edition of your "Review of Sir William Hamilton," and to notice some objections to it, I should hardly have thought it fair to trouble you with my notes in so crude a form.

     Yours, very truly,
          R. G. HAZARD.
To J. STUART MILL, ESQ., M. P.

APPENDIX.

ON receiving this letter, Mr. Mill hastily replied to some of the positions taken in it. I will now notice only one of his objections, and that for the purpose of correcting what appears to be a very common error in another department of thought. In respect to the others, I will wait that more mature examination of this and the subsequent letter which Mr. Mill has kindly promised.

The correction alluded to appears in the following correspondence. I am glad to have my view confirmed by one whose authority will be so generally recognized as that of Professor Rood, and especially, as since these letters were written, some physicists have suggested that the point had been too long settled to be now disturbed.

PEACE DALE, R. I., February 5, 1867.

MY DEAR SIR: You may recollect that, in a letter (printed for private circulation) which I addressed to J. Stuart Mill upon the subject of our differences in regard to the "Freedom of Mind in Willing," involving our notions of "Causation," I essayed a demonstration, that an effect must be simultaneous with the action of its cause, and thence argued that succession did not enter into our idea of Cause, and that, therefore, the definitions of it given by him and many others, which make Cause only a uniform *succession* of consequents to antecedents, was invalid. To this point he replied: "Then sunrise is not the cause of day, for the actual sunrise has taken place for some time without producing day, namely, the time necessary for a ray of light to travel

APPENDIX. 61

over the intervening distance." If this were true, it would not affect my position. This is obvious when we correct the expression, and say it is our reaching the light, and not the position of the sun (absolute or relative), which causes day. But, as I was about thus to reply, it occurred to me that this travelling of the light made no difference ; but that, so far as regarded it, the apparent and actual time of sunrise were the same. Mr. Mill said that, on this point, the physicists were all against me. Several of them, with whom I have conferred, agreed with him as to the general belief. Some of them have argued the point, but in every case have finally yielded it. The problem may be thus presented :

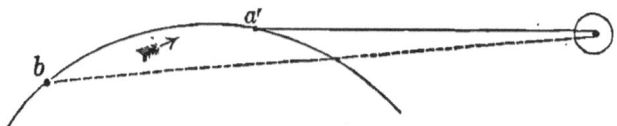

Let ☉ be the sun, a' the point on the earth's surface which has just reached the position at which the sun's light can reach it. It is now actual sunrise at a', and a person, on reaching that point, will immediately see the sun by means of a ray of light which left it $8'$ before. As there is always a ray of light reaching from ☉ to a' (though a flowing one), it is as constant and instantaneous in its action at a' as if it were a rod of iron which each person came in contact with at that point. The sun is also seen in the direction in which it really is (refraction and a slight aberration excluded). The general impression seems to be, that we see it in the relative position to us which it occupied $8'$ before. This would be in the direction b ☉. Several of those with whom I have mooted the point have so stated. Both these errors arise from considering the sun as moving around the earth, instead of the earth around its axis, and are the only cases which occur to me in which it makes any difference to the result whether the one or the other of those hypotheses is adopted. These views have no bearing upon the problem of the aberration of light, which, so far as it arises from the rotary motion of the earth, is almost inappreciable.

It seems a little remarkable that these errors, so purely physical, should have been brought out in discussing a question so purely metaphysical as that of our "Freedom in Willing;" perhaps the very last in which people generally, and especially you physicists, would expect to find anything touching, or even approaching, daylight.

Yours, very truly,   R. G. HAZARD.

To Professor OGDEN N. ROOD,
   Columbia College, New York.

COLUMBIA COLLEGE,
NEW YORK, November 23, 1867.

MY DEAR SIR: After the reception of your letter concerning the erroneous idea entertained by many relative to the real time of sunrise and sunset, I made the experiment of putting the question, point blank, to a number of educated, and even to some scientific, persons.

At first they all, I believe, without exception, were disposed to answer that the sun's disk is perceived about 8' after it is really above the horizon; and, conversely, that it remains visible for the same interval of time after it really has set.

The instant, however, I presented the real facts of the case, so clearly set forth in your letter, naturally they all were at once convinced.

In two or three text-books on astronomy into which I looked, it appeared that the point was not at all touched on.

To your last remark, I think most physicists would reply, that, while they have no fear of metaphysics, as such, yet that individual metaphysicians are sometimes quite keen-sighted in discovering the unprotected joints of their "gross material" armor!   Very truly,

OGDEN N. ROOD.

ROWLAND G. HAZARD, Esq.
   Peace Dale, R. I.

LETTER II.
FREEDOM OF MIND IN WILLING.

AFTER a long interruption, from causes to which I have occasionally alluded, I return to the consideration of your objections to my positions in "Freedom of Mind in Willing," etc.

In a former letter, as preliminary to this, I discussed our notions of Causation, in the diversity of which I think many of the differences in our views upon the Will have their root.

In coming, now, more proximately to consider these differences, I will re-state my definition of Freedom, to which I understand you to assent, namely: "Everything in moving or in acting, in motion or in action, must be directed and controlled in its motion or its action by itself, or by something other than itself; and that of these two conditions of everything moving or acting, or in motion or action, the term freedom applies to the former; . . . hence, self-control is but another expression for the freedom of that which acts, or of the active agent." [1] I also understand you to agree with me that the faculty of Will is simply a faculty or ability to make effort, and that an act of will or volition is the same as an effort.[2]

[1] *Freedom of Mind in Willing*, etc., Chap. IV.
[2] *Ibid.*, Chap. VI.

I would next notice your objections to the use of the term " necessity," which seems to me, also, to be unfortunate; and I think the advocates of freedom have even more cause than their opponents to complain of its being used in the argument in various senses. In your chapter on the " Freedom of the Will," you say, " necessity, . . . in this application, signifies only *invariability*, but in its common employment, compulsion."

Such common employment would seem to justify its use as the antithesis of freedom: compulsion and constraint being the terms which are generally used as antagonistic to that self-control which, under my definition, and as I believe in the popular apprehension, constitutes freedom. But neither invariability nor compulsion seem to me to express our ultimate idea of necessity, which, in its relation to action and to any succession or change, more properly indicates *that which must be and cannot be otherwise.*

In the idea of necessity, as thus defined, invariability is not an element at all, but is only an inference from it, as *that which must be and cannot be otherwise*, admits of no variation.

Neither does compulsion properly enter into this idea of necessity, but is associated with it, because, in some cases, and only in some, it is the occasion or the cause of the necessity, or that the event or thing must be and cannot be otherwise. We observe, then, that the idea of necessity, though distinct in itself, lies between, and is associated with compulsion on the one hand as frequently its antecedent and cause, and on the other with invariability as its consequent.

A term thus situated is liable, in use, to slide into and partake, sometimes on the one hand and sometimes on the other, of the meanings of the terms with which it is thus associated.

In what I have deemed its proper signification, necessity is not the antithesis of freedom. The addition of 2 to 2 will of *necessity* make 4, *i. e.*, *it must be so and cannot be otherwise ;* but, as there is no tendency to make anything else, no compulsion or constraint is needed as a cause to insure the result, it will be without compulsion or constraint. It is so in its own nature, and no appliance of power is requisite to make it so; nor could any such appliance of power make it otherwise.

Again, free action is of necessity free, *it must be so and cannot be otherwise ;* and if such necessity is the antithesis of freedom, free action is not free.

Still more obvious is it that necessity, when it "signifies only invariability," is not the antithesis of freedom. Free action must be *invariably* free, and if invariability is the antithesis of freedom, or excludes it, then free action cannot be free, and cannot be free for the reason that it invariably is free.

Such propositions as the two just stated are advanced only a very short step beyond the truism, that what is, is ; but if we enlarge the sphere of our examination so as to take in the statement, that the volition is *invariably* as the inclination of the willing agent, and still assume that invariability is the negation or disproof of freedom, then, the volition thus conformed to the inclination is not free. The fact of the invariability, in itself, affords no ground for such a conclusion, for the question still arises, Is the volition thus invariably conformed to the inclination by the agent willing, or by some agency without him?

It is obvious that there may be invariability in free

action, and, conversely, that there may be variability in coerced action. To say that free action may be just as variable, or just as invariable, as that which is coerced, is only to assert that what has in itself power to act may vary its own action or movement as readily as it can vary the action or movement which it causes in anything else; and this, in view of the fact that to vary its effects in the anything else it must first vary its own action, becomes self-evident.

Hence, invariability does not of itself indicate either the existence or the non-existence of freedom. It is probably only by its association with the term necessity, and, through it, with the many cases in which necessity and a consequent *invariability* are the result of compulsion, that invariability has come to be regarded as the antithesis of freedom. As already shown, it is only in cases in which compulsion is its cause that necessity itself can be so regarded.

Necessity, in such cases, presupposes the action of some power or force capable of compelling; and unless the word *necessity* is thus used, there is no radical ground of dispute between some of us who contend for freedom, and some of the advocates for necessity. There can be no more argument between one who asserts that the mind in willing is free, and another who asserts that its action is in some respects invariable, than between one who says that a lemon is sour, and another who merely says it is yellow. In further illustration of the latitude with which the term necessity is used, it may be noticed that whatever exists without the exercise of any power or cause is said to be necessary, as space; and that which exists in virtue of the exercise of a sufficient power or cause, is also said to be necessary. That which any specified power cannot prevent, is said to be necessary as to it. This last, as applied to volition, must mean an effort of my own, which by my own effort I can not prevent, involving two counter efforts at the same time.

I may have occasion further to comment upon these and some other ambiguous terms, when I come to their application in the argument; and even if it should appear that the differences in the views of the contestants of this question of freedom in willing are often rather in the definitions than in the facts or inferences from them, still, to ascertain that this is so, and to reconcile such differences of nomenclature, are objects well worthy our attention.

But some real and important problems remain to be elucidated or settled. Prominent among these are the questions, Is intelligent effort a beginning of the exercise of power, or is it a product or effect of some previously exerted power? And closely allied to this, the further question, Is the being that wills an independent power in the universe, which of itself performs a part in producing change, thereby contributing to the creation of the future, and making it different from what, but for this independent exercise of its power, it would have been; or is its action by will — its effort — really only an instrumentality through which the action of some extrinsic power or force, existing among the past or present conditions, is transmitted and made effective in producing and determining the future? My thought has led me to the affirmative of the alternatives first mentioned in each of these double questions; to the conclusions that every being that wills can begin action, and by effort produce such changes, — such events as its finite power is adequate to, — that to such effort no previous exercise of power is requisite, and that no events or extrinsic power or force can produce or direct the volition or effort of any being, but that every being that wills is an independent power in the universe, in conformity to its own intelligent design or preconception, by its effort, freely doing its part in the creation of a future, which, when reached, is the composite result of the action of all such beings upon the previously existing passive conditions, and also upon that flow of events which other causes (if any such) may be producing: intelligent being, by effort, thus acting upon, and so changing, either the fixed things or the flowing events, that the future will be made different from what, but for its effort, it would have been. In other words, I hold that every intelligent effort (and we know of no other) is an exercise of originating creative power; that even the oyster, if it acts by will, is a co-worker with God, and with all other intelligent agents, in *creating the future*, which is always the object of effort. The oyster *wants* to produce some change in the future, and directs its effort to that end, in some mode to it known. Its knowledge may be limited even to a single mode, neither requiring nor admitting of intelligent choice as to the mode, and this limited knowledge of the mode may be innate, never having required any exercise of its own intelligence to discover it, and its action, consequently, be purely instinctive; but having in itself the power of effort, the intelligence to perceive an object, and the knowledge (innate or acquired) to direct its effort to that object, it has all that is requisite to constitute a self-acting and self-directing agent.

But while, in the final effort to change the present, or influence the future, every conative being acts thus independently of control by others, there is an interdependence growing out of the exercise of this independent power, by which each one varies the conditions upon which others are to act, and may, so far, induce a variation in that action; or, to bring it under our general formula, each may thus, by his own effort, make the future action of others different from what it otherwise would have been; the power of each to vary the future thus indirectly, extending to the free actions of other intelligent beings, as well as to passive things and flowing events.

As every intelligent effort to change or convert the present into a future must be made with reference to the conditions to be changed, every change in the conditions tends to vary all effort. In merely opening its shells, an oyster changes the sum of the conditions to be acted upon, and may thus modify the action of all other beings, as a pebble dropped into the ocean tends to move every particle of its waters. Even the Supreme Intelligence must be presumed to conform His action to the existing conditions, and as the oyster in opening its bivalves does thereby change the conditions, it may, in so doing, change the action even of Deity.

We can likewise increase or vary the knowledge of others, and, to some extent, their wants also, and thus induce variations in their action, or cause it to be different from what it otherwise would have been.

The power which one may thus exert to influence the action of another, does not interfere with the *freedom* of the action of the agent thus influenced. If he is influenced by changing the conditions to be acted upon, then the action, upon the changed conditions, may be as free as it could have been upon them before they were thus changed; and that a being conforms its action to the existing conditions (or rather to its view of them), does not argue any want of freedom, but the contrary. In a game of chess, each player influences the moves of his opponent, who still moves freely. The move of one changes the conditions upon which the other is to act; but, this done, the one exerts no control upon the volition of the other, who now wills as freely, in view of the changed conditions, as he could have done had they not been changed. One has merely presented different circumstances for the free action of the other.

If a being should go on acting without reference to any changes in the conditions, as a steam-engine would go on pumping after all the water in the well or mine was exhausted, this would indicate that the intelligence — the mind — of the actor did not, and that some extrinsic power did, control its action. The question is not as to how the conditions came to be as they are, nor whether the action would have varied if the conditions had been different, but, being as they are, does the mind act freely upon them?

So, too, as to any changes which one may make in the knowledge and wants, or any of the characteristics or attributes of another being; the question is not how it came to be such a being as it is, nor whether its action would have varied if its characteristics had been different; but, before such a being as it is, does it now will freely?

In support of these views, I urge [1] that every being that wills has in itself a faculty of effort, wants which require effort for their gratification, and the knowledge to direct its effort with more or less wisdom to this end. To beings that cannot create from nothing, with this faculty of effort, the perception of an object in the

[1] *Freedom of Mind in Willing,* etc.

future, and the knowledge of a means of attaining it, there must be present conditions to be acted upon and changed, to be converted into the desired future.

I have also endeavored to show that every being, having in itself these attributes of will, want, and knowledge, has all the attributes essential to self-action, and may, from its own inherent faculty, act upon any existing conditions, and direct its action by means of its own knowledge, independently of any extrinsic power or force, and hence, under my definition, in this ability to direct and control its own action, may act freely.

The ability to act freely does not, however, of necessity, imply that it does in fact act freely. Hence, I have further attempted to show that an act of will or effort *must* be free.

That, it being impossible that anything which is inert and cannot act at all, should itself act by will, or act upon the mind, and cause it to will, or that what is unintelligent should always conform the volition of a being to that being's view, sometimes its mistaken view, of the mode of attaining its object, the will of the being cannot be moved or directed by that which is inert and unintelligent.

Nor is there any conceivable mode in which one intelligent active being can directly move or *act* the will of another; and if any such moving or acting by an extrinsic being were in fact possible, then the willing — the effort — would also, in fact, be the effort of the extrinsic being.

The idea, that one being may directly control the volition of another, involves the assumption that the will is a distinct entity, which may be appropriated by any one strong enough to seize and wield it for the purpose of willing, whereas it is only the mind's faculty of making effort or exerting power, and the willing is only the effort or immediate exercise of power — a state of the active being — and not a thing which has power, or which power can use as an implement, nor even a medium through which power may be transmitted.

I have also, in this connection, urged that, as the being always conforms his action to his perception or knowledge of the means of attaining the object, the only indirect mode in which the willing of any being can be controlled is by so changing his knowledge, including his knowledge of those sensations and emotions which are elements of want, that, as a consequence of this change of knowledge, he comes to a different conclusion as to the object to be attained, or of the mode of attaining it, and wills differently, and that this indirect control is predicated upon the assumption that the being that wills controls its own act of will; otherwise there is no ground for presuming that the action will be conformed to its changed knowledge, or vary with it. Hence, as the willing of any being cannot be directly controlled by the action of extrinsic power or force upon it, nor yet indirectly influenced except through its own self-control, or freedom in action, it follows, that if it wills at all, its action in willing must not only be free, but that its effort is an independent exercise, and beginning of the exercise of its power, and not an effect of power previously exerted upon it.

In the common acceptation, too, of the terms, and the ideas they represent, compelling or constraining the act of will by prior exercise of power or force, involves the contradiction of willing when we are unwilling or not willing.

That you agree with me that mind does will — does by effort put forth power — producing effect, I infer from your saying "your view of what the mind has power to do seems to me quite just." You add, "But we differ on the question, how the mind is determined to do it," and in effect argue that volition is an effect which is controlled and made to be as it is by previous conditions.

If the volition is regarded as a distinct entity, the freedom of which is in question, then the control which you assert would negative its freedom, for the conditions which precede a volition cannot be that volition itself, and, hence, such control would not be by itself, but by something not itself, and therefore such *volition* would not be free, and upon this I presume we do not differ.

But, if this control of its action or volition is by the active being itself, then, even though the volition be still regarded as a distinct entity, the control which enslaves the volition, establishes the freedom of the being in willing, *i. e.*, its freedom in the use of this distinct entity as its instrument. To meet the issue, then, it is necessary to show, not only that the volition is controlled, but that it is controlled by some power other than the being that wills, for if by the being, its action is self-controlled, and consequently free.

In this view, your agreeing with me as to "what the mind has power to do," must be taken with some limitation. I, holding that the mind has of and in itself power to begin and direct its action in the absence of all other active power or force; you, that it must be moved to act, and determined in its action, by some prior exercise of power or cause. In this relation, you sometimes, and perhaps always, use the term *influence*, upon the vagueness of which I may hereafter have something to say, and will now only remark, that if it does not imply the exercise of any power or force, then it does not imply any compulsion or constraint upon the being in willing, and does not interfere with its freedom in willing. That which acts without compulsion or constraint acts freely, and compulsion or constraint implies the action of some power or force which is sufficient to compel or constrain.

Your expression, "we differ on the question, how the mind is determined to do it," might be taken as meaning that, in your view, the mind's action is directly determined for it, and not by it, or, it may mean that while the mind does determine its immediate act, it is determined to determine by the operation of prior causative power or influence.

I admit the position of Sir William Hamilton, as quoted and commended by you, that "it is of no consequence in the argument whether motives be said to determine a man to act, or to influence (that is to determine) him to determine himself to act;" and I would apply the same remark to anything else which is said to influence a being to act as well as to motive. I not only admit that it is of no consequence in the argument, but I am in doubt as to whether there is any real difference in the two positions; and whether saying that a being is himself determined to determine as to his act, is not exactly equivalent to saying a being is himself determined as to his act; as to say, I know that I know, is no more than to say I know.

In another aspect, there seems to be not merely a futility, but an incongruity in the addenda to the original idea. In the latter part of the expression, Hamilton asserts that the being determines himself to act. Hence, in that act, he is self-determined; but can one whose determination is determined by something else be self-determined? Is there not a contradiction, or at least an incompatibility of ideas, involved in the expression, "determined to determine himself." If, using other terms, it be said that the mind does control its own effort, but in the exercise of this control is itself controlled by something else, the same difficulty remains. It is, perhaps, intended to exhibit the mind as placed in a position analogous to that of the ivory ball between the one from which it receives and that to which it communicates the impulse. The result would be the same if it were wholly left out. Under this view, the mind has the faculty of effort, but can exert it only *when* and *as* it is moved to do so by some other power, as a steam-engine (including in itself the expansive steam confined in the boiler) has in itself the power to operate and to turn the millstone, which crushes the grain, provided some extrinsic power first changes the existing conditions, under which it is motionless, by opening a valve, and letting the steam press or impinge upon the piston ; and the manner or direction of its motion will depend upon the manner of the connection of the valve which is thus opened. The whole might be so contrived that the pouring of the grain into the hopper of the mill would, either by its motion in going in, or by its weight when in, move the valve, making an aggregate apparatus in which the movement to crush the grain would depend only upon the condition that there was grain in the hopper, ready to be crushed, or upon the change from its not being to its being thus ready. In this case, however, the power which moved the grain into the hopper is still, really, the power which, acting through intermediate instruments, moves the valve, and is a power extrinsic to the engine, acting independently of it. If the engine, in addition to power, had intelligence also, so that, when it *perceived* or *knew* that there was grain in the hopper, it could, without any other change of the existing conditions by other power or force, itself move its valves, and at its own pleasure produce the proper motion to crush the grain, the whole combined apparatus, with its power of self-movement and intelligent exercise of that power for the purpose of accomplishing the end to which it was pleased to apply its power, would then be free in its action.

But at this point of intelligent action — at the very gist of the question — the analogy, like all possible analogies drawn from movements of unintelligent matter, practically fails, and leaves the disputants to recur to and reason upon the actual facts of intelligent action to which there is no known similitude in the universe.

The arguments which you adduce in support of such of your positions as mine conflict with, I think are all embraced under the following heads: —

1. The argument from cause and effect, or the assertion that volition is itself an event which is a necessary consequent of its antecedents, and hence really controlled and determined by the past events.

2. The influence of the present external conditions, or of things and circumstances including the action of one conative intelligence upon another.

3. Influence of internal phenomena, as the character, knowledge, disposition, inclination, desires, wants, and habits, which make up the attributes or conditions of the mind that wills.

4. The argument from prescience, or the " possibility of prediction."

Of these, the first three are more or less blended in each other, all of them assuming that the mind's acting

CAUSATION AND FREEDOM IN WILLING. 77

is always but a consequence of some prior action upon it; motive being predicated of external and also of internal conditions, its supposed controlling power is embraced in both the second and third.

The fourth is a wholly distinct and very different argument, for it cannot be contended that prescience of a volition is in itself a power which compels or constrains that volition to be; but only that the possibility of predicting a volition proves, or at least indicates, its connection in some way with something already known in the past, present, or future. Either will suffice equally well for this purpose.

The argument upon these points should be based upon the phenomena and characteristics of voluntary action, to some of which I will now recur.

The action of a being is by volition, or effort, which is always *intended* to make the future different from what it otherwise would be. This is the object and design, without which no intelligent being would make effort. Hence, effort can be predicated only of an active, intelligent being; of a being that can act, and that has intention or design.

An intelligent being will not make effort to do when it does not want to do, and hence want, in such being, is also a condition necessary to its effort. The effort itself may sometimes be the thing wanted, and, in such cases, the making of the effort is the thing to be done, is the ultimate object.

Any being making effort to vary the future, must have some knowledge, or belief, or expectation as to what the future would be without such effort, and also as to what change in it will be wrought by his effort. For convenience, we will call the perception or expectation of any being of what the future will be, if uninfluenced by his action, *his primary expectation*; and that of what he supposes it will be made by his action, *his secondary expectation.*

The expectation of future effect is the foundation of our action, but whether this expectation is or is not realized, in no way concerns our freedom in acting. That which will be in the future cannot change that which now is, or which has been. An unsuccessful effort is just as freely made as one that is successful. The expectation is merely knowledge more or less certain, positive, or confided in, as to the states or conditions of things which will be in the future.

If one knew that he were, himself, the only agent of change in the universe, and that everything else was passive and quiescent, he would know, with assured certainty, that in the absence of any exercise of his own power, the future would be the same as the present; and his effort, if any, must be to change the existing conditions and make them different from what they are.

If he know that there are other agents at work changing the present into, and thus creating, the future, the problem becomes to him a far more complicated one. To ascertain what the future would be, is now the most important and difficult process in determining as to his own effort to vary it. He must have some expectation of what the future, if produced by the composite action of all *other* powers of change, will or will not be, or he can have no reason for putting forth his own efforts to make it different. He must, also, have a secondary as well as a primary expectation, or he can have no ground of choice between them, and, hence, no sufficient knowledge to direct his action, nor any reason to act at all.

There may be cases in which one, dissatisfied with

the present condition of things, may act at random, on the presumption that any change must be for the better; but, in such case, he expects some change from his own effort, which he does not rely upon others producing.

The conditions of the hypothesis of a sole active agent of change relieves him from much difficulty in determining his primary expectation, but involves that of accounting for his changing from the passive to the active state when all other conditions are the same, and all passive.

If universal passivity should once obtain; if all material motion should cease, and all changes in thought, feeling, and perception be suspended, there would be an end of all change, including that from rest to effort, by which intelligent beings begin to influence the course of events, after having refrained from doing so; for intelligent beings would not make effort except upon a perception of some desirable and sufficient object of effort; and, if the existing perception had not already proved to be a sufficient ground for action, it could not, without some change, become so, and all such change is excluded by the hypothesis. Hence, if a universal passivity once obtained, there would be no conceivable way out of it into activity or change again; all matter would be motionless, all spirit inactive, and satisfied with the existing conditions of universal repose.

This is only a phase of the general case which I before reached, that fixed existences, or fixed conditions of existence, cannot of themselves be cause of subsequent change.

This difficulty in conceiving an absolute beginning of activity is analogous to, if not identical with, that of conceiving an absolute beginning of existence. Both involve the idea of an absolute beginning of change, or a sudden starting of power into existence as a cause of that change, when there was no acting power or cause to produce change, nor any perceived reason for the exercise of any existing potential power, or for bringing power, or anything else, into existence.[1]

In the supposed case of a universal passivity, there might be beings with sensations and perceptions, with feeling and knowledge; but, if these involved no want, there would be no effort for change till there was some change in them, and to produce this there is no existing cause or power.

It is, perhaps, conceivable that the continuous monotonous sensations and perceptions known by the mind to be such, might create a want for variety. Waving this last consideration, the perception of objects of effort might arise either from a change in the conditions perceived, or a changed view of the same conditions or of their relations; but, if all spirit causes were quiescent, such change could only be effected by material movement.

Admitting that matter in motion may be cause,[2] we have an apparent similarity in the formulas which express the necessary conditions to the beginning of the motion of matter and the beginning of the action of mind, viz., that if all matter is quiescent, the action of

[1] May not this difficulty of supposing a beginning of power be the foundation, or the suggestive idea of Sir William Hamilton's doctrine of Causation, in which every actual exercise or exhibition of power presumes the preëxistence of an equivalent potential power? If so, his theory merely postulates the existence of power from eternity, as one of the alternatives in the dilemma, of which an absolute beginning of power is the other.

[2] For the discussion of this point, see *Freedom of Mind*, etc., Chap. VIII.

CAUSATION AND FREEDOM IN WILLING. 81

intelligence is necessary to its motion, and if all spirit is quiescent, the movement of matter is necessary to its action. But, though at this initial point there is this apparent similarity, there is a wide difference in the actual phenomena in the two cases. The change, by which matter, before quiescent, begins to move, must be a change by which power or force is directly applied to it, not only compelling movement, but the direction of the movement. The material change which, in the other supposed case, is essential to the action of mind, does not directly make nor compel the effort, but only so changes the conditions that the mind perceives a reason for itself making a voluntary effort, and, in this case, the mind must also determine what effort is adapted to the changed conditions, or rather to its changed view or knowledge of them. In doing this, the mind determines its action, conforming it to its changed knowledge of the existing conditions and the changes it desires in them. There is a further difference, already suggested, and one which perhaps is sufficient to except mind from the necessity of any external change to enable it to begin action. Mind can observe or know what is, and also remember what was, without effort; and if an observed monotony is such a perception that the mind, by the mere lapse of time, misses the pleasurable excitement of variety, which it recollects to have experienced, and, hence, wants variety or change, this would be a sufficient ground for effort to an intelligent being which, previous to the universal passivity, had experienced variety, and if such knowledge of the pleasurable excitement of variety, or the want of variety, is innate, then there is in the constitution of the being — in its aggregate characteristics — a provision for a beginning of activity from wholly quiescent conditions, and it could *begin* effort to change this universal passivity. In like manner, if continued repose or quiescence leads to a want for activity, this would be a ground for action. In these cases, the mind could make effort for change, even though it expected in the one case only to gratify its want for change, without reference to the character of the change, as in the other to gratify its want for activity, without reference to the value of the results of its activity.

No such constitutional element by which the mere fact of a continued monotony, or passivity of conditions, not at first sufficient to move, may become a ground, or occasion of movement or action, can be predicated of matter; for such action, upon such ground, would constitute it a conative intelligence acting from its own perception of a reason for acting, and not moved or acted by another power or force.

If, further to illustrate this difference in the genesis of material movement and of mental action, we suppose the first change from a monotonous passivity to be merely the advent of a quiescent material formation, it must remain quiescent. It cannot move itself, and there is no other movement or activity — no other power or force — to move it. But, if we suppose the first change from the monotonous passivity to be the advent of a conative intelligence, also in a passive state, and any supposed cause of such advent, and all other power or cause to immediately cease to be, then, in his passive perceptions of the existing passive conditions, including his own feeling and desire or want, this conative intelligence may at once find objects of effort, and make effort to attain them, and with each change he effects in the passive conditions, new objects of ef-

CAUSATION AND FREEDOM IN WILLING. 83

fort may arise. In such case, the newly created conative intelligence is a sole power and cause of change, and of course cannot be dependent upon any other power or cause, but, in virtue of his inherent attributes, is, at his creation, and continues to be, a wholly independent power, acting in conformity to his own views, and to his own designs to create or vary the future.

If we now suppose this sole causal power by his effort to create, or bring into action, other causal power or force; for instance, that he puts matter in motion which in turn produces other changes, this will vary the conditions upon which he acts, but does not interfere with his own inherent power of acting, nor with his freedom in the genetic exercise of this power. On the contrary, he may now suspend his own action, and resume it again whenever, in the changes effected by this other causal power or force, he perceives a reason for putting forth his own effort to influence the course of events. Even if he is unable to overcome, or in any degree to counteract this extrinsic power or force, he is no less free to make effort, and to begin to make it for this object, than he was to try to change the passive conditions which he found existing at his own creation. Nor can it make any difference whether this extrinsic power or force, which is thus varying the conditions upon which he acts, is intelligent or unintelligent, nor whether it was brought into existence by his own efforts or otherwise; nor whether it has always existed, or has had a beginning. He is as free to act upon his knowledge of the actual conditions, including his immediate sensations or observation of what other powers or forces have effected, and the preconceptions of their future effects, which he passively perceives, or by effort deduces from these present sensations, as he was when no other power or force existed, and he was acting only upon existing passive conditions. In both, and in all cases, he is free to act and to begin to act, whenever, either in fixed or flowing conditions, he perceives a reason for acting.

He always acts to make the future different from what it otherwise would be, and directs his action by his knowledge of means to the result, which, on comparing his primary with his secondary expectations, he chooses and desires. When he ceases to be a sole cause, he is more liable to be mistaken in his preconceptions of what the future will be, and to misapply his effort, and fail of effecting his objects; but he is equally free to make the effort; equally free to try to do, and to conform his effort to do, to his own notions, whether they be true or false, wise or foolish. There may be cases in which, even in regard to extrinsic matters, we act as a sole cause. There may be passive conditions around us, among which we perceive that by effort we can effect desirable change; but, even in such cases, we count upon the continuance of natural laws, or the uniformity of cause and effect, which, in my view, are only expressions for the uniform action of some other intelligent power or cause. This reliance upon the action of other causes to aid us in our efforts is not the same as a prior action of power causing us to make effort, or controlling the direction of the effort, but is only one of the elements of our secondary expectations, and does not prevent our acting as an independent cause. nor even, in relation to the particular effect we seek to produce, as a sole cause.

If all within the sphere of one's action were quiescent, he could still act, and the future effects, including the action of other causes and their influence upon

CAUSATION AND FREEDOM IN WILLING. 85

these effects, would all primarily be the effects of his action. Even in these cases, then, in the preliminary examination to determine our own action, we look to the action of others as an important element. It, however, oftener happens that we do not thus take the initiative, and make occasion for the action of other causes, but by our efforts seek to modify the effects of other causes, already active, rather than wholly to create the future.

The hypothesis of a universal passivity is wholly foreign to our experience, and does not come into the practical question of our freedom of action in the actual conditions of our existence, in which we find that, even when one is wholly inert himself, changes are continually taking place around and about him, which vary the sensations and perceptions of which he is only a passive recipient, bringing to his notice objects of effort; that either by the constitutional continuous movements in his own being, or by the action of some other extrinsic cause, hunger comes from abstinence, that even what in itself is agreeable becomes a wearying monotony, inducing a desire for variety, and that the wants of repose and of activity reciprocally follow each other. These last two I have suggested may, perhaps, spring directly from the attributes of intelligent being without its own effort, and without the action of any extrinsic power.

Assuming, now, that to each individual there is without him a certain flow or current of events, produced by other causes than himself (material or spiritual, or both), we come to the question, has he an independent power or faculty of effort by which he can of himself begin action, and thereby so influence this current of events as to make the future different from what, but for its efforts, it would be? If he has such power, and in the exercise of it is free from external compulsion and control, — if this current of events does not determine, but he himself determines his effort, by conforming it to his own view of what, under the existing conditions, suits him best, — then, under my definition of Freedom, he is a free agent, in his finite sphere, and to the extent of his finite power as freely doing his part in creating a future, as God, in His sphere, and in the exercise of His power, is in doing His part of the same work of creating that future, the creation of which is the composite result of the efforts of every being that wills.

This question of freedom in willing, however, does not involve that of our actual power to do, for we may be free to make effort, *i. e.*, to try to do what, from deficient ability, we may not succeed in doing. This freedom in making the effort, or in trying to do, is the question at issue, and is wholly distinct from that of our power to do what we attempt.

The speculations in which I have indulged upon the hypotheses of a sole cause, and a universal passivity, however foreign to our own actual experience, I trust, have thrown some light upon the more practical question of the ability of each individual to begin action when, though himself quiescent, he is the percipient of changes effected by other causes.

The question as to the mind's ability to begin action covers the same ground as the first of the four arguments, or categories, on page 76, involving the asserted influence of the past and its causal influences, which again involve that of the uniformity of cause and effect.

The necessitarian argument, on this ground, assumes that the mind must be acted upon by something before it can itself act, and then finds this something in a causative agency of the past, which it generally designates as *a motive*.

This argument, in various forms, is applied to all of the four categories, and the different phases in which it appears will be most conveniently treated as they arise in the discussion of each of them.

We may, however, observe, generally, that the past is always that which has already been changed into the present, and having now no actual existence, cannot, of itself, be a cause of anything in the present. We remember it as that which has been, but it no more exists in the present than does the future, of which we have a prophetic conception. That our knowledge of the one is more certain, more reliable, or more perfect than of the other, does not give it extrinsic causative power. Knowledge, however perfect, is not itself knowing or active, nor does it confer the power of activity upon that which is known. It may be said that the past is not necessarily changed in the present, but may flow into its future without any change. In this case, the past has not produced the only effect of its causative power which can possibly be attributed to it, that of changing itself into its future, for the only effect of the action of any cause is to make the future different from what it would have been, and the moment it flowed into its future, without change, it would become a fixed existence, which, as before shown, would then of itself have no power to produce subsequent change, and, of course, could not change anything or any being from passive to an active condition ; could not impart motion to matter, or volition to intelligence. It would only be a subject to be acted upon, and not a thing that could act.

It may be said that though no effect was produced by these causative powers of the past, they did exist, but that they exactly neutralized each other, and hence no change was effected by them. Still this no-effect must continue, unless some new power is added — some agency — which, like that of intelligence, having a want for variety, can, on perceiving this universal passivity, put forth power, and begin change, without being first acted upon by any other activity or power. By the hypothesis there is no such other activity, and if there is nothing to which passive conditions, as want and knowledge, furnish a ground for action, no action can ever be. If the past has already applied its causative power to change itself in passing to its future, and failed, then, the conditions being all the same, it can never succeed in doing this, but must forever remain in this condition of unsuccessful appliance without any effect or change. There are only two conceivable modes in which the effects of the exercise of any causative powers in the past can be extended to the present. One of these is by putting matter in motion by which those past causes may have developed a self-continuing power, which will extend the effects of their own action in time.[1] The other is through the action of some intelligent being, which has either the ability to continue its own action from the past to the present, or to begin new action in view of the fixed results of past causative agencies, and to adapt its action to these results, which now constitute the conditions to be acted upon ; but it is obvious that no motion could be imparted to matter from a past in which everything had, even for an instant, become quiescent, and if, at the

---

[1] On the question of the possibility of such causes, see *Freedom of Mind in Willing*, Book I. Chap. VIII.

CAUSATION AND FREEDOM IN WILLING. 89

moment of such quiescence taking place, the existing conditions did not present a reason for effort, they could not, while continuing the same, present any such reason to any intelligent being in which also no change had taken place

Of these modes of continuing the influence of causative power, it may be remarked, on the first of them, that any effect in the present is the result of the present action or impact of the moving body, and not of its *past* motion; and of the second, that it is not the *past* existence of the intelligent being with his attributes, but his present effort that produces the effect. As heretofore shown, the effect must result from causes in action at the time it occurs, and not from prior action.[1] There are also two conceivable modes in which the causative agencies of the past may effect the present action of the powers of the past thus continued into the present. The one by the state to which the past has brought the conditions to be acted upon, and the other by the characteristics it may have imparted to the powers which are to act upon these conditions; for instance, the direction which it may have given to any matter in motion, and the changes it may have made or left unmade, in the character of any intelligent being.

The action of these powers or forces, intelligent and unintelligent, must be affected by their relations to the conditions which the past has entailed on the present. Though the past agency, which put a body in motion, may have no present control of its movement and effect, still the *effect* of that movement may depend upon certain material being in the line of its movement, so that it will come in collision with it, and the

[1] *Letter on Causation*, page 25.

position of such material, or that it is in the line of the body's movement, may have been determined in the past.

But the consideration of the influence of all the extrinsic conditions upon the mind's freedom in willing belongs under our second, and that of any changes in the intrinsic conditions of the being by the past, under our third category or head; and this last especially so, as we are only thus influenced by the past through our *memory*, which is a form of our knowledge. That habit forms no exception to this, I think, is shown by my analysis of it in "Freedom of Mind," etc., Book I. Chap. XI.

In the first category, the controlling influence of the past is put forth in the argument from cause and effect, or that for every event or thing which begins to be, there must be a prior cause for such beginning, upon which it is dependent for its beginning to be and for its being as it is, and not otherwise, and, hence, volition, being an event or thing which begins to be, is dependent upon a prior cause, which, under the admission that the same causes must produce the same effects, of necessity causes it to be and to be as it is, and not otherwise.

In regard to the dictum, "The same causes of necessity produce the same effects," I have already stated my views pretty fully,[1] and have also remarked that the very object of volition is always to interfere with and change the uniform result which would otherwise recur; and will now add that the determination of a volition, by any causative power in the past, is no less an interference with our freedom if its action be variable than if it be uniform. It is not, then, the uni-

[1] *Freedom of Mind in Willing*, Book II. Chap. XI.

CAUSATION AND FREEDOM IN WILLING. 91

formity of the effects of the action of past causes which interferes, or indicates any such interference, with our freedom. Such uniformity, by association, induces the idea of necessity, though, as already intimated, by enabling us to anticipate, it, in fact, aids our own efforts to thwart or vary the results of causation in the past.

As already suggested, if this argument from the necessary uniformity of cause and effect is applied to volition as a distinct impassive entity which begins to be, it proves that such entity is not free; but, if it is applied to a mere state or condition of mind, it does not prove that the mind in such state is not free, or that mind, as itself a cause, may not change itself from the passive to the active state without any extrinsic appliance of power or cause to it. To avail anything, then, this argument from cause and effect must assume, not that effort itself, but that *mind* in its effort is controlled by the antecedents, and cannot itself begin action or inaugurate change. It is common to illustrate and enforce this argument for necessity by reference to the phenomena of matter in motion. Little aid should be expected from the comparison of phenomena so essentially different as material movement and intelligent effort, and there is much danger in transferring the observations and deductions which we may make in one of these fields of inquiry to the other. The difficulty of explaining the phenomena of mind in effort, by reference to the facts observed of matter in motion, is really not less than that of explaining the motion of matter by reference to the phenomena of the mind's effort. Indeed, as motion is one of the direct results of effort, while effort can never be produced by motion, we might more logically refer the material phenomena to the mental than the converse. Still, as a means of illustration, the phenomena of motion cannot well be dispensed with. Matter in motion may at least be conceived to be, and to most persons does in fact appear to be, a cause of change. In this one respect it resembles effort, to which there is no other known thing in the universe that has any similitude whatever. If, then, we would illustrate effort by analogy at all, we must admit the phenomena of motion as a means of doing it, and do the best we can to avoid sliding into the errors to which, in following such analogies, we are exposed. This resemblance, seeming or real, lies not at all in the things themselves, nor in their modes or actings, but only in the one circumstance that both do produce effects. Still, from the close association, in the popular mind, of material causation by motion with intelligent causation by effort, the ambiguities and the confusions arising from the vague expressions common to such subjects, have been much increased by an indiscriminate application of the same terms to both of these forms of causation. The phrase, "that which moves," has two very distinct meanings, sometimes indicating that which causes the motion, and sometimes that in which motion is caused, or that which is actually moving, without any reference to the cause of its moving. The horse is *that which moves* the carriage; the carriage also is *that which moves*. In like manner, the phrase "that which acts," is applied to intelligent beings in the state of willing, and to matter in the state of motion, and through this last application readily partakes of the ambiguity which attaches to the phrase "that which moves." We speak of the action of the mind in willing, and of the action of the muscles, meaning,

CAUSATION AND FREEDOM IN WILLING. 93

primarily, that the mind is itself active, and that the muscles are acted or moved by it.

The phrase, "that which acts," as compared with the phrase, "that which moves," is an approach to the idea of a self-active power, excluding to some extent the idea of that in which action or motion is only caused. We may properly say that A moves a piece of lead, or a piece of lead is being moved by A; but not that A acts a piece of lead, or that a piece of lead is being acted by A. That which moves may mean either the power which produces the motion or the passive thing which that power moves; but that which acts is always the active agent or the actor. *That which moves* (*i. e.*, the entity moving or in motion) may be wholly passive in moving; that which acts (*i. e.*, the entity acting) cannot be said to be passive. But action and motion are liable to be confounded. By using the word *effort* to indicate the mind's exercise of power, we avoid much of the confusion to which the word *action*, with its analogies and associations, exposes us; for though we sometimes use the phrases, "motion of matter," and "action of matter," as convertible, as also the phrases, "mind's action," and "mind's effort," thus applying the term action both to mental effort and material motion, we never (in this sense of the word) think or speak of the *effort of matter*. All effort is of the mind, which has no other mode of exerting its power. But, in the exercise of this power, it has two very distinct objects: the one to produce change in the external world, the other to extend its own knowledge beyond the mere passive perceptions of phenomena. By effort, we draw inferences from present facts, anticipate the future, reproduce the past, or so arrange our ideas that new relations and new truths become apparent. To produce external change, we always begin with an effort to move the appropriate muscles of our own bodies; this is the case even when we would change the knowledge, thought, or action, of our fellow-beings, for there is no known mode of communicating our thoughts to them, except through material changes, which we cause for that purpose. The case would be different if we sought to produce change in beings that could directly perceive our thoughts without the aid of such external manifestations. Prayer requires no material medium; but as God is everywhere, is within as well as without us, this hardly makes an exception; and any intelligence, which is not so far within us as to have an immediate cognition of our thoughts, must learn our thoughts through external changes. We may then say that, in all our efforts to change the external world, including the actual experiments by which we add to our knowledge of it, and the modes by which we impart our knowledge to others, we begin with an effort to move our muscles, while in attempting directly to increase our own knowledge, including that of the modes or means of producing changes, we often begin and end with an exercise of the mind's intrinsic power, without resorting to experiments in matter, and, hence, we use the phrases "muscular effort" and "mental effort," not to indicate efforts made by the muscles, and efforts made by the mind, but to generically distinguish the *objects* of the mind's effort in each particular case. We cannot distinguish these two classes of actions from each other by reference to the actor, for the actor is the same in both; but we name them from the subjects of the action, muscular efforts always meaning efforts of the mind to change what is extrinsic to it, and mental efforts meaning efforts of the mind to change itself, i. e., to increase its own knowledge, there being no other mode in which it can effect change in itself. Still, this use of the phrase "muscular effort" leads some persons to attribute original intrinsic power by effort to the muscles, laying a foundation for a belief in material causation, and increasing the confusion in regard to power in matter which the use of the word action has occasioned.

I trust that these remarks upon the use of the terms *motion*, *action*, and *effort*, may, at least to some extent, prepare the way for the proper use of the phenomenon of matter in motion as an illustration of that of mind in action, and aid to make both the agreements and disagreements in them available for that purpose. I have already stated some of these, and noted that the analogy wholly fails at the very point which concerns the question of the mind's freedom in effort; but, as such analogies may still be useful, and are, in fact, very generally used in the discussion, it may be well still further to trace them out, and note their bearing upon it.

Spirit is the only thing which can make effort, or exert intrinsic power. Matter is the only thing that can be directly changed by power extrinsic to itself.

Power to effect change by effort is a part of the constitution of intelligent, active beings; the susceptibility to be changed by power is a part of the nature of things. The phenomena of spirit, as knowledge, perception, sensation, emotion, are only indirectly affected by extrinsic power, and cannot be directly acted upon by it.

96 CAUSATION AND FREEDOM IN WILLING.

Matter, in being moved by a force extrinsic to it, is wholly passive in its movement; my hand, in being moved by a mental effort, is, in itself, as passive as when at rest. So, too, if my mind, in acting, were *acted* by something extrinsic to it, it would be as passive in acting as when not acting. If the effort is produced or caused by power extrinsic to the agent, then the agent is passive, and does not act or make effort. Any expression of the idea that the effort is produced or caused by a power extrinsic to the being making it, involves the contradiction that the actor is not active, or that he is both active and passive at the same time. The idea not only necessitates this solecism in expression, but is contradictory in itself.

That which produces motion in matter is the cause of the motion, and if matter *moves* itself, or produces motion in itself, it is self-moving. So, too, that which produces action is the cause of the action, and if a being *acts* itself, or produces action in itself, it is self-active.

The action of mind is wholly in the mind's effort, and not in the antecedents or the consequents of its effort; and, hence, a being with a faculty of effort is self-active, needing only an occasion for action.

So long as a substance is caused to move by some extrinsic power or force, it is but the passive subject of the action of that power or force, or a passive instrument, or a medium, through which that power or force is transmitted and made effective in something else. It is not till the moving power or force ceases to control the movement of such substance, that it can itself become cause. If, after such power or force has ceased to produce, or to control the movement, this substance continues to move by some inherent quality or property in itself, then, in virtue of this inherent attribute, it has power, and may be, in itself, a cause. In such case, the prior extrinsic exercise of power by which it was put in motion, has, from what was before inert and powerless, created or developed a moving power capable of acting independently of, and either in concurrence with, or in opposition to, the power which has thus produced it. So, too, the creation of a being with a faculty of effort, wants to be gratified by effort, and the intelligence to put forth and direct its effort to their gratification is the creation of a power or cause, which, in virtue of its own inherent attributes, is self-active, and can go on to produce effects wholly independent of the power which created it, or of any other power. The matter, though fully developed in existence, if at rest, requires extrinsic force to put it in motion; but mind can itself begin action, and change the direction or intent of its action whenever it perceives a reason for so doing.

All the arguments against the freedom of the mind in willing, which are embraced under the first three heads, assert, or assume, that the mind must be acted upon before it can itself begin to act; and this, to avail, must assert that it is acted upon by some extrinsic power, which is sufficient to produce the effect and cause the mind to act, and to act in the manner in which it does act; for, if acted upon by some power which produced no such effect, its freedom could not thereby be interfered with, and for stronger reason, if it were conceivable that it could be acted upon by that which has no power at all, such action could in no way interfere with its freedom. I can see no reason for asserting that a volition is not free merely because it has had antecedents, uniform or otherwise, *i. e.*, because something has been before it.

In each of the three positions named, then, and especially in the first, which relates to the influence of the past, and the application of the law of cause and effect, it is virtually asserted that the mind, in its act of willing, is caused to act, and to act in a particular manner, by the prior action of some causal power or force.

Having noted what, in this connection, seem to me the more important of the resemblances and discrepancies between the phenomena of matter in motion and of mind in action, I will proceed to consider this question of the mind's being caused to act, and controlled in its action, as an effect of a prior exercise of power or force. And, on it, I would first remark, that we not only have no experience of any *direct* application of such power or force to the mind's act of will or effort, but that we cannot even conceive of any mode or manner in which such power or force could be applied to it; but, on the contrary, our experience is, that from a state of inaction we can of ourselves begin action without any such power or force first acting upon us, and with no other essential antecedent than our perceptions of the present and expectations as to the future, both of which, being forms of knowledge, are passive in their nature.[1] If these have been attained by prior effort, that effort has been exhausted in the effect, leaving the mind, so far as such effort is concerned, in a passive state with its increased knowledge of the present and future, which is all that it requires, and all that it uses, to itself determine as to its exercise of its own power of acting, and the manner of such exercise.

[1] Knowledge and our perceptions are always passive. See *Freedom of Mind in Willing*, Book I. Chap. III.

CAUSATION AND FREEDOM IN WILLING. 99

I have already remarked that the ability of the mind to start from a fixed condition of universal passivity into action, is, at least, doubtful, and that such condition being wholly foreign to our experience, the problem is not practically important.

The more practical question is, can the individual, himself passive in the midst of changing conditions, of himself put forth effort, and thus begin action. Upon the general question of one's power to begin action, it does not make any difference whether the conditions, which by effort he seeks to change, are fixed or are in process of change by the action of some other causal power (provided that in case all other conditions are fixed he has not passed into the fixed state himself). In either case, he acts upon his expectation of the *effect* of his effort upon the future, and any change in his expectation by the action of other causes is, of course, a change in his knowledge, which will be considered under its proper head. Assuming, then, that in actual life, other causes are continually producing changes around us, our experience is that we may be passive observers of the course of events — mere recipients of the changing sensations and emotions they produce — till we perceive [1] that they are tending to some undesirable result, or that by our own effort a more desirable result may be obtained, and then put forth our power by effort to prevent or to modify the result to which the action of extrinsic causes is tending.

This change from a passive to an active state is as much a matter of observation and experience as the changes in our sensations and emotions are, and the change from a state of non-effort to one of effort is as

[1] *Freedom of Mind in Willing*, Book I. Chap. III.

well attested, in both these modes, as the change from a state of not seeing to that of seeing, or from that of not feeling to that of feeling, and the *beginning* of an effort is as marked as the beginning of a sensation. The necessitarian argument from cause and effect itself asserts, as one of its essential links, that volitions do *begin to be*, but, as this may only mean that different volitions constantly succeed one another, it does not necessarily assert that we are ever in that state of non-effort which is a prerequisite to a *new beginning of effort*, though not to the *beginning of a new effort*, and, admitting that every volition has a beginning, the necessitarian might still argue that each one in succession is a consequence of that which preceded it, the whole being an uninterrupted series, dependent upon the first term, or upon it and such extrinsic forces as might combine with it to vary the subsequent volition ; or, admitting the total suspension of action in the individual, assert that his resumption or beginning anew was the result of some causative power in the past ; in either case making the whole destiny of the being depend upon the time, or, as it is asserted that the causative powers of the past are divided in space, upon the time and place at which it was dropped into the current of events.

Any reasoning upon these questions must ultimately rest upon the consciousness. There is no bringing the argument, either for the mind's freedom or for its necessity in effort, home to one who has no consciousness of effort. If he has not this direct intrinsic cognition of it, he cannot know it at all, for, as there is nothing with which it has in itself any similitude, there is no extrinsic mode of imparting even a conception of it to him. Such a being, however, though he might have knowledge and feeling, and might be the passive subject of action, could not himself act, — could not make effort, — for an unconscious effort is in thought as absurd as an unfelt feeling. But, while the fact of effort involves the consciousness of it as a necessary concomitant, it is not so certain that the consciousness of effort is conclusive as to the fact of effort. A feeling, either in the form of a sensation or an emotion, cannot be merely representative. That I feel, is itself the ultimate fact in the case for which no other can be substituted, and which no other can account for on the ground of mistake or otherwise. But it seems conceivable that our conception of an effort may so represent effort in us as to be mistaken for it; in other words, that we may have the feeling of effort without actual effort, the feeling being conclusive only of its own existence, and not of the effort to which the feeling is attributed, as the sensation of material resistance is proof only of the existence of the sensation, and not of the existence of the matter to which we refer it as its cause, or even of any actual resistance whatever. One's consciousness or internal perceptions are the best possible, if not the only, ground of belief to himself, but not to others. One cannot be mistaken as to his own actual consciousness, or his actual sensations, but he may draw erroneous inferences from either.

In this view, I could not, as against any one denying the fact, insist that our consciousness of effort is conclusive proof even that we make effort, much less, the fact of effort being admitted, urge any dicta of consciousness as proof that such effort is either free or not free. Hence, too, I deem your objection to Sir William Hamilton's position, that freedom is directly proved by our consciousness, well founded; but it seems to me that your objection, if not actually too broadly stated, is liable to be so construed. You say, "consciousness tells me what I do or feel. But what I am *able* to do is not a subject of consciousness. Consciousness is not prophetic. We are conscious of what is, not of what will be. We never know that we are able to do a thing except from having done it, or something equal and similar to it."

In regard to that for which effort is made, it may be true that we can only know or judge of the probability of our actually doing it by our experience in similar cases. But, if the effort itself is the thing to be done, I contend that we must be conscious of our ability to do it, and must have an expectation, a "prophetic" anticipation, that we can or may accomplish that which is the object of the effort, otherwise the effort would not be put forth, and for our first actions we must have these prerequisites prior to experience. I have before given my reasons more fully for the position that the knowledge of a mode of effort, and also that by effort we can move our muscles, must be innate, preceding all experience.[1] If, in this, I am right, the present existence of the knowledge of this *ability* is a matter of consciousness. It is still, however, only a perception of feeling of our being able to move our muscles, and we might yet be mistaken in inferring an actual ability from this perception or feeling of it. Our *knowledge* of this ability, however, whether it conform to the fact or not, is still innate, and a direct revelation of consciousness.

We agree that the mind does make effort, and in discussing those questions of its freedom in which we

[1] *Causation*, page 16.

differ, I shall endeavor to postulate nothing from consciousness which you will not admit.

You have adopted a position which seems to be a common one on both sides of the controversy; viz., that freedom in any act of will requires that we should, at the time of willing, be able to will the contrary. This raises the question, are we thus able? And as both parties agree in bringing this to the test of consciousness, I will consider it here, deferring for the moment the question of our ability to begin action, to which I was about to apply the foregoing views.

As against Sir William Hamilton's inferring freedom directly from consciousness, you say, "To be conscious of free will, must mean to be conscious before I have decided that I am able to decide either way." I would say that, to be conscious of free will must mean to be conscious, before I have decided that it is I that am to decide; that I am to determine my own act of will at my own pleasure, or as on examination I shall find will suit me best. The case you state, whether one will prefer to murder or not to murder, does not raise the question of freedom in willing, but only of preferring or choosing, which, though heretofore held to be the same as willing, you agree with me is something entirely different. The willing to murder is just as free as the willing not to murder, and the only question touching the freedom of the willing is the same in either case; viz., Does the being as he is, good or bad, himself determine to make the effort to murder, or not to make it? Whether he determine to make, or not to make, may indicate what his character is, but has no bearing upon the question of his freedom. As the relations of *character* to freedom will hereafter be considered, I will not here comment upon them.

Your analysis of the phenomena of consciousness, and of the manner in which, through it, the belief in an ability "to do or abstain," or to do "the other way," as you state it, but which is often stated as an ability to "do the contrary," is induced, does not conflict with my positions, but is in accord with them.

That this ability to "do the contrary" is essential to freedom, seems also to have been reached through a logical error in this wise. Freedom and Necessity being assumed to be directly opposed, the one of necessity excluding the other, it follows that the freedom of an act requires that it should not be of necessity; and then, as necessity implies that which must be and cannot be otherwise, it becomes essential to the freedom of an act of will that it could be otherwise, which, as between it and not acting, or between it and any other contemplated act, is to say it could be the contrary. It is hardly necessary to urge that the conclusion is vitiated by using the term necessity in two different senses. So far is it from being true, that to be free in willing one must be able to will the contrary, that if it could be proved that an effort could be otherwise than in conformity to the intent, design, and object of the actor, it would tend to prove him not free in his effort. Our freedom in willing is evinced by our willing to do what we want to do, and it cannot be necessary to this freedom that we should be able even to try to do what we do not want to try to do.

The expression "ability to *do* the contrary," so often used, has a vagueness which is not wholly removed by a change to ability to *will* the contrary. The question, what is the "contrary"? still arises. If the question is only between doing and abstaining, willing or not willing, there is no doubt as to which is "the

CAUSATION AND FREEDOM IN WILLING. 105

other," or what is the "contrary." But, as between positive acts, the "contrary" is not always so clear. Going down stairs is the contrary to going up stairs. If I am already at the foot I cannot go down, but I may go up. But this inability to go up is not a deficiency in the freedom of willing, but of the knowledge of a mode of willing. The inability attaches as much to unfree as to free will. If the willing is free, *i. e.*, if I control and direct my own act of will to the doing of anything, I must know some possible mode of doing it; I must have a plan of action by which to direct my effort to the doing; and if, on the other hand, my act of will is not free, *i. e.*, if it is controlled and directed by some extrinsic intelligent agent, that agent must direct it in conformity to some plan known to it, and in either case the want of the knowledge of a plan renders the act of will impossible. If it be said that this reasoning does not apply to control by unintelligent power, it may be replied that such power, even when exerted without intelligent design, must still conform the willing of the controlled being to some plan of doing the thing, and there being no possible plan of going down stairs from the bottom, such conforming is impossible. It is not a question of power, for infinite power could not overcome the difficulty.

Reducing the case to its lowest terms, if the actual willing is a free willing, then the freedom to will the contrary would be a freedom to will unfreely; and to assert that the mind is not free because it has not the liberty to be unfree, or because it cannot be otherwise than free, is the sophism to which I have heretofore reduced some of the necessitarian arguments, and upon which I need not now comment. Under my definition, the freedom to will the contrary of an actual free act would be freedom to will counter to one's own control or direction, which, again, would be a freedom to be unfree; and the position is here again reducible to the same sophism and absurdity as the more radical case of it just stated.

Returning, now, to the question of our ability to begin action, I think it will be admitted that we are at times unconscious of effort; and if, as I have endeavored to show, the existence of an effort involves the consciousness of it, it follows that at such times we really are inert, — that, in fact, we sometimes are in a passive condition. And, in reference to the mind's ability to put forth its power, and begin effort in the absence of all other causative power or force, and of course when no other such power or force is acting upon it, I suggest this case: Suppose one, while in an unconscious and consequently passive state, to be taken by a tornado into an unknown forest where everything was wholly passive, and that the last effect of the tornado, or the effect of its ceasing to exist, was to awaken him from the unconscious to a conscious state, in which he felt hungry or lonely, can it be doubted that he could immediately make effort to pluck any fruit in sight, or to get out of the uninhabited district? It will be borne in mind that his perception of the conditions is passive, and that in the premises there is no power to act upon him prior to his own acting, and hence, unless he can thus begin action, everything must there remain passive until the ingress of some other power.

Strictly speaking, there is perhaps no difficulty in conceiving an absolute beginning of action, the real difficulty lying in conceiving of the creation, or even

CAUSATION AND FREEDOM IN WILLING. 107

the existence of anything to act, before there has been any action to produce it. However this may be, there is no difficulty in conceiving the beginning of action by each individual intelligence after it comes to exist, nor of the beginning of each particular action of such individual. We cannot conceive an absolute beginning of time, but have no difficulty in conceiving of a beginning of any designated portion of it.

In our notions touching the beginning of effort, we are misled by the analogies of material phenomena. When matter is quiescent, it requires the direct application of force to put it in motion. When mind is quiescent, it requires a change in its knowledge — in its perceptions. As a prerequisite of action it must obtain the perception of a sufficient reason for acting; but this, as before stated, it may passively obtain. A conative intelligent being, in virtue of its intelligent perceptions, can design a future effect, and at pleasure apply the power, which, in virtue of its inherent faculty of effort, it possesses in itself, to produce the effect. Having, in itself, all the requisite attributes, it can, of itself, begin action, and stop or change its action to conform to its changing perceptions of future effects, and to any change in its design; while unintelligent matter must be moved by something not itself, and then cannot stop its motion, or change its direction; but for these also requires to be acted upon by something not itself. A combustible material does not stop or change its course to avoid a consuming fire. An intelligent being will, of itself, stop or change its action to avoid painful consequences.

To the action of a being with a faculty of effort, wants demanding effort, and knowledge to apply its effort to the desired ends, no extrinsic or prior application of power or force is requisite, for all that is necessary is, that it should perceive that there is an occasion — a reason — for putting forth its own inherent power. This reason is always the present perception of some desirable result in the future. It is thus isolated from the forces of the past. The past may have made the being what it is, with its knowledge and its wants; but how or when it came to be such a being as it is, has now nothing to do with its power to begin action, or with its freedom in acting. The question is not, how it came to be such a being as it is, but whether, being as it is, it now wills freely, or is capable of self-activity, and of beginning action. Such a being, if created and thrown among the existing conditions at this instant, could immediately begin action — could make effort to change the present, and conform the future to its wants, whether (in the absence of its own effort) it expected that future to be the same as the present, or to be varied by the action of other causative power; in short, could act upon and vary the fixed conditions, or flowing events, to make the future different from what, but for its action, it would be. As to the fixed conditions he could do this if there were no other power in the universe, and, as to the changing or flowing conditions, he could do it though all the other powers in the universe were wholly absorbed in changing the conditions, leaving no extrinsic power to act upon himself, and of course, in either case, there is no power to control, or even to act upon the being thus making the effort, and he must, therefore, act of himself, and so acting, without being in any wise acted upon, act freely.

Nor could it make any difference when the existence of the conditions commenced, or whether they ever had any commencement; whether they have existed in their present or in some other form from all eternity, or are the immediate creation of the instant, constituting, with the like instantaneous creation of the conative intelligence, an absolute commencement of creation, having no past. The question as to action is still the same. What, under these conditions, as they now actually are, is the active being, with its existing knowledge and want, to do or attempt to do? In either case, the power of such being to change, or to attempt to change, the existing conditions, is the same.

It may be objected, that we have no experience in regard to action in the supposed cases of the creation at the instant of action, either of the active agent, or of the conditions to be acted upon, or of both; but even if this is true, such hypothesis would still be allowable to eliminate the accidental phenomena and associations from the essential elements of volition, as in demonstrating a property common to all triangles we eliminate, in our reasoning, all the conditions except those which belong to all figures with three sides, and reason exclusively from these. But, as before shown, on every occasion for action there is some change, either in the knowledge or wants of the active agent, or in the conditions to be acted upon, and with every change, whether effected by the past, by the power and forces of the past, or by any other cause whatever, or by no cause, the aggregate existence regarded as an entirety, is, at the instant of change, a new and immediate creation, in which the intelligent being finds himself suddenly placed, and often under circumstances wholly unexpected, but still is ever ready to put forth his inherent power of effort, if in the conditions of this new creation he perceives a reason for so doing. Every intelligent being has, in fact, continually to adapt its efforts to the various circumstances of the new creation of each instant, and in so doing meets with no compulsion or constraint. He may always freely try to do, though he may not always have power to do. Though at each instant there cannot be an absolute commencement of creation, there is in each a commencement of a new creation, and if, at any one instant, all the causative powers and forces, which brought about the then existing conditions, should cease to be, having just introduced, as their last effect, one single conative being, this one could still put forth effort to change the quiescent conditions, and conform them to his want. The effort, in such case, is a *beginning* of the exercise of power. In the quiescent phenomena, and in the mind's perceptions of them and of the requisite changes in them, there is no power, but only subjects upon which to exert it, and passive perception of desirable objects to be obtained by its being exerted. For these the mind puts forth its effort, and doing this in the absence of any power to act upon it, manifests its own power of self-action — of acting as an originating first cause.

If, instead of all the other causative powers ceasing to be, we suppose them to continue active, but in such manner as not to affect the action of the particular conative being, the result is the same. He must then act of himself upon his own perceptions of a reason for acting, and without being first acted upon by any extrinsic power.

It cannot be said by the advocates of the controlling power of the past, that this hypothesis of the non-influence of existing causes is either inconceivable or inadmissible; for, if they contend that the volition of the being is at any and every instant the effect of the *whole* past, then, as the whole past is the same to all, the volition of every being would be the same at the same instant;[1] and if, to avoid this consequence of their assertions of a causative power in the past, and of the necessary uniformity of causation, they say that the whole past does not act upon each individual, then they admit that portions of the past may not affect the volition of this individual being; and if portions may be dispensed with, it is conceivable that any and every portion may be so eliminated; and, further, that nothing of the past of *necessity* affects the volition of any particular being, and hence, such being may act uninfluenced by these past conditions. Upon the efforts of the being to make his way out of the forest, into which he had been hurled by a tornado, the changes originating in the past, such as the present growing of the trees, or the motion of the foliage, may have no influence, and all such changing elements being eliminated, he, as he now exists, with his knowledge and his wants, acts as a sole agent of change upon his own perceptions of the passive conditions of the present, and without the appliance of any extrinsic power of the past or present.

Having in himself a faculty of effort, and the knowledge of a mode of directing his effort to a desirable result, he himself puts forth and directs his effort; and it is of no consequence how or when he acquired this faculty and this knowledge, or whether to them there has been any past. It is sufficient that he now has them.

[1] For a more general statement of this position, see *Causation*, page 43.

In the cases of instinctive action, the being is created with the knowledge of the mode of action, and has not acquired it by any experience in the past. It need not know, and probably does not know, that the conditions upon which it first acts had any existence prior to its own, and so far as its action is concerned, there is no necessity that they should have had any prior existence whatever. Their *present* existence is all that is essential to their being acted upon; as the present existence of the being with its faculty of effort, its want of change, and the knowledge of a mode of directing its effort to produce the change, are all that is essential to his acting upon them. The same is evidently true in all other cases of action. Whether the faculty of effort, the knowledge by which it is directed, and the want, are any or all of them innate or acquired, or whether they existed in the past, or not till the instant of the effort, can make no difference to the freedom of the being in the effort.

It is not, then, necessary to a volition that the active being should have had a prior existence, or that, so far as the being and the existing conditions are concerned, there should have been any past — their immediate creation at the instant serving equally well for all the purposes of voluntary action.

Nor does it matter by what power or cause the present existing conditions have been, or are brought about, whether by the effort of the actor or other intelligent power, by matter in motion, by some mysterious power of "the past," or as the last result of a continuous series of antecedents and consequents in a chain of causes and effects. The prior cause of the existence of the present conditions does not, in any respect, vary their power, or give them any power to produce or hinder a volition. The intelligent being acts neither more nor less freely upon the existing conditions as they are, under any one of these hypotheses, than under any other of them, and, in fact, really acts upon them without any reference whatever to their causes, and just as freely as if there never had been any prior cause of their existence; but they had either existed from all eternity, without any beginning or any coming into existence, or had, at this instant, begun to be without any cause. He has no occasion whatever, in deciding his action, to take into account what has been in the past, but only what, in view of the *present*, will be in the future, or what may be expected. He acts entirely upon his present expectations, and looks to the past, or rather to his present memory of the past, only to increase his knowledge, and form more accurate expectations. It may be said that the knowledge of the past causes of the present conditions enters into, and becomes the possession or attribute of the being that is to act upon them, and that his action is influenced by this knowledge. The consideration of any such influence belongs to our third category. The fact, however, is, that even the most intelligent finite being generally knows very little of the causes in the past which have produced the present, and for the purpose of determining his own actions, seeks to divine them only to increase his knowledge, and enable him more certainly to foresee the future, and to avoid mistakes in his action. But were these causes ever so well known, that fact has no bearing upon the question of the ability of the being to begin action; for, as before suggested, he might have this same knowledge at the instant of his creation without there having been any past, and his action would be just the same as if it had been acquired by past experience. It is his *present knowledge* of the relation of his action to the future effort, and not the knowledge of past relations, that he acts upon. Though in the past he may have acquired the knowledge which enables him more correctly to judge as to what the future will be, he is, in the present act of will, with this acquired power of divining the future, entirely isolated from that past. So far as his present action is concerned, the whole past has culminated, and been concentrated in the knowledge (including that of the existing conditions) which has now become the possession or attribute of the knowing being, and not the possession or attribute of the past. Neither the past nor the things or events of the past can know, or could, in the present, use knowledge to direct a volition, as to the future, in itself, or in anything else.

It appears, then, that, to each individual, it makes no difference whether the course of events, or the future conditions which would obtain in the absence of his own action, will be produced by intelligent or material causes, or by the absence of all causes of change. He is only interested in knowing what they would be, and by what means he can, by his own action, make such differences in the future events and conditions as he deems desirable. With this knowledge, and an inherent faculty of activity, he can act independently of any other power or force, and resist or coöperate with any others, and if he, with such knowledge and faculty of action, and also the conditions to be acted upon, were the immediate creation of the instant, and had no past, he could still immediately begin action, and put forth effort to change the conditions. If

CAUSATION AND FREEDOM IN WILLING. 115

there were no other power in existence, he could make effort to change the existing passive conditions, and, if there were other powers, he could himself conform his own action to the expected results of these coexisting causes of change without being first acted upon by them, and even though all other past causation had been wholly exhausted in producing the extrinsic conditions, and without any action upon himself, except such change in his knowledge as would result from the changed conditions.

This power to begin action is the peculiar attribute of an intelligent being, with a faculty of effort, and with wants demanding effort. It is an immediate consequence of the fact that a being, having such faculty of effort, intelligence to perceive an object of effort, and to direct its effort to that object, or rather, with a view to that object (for the degree of sagacity with which it does it has no bearing upon the question of its ability to make, or of its freedom in making the effort), has in itself all that is essential to action, and let it have come into existence when and how it may, can now of itself act upon any existing conditions, wholly independently of any powers which brought it into existence, or of any other power past or present; and the past, as such, has no necessary relation to its present ability to make and direct its own effort. By means of its intelligence — its perceptions at the moment — it uses and directs its inherent power by effort to produce such future change, as in its view of the existing conditions it deems desirable. All experience attests that the moment we perceive a mode of effecting change, combined with a sufficient reason for adopting it, we are ready to make effort, requiring no prior action of power or force upon us to change us from the passive to the active state; but only that in the present conditions we shall perceive a sufficient reason, now existing, for putting forth our power to affect the future.

It is in view of this power to begin acting, and not as a *first actor*, that I regard every being that wills as a " creative first cause," and hold that the future is always the composite effect — the joint creation — of all these first causes, acting upon such fixed material as there may be to act upon, and modifying any necessary results of matter in motion.[1]

It may perhaps be said that even admitting that a conative intelligent being is thus independent of any exercise of power in the past, — can thus begin action, — still, that it does so is now the very thing to be accounted for — that the exercise of its inherent power is an event which now begins to be, for the existence and manner of existence of which there must be some cause. That though the volition or causative action may account for the existence of other phenomena, and for their being as they are, and not otherwise, its existence does not account for itself, nor for its being as it is, and not otherwise. To account for anything is to ascertain the cause of its being, and for its being as it is. It is unfortunate that in this connection the

---

[1] It is from not recognizing this power of mind to begin action, that Sir William Hamilton gets into all his difficulties, in regard to the alternative of "an absolute commencement" on the one hand, and "an infinite regress, a chain of causation going back to all eternity," on the other. The argument from this assumed necessity of an infinite regress, or an absolute commencement, is used by Edwards as especially applied to volition, and also generally as involved in the law of cause and effect, or the necessity of a causal antecedent to every event. I have endeavored to point out the fallacies involved in his application of it in both these modes. See *Freedom of Mind in Willing*, Book II.

CAUSATION AND FREEDOM IN WILLING. 117

word *cause* is used to designate both the action of a power which makes or compels the existence of the event or thing, and also the perception of beneficial result, which is not itself power, but merely the reason why an intelligent being puts forth or exerts its power to bring an event or thing into existence. The facts and their relations, which are perceived, have in themselves no power. They might have existed unperceived for any length of time, and in connection with all other contemporary circumstances, without producing, or having any tendency to produce, any effect or change, and certainly could produce no volition in a being which did not recognize them. This added circumstance of recognition, this *perception* of the existing facts and their relations, has not, in itself, nor when combined with the other circumstances, any actual substantive power. This inheres in, and is put forth or exerted, not by the circumstances, nor by the perception of them, nor by the reason perceived, nor by any combination of these elements, but by the perceiving being, which, as a *self-active power*, does not require the previous exercise of power upon it, but only that it shall perceive that the present or expected conditions admit of desirable changes, which, in its view, are a sufficient reason, or offer a sufficient inducement, to put forth its power by effort to effect these changes.

Matter in motion being the only known means by which the effects of causative power are extended, either in time or space, it is through such motion that we seek to connect any motion or change in that which cannot move itself with a self-active or originating cause; and, as intelligent being, with a faculty of effort, is the only self-active or originating power known to us, we seek to trace back any such motion or change to the exercise of this power, and having done this, there is no further inquiry as to what power produced the phenomenon. A volition or effort differs from the phenomena, which we thus trace back to their primary cause, in being itself the exercise of the power, or its immediate manifestation in action. It is that particular state of the existence of the being in which it acts as power, and is embraced in that existence without any connecting link; and hence no tracing through such link in the case of volition is possible. We have accounted for the motion or change by tracing it to the exercise of a self-active, self-directing, originating, or first cause; and no longer look for its antecedent power, or for the power of this power, though we may still seek a solution of the very different questions as to how this power came to exist, or under what conditions it exists, or is productive of effects.

To the first of these, how intelligence, as manifested in a conative being, or otherwise came to exist, no intelligible answer has yet been given. The conditions of its existence are knowledge and feeling combined with a faculty of effort, all these being essential to the exercise of its power by effort. When we seek to account for the action of such being, we do not look for any extrinsic power that makes the effort or compels and gives direction to it, but we seek the reason which the being itself passively perceived for putting forth its own power, and this perception of a sufficient reason, which is the only prerequisite of its effort, is as distinct from power or effort, as the sensation of vision is from its object. When we find that the being had a want, and perceived that by effort he could gratify that want, we have found the elements of this sufficient reason. There was no power in these elements, singly or combined, and power here commences — begins to be — without previous power to cause it to begin to be. With want and knowledge, both in themselves passive and incapable of effort, or of manifesting power in any way, the intrinsic potentiality is developed, genetic power is evolved, and action begins to be.

We trace back a river towards its source, and find each portion of it preceded by what is also a portion of a river, and which, in its flow, makes the succeeding portion, but at length come to where the supply of water is no longer from a section of the river; and continuing the regressive examination, we find that the action of heat, a thing entirely different from a river, is among the essential antecedents of its existence. So, too, tracing back any change in matter, we may find that each successive phenomenon has, for many steps, been caused by antecedent motion of matter; but at length we come to where the antecedent is not a movement of matter, but a volition or effort, and continuing *this* regressive examination, find that knowledge and want, or rather the perception of reasons founded upon them, are among the prerequisites of the volition or effort, and all these prerequisites being wholly passive, with no element of action, are as different from volition as the heat of the sun is from the water of the river; but by this combination of intelligence with a faculty of effort, activity is generated directly from passivity, without the necessity of any prior action of power upon the combined elements which characterize the conative being.

The views now presented, I trust, are sufficient to establish the ability of the mind of itself to begin action without the application to it of any prior power or force constraining or compelling it to act; but, be this as it may, I presume it will, at least, be admitted that neither the Past, nor any causative Powers or Forces in the past, *directly* act upon the mind in the present, causing or compelling it to act, and to act in a particular manner; but that the Past and its causative agencies only *indirectly* affect the mind's action, by having already changed either the mind itself, or the conditions upon which it is to act; thus changing the elements in the relations of which the mind perceives the reasons and inducement for effort, and for the particular effort which it puts forth.

It is in these external and internal conditions, and the inducements which grow out of their relations, that, admitting that the mind does determine its own action, you find a power or *influence* which determines it to determine. This word *influence*, perhaps, occasions as much confusion, and underlies as much fallacy, as any one used in this discussion, *cause* and *choice* excepted. Like cause, it is applied to power itself, and also to the perception by a sentient being of a reason for exerting its power; neither the perception nor the reason perceived being in themselves power. As distinguished from the actual appliance of power, influence always implies the mind's perception of a reason. It is admitted that any changes made in the conditions in the past may vary the mind's perception, but such perception or reason being but a form of knowledge, the consideration of its effect on the freedom of the mind's effort will properly come under our third category, and leave us, in the second, only to consider the *power* of external conditions to produce, control, or determine the mind's effort; or to control or determine it in its own act of determining ; or in any wise to interfere with its freedom in acting.

If the external conditions have such controlling power, then, it must be admitted that the mind, in its action, is controlled by something which is not itself, and is, therefore, not self-controlled, and not free in its action. This is the question involved in our second category.

The first difficulty in arguing this point is that of fixing upon any conceivable mode in which these external conditions (the influence which belongs to the mind's perception or knowledge of them, and not to the conditions themselves being excluded) can act upon the will itself, or so act upon the mind that wills as to control its action, or in any way interfere with its freedom in effort.

Some conception or idea of what is asserted is essential either to sustaining or refuting it.

It cannot be intended to assert that some *particular kind* of extrinsic conditions prevent free action, while others do not, for this would, in some cases, admit the freedom which is wholly denied as impossible. The assertion, then, must be, that the mere existence of conditions of any kind excludes freedom. The position seems to be, that as the mind must conform its efforts for change to the conditions to be changed, those conditions do control and determine its efforts; and, conditions to be changed being always prerequisites of the mind's effort, it is always thus controlled and determined by them, and the mind being so controlled in its effort by something extrinsic to itself, is not free in its effort. The argument assumes that the action is invariably conformed to the existing conditions, and that the conditions or subjects to be acted upon, control and determine the action of the agent that acts upon them.

If only unintelligent external conditions and the intelligent active agent are taken into consideration, and the control of the volition must be attributed to the one or the other of these two, it would be more rational to attribute it to that which wants change, or which can perceive the relation of its effort to the expected effect, and of that effect to its want, than to the conditions *which resist the change* for which the effort is put forth, and which cannot know the want nor the changes required for its gratification, nor the effort fitted to produce them; in short, to attribute the effort for change to that which desires change and knows how to effect it, rather than to that which resists change and does not know. The external conditions are related to the mind's effort only as objects to be acted upon, and altered by the effort. To say that they cause the volition, is to say that what resists, and is to be overcome, causes the effort which overcomes it; and the word *cause* is thus applied, not to that which has *power to change*, but to that which is *to be changed*. The power to act is attributed to the passivity to be acted upon, and the passive subject of the action is deemed the active cause.

It is essential to the gratification of the want of the actor that certain changes should be effected in these conditions; but this does not imply any *power* in the conditions to act upon, and produce, control, or direct the effort of the actor, any more than it does to directly act upon and change themselves without any such intermediate effort. We can, *at least*, as well conceive of their acting directly upon themselves as upon anything which is extrinsic to them. The per-

CAUSATION AND FREEDOM IN WILLING. 123

ception by the active being that the change is essential to his gratification, is to him a *reason* for acting; and from the vague manner in which reason and cause are used as interchangeable terms, and the further confounding of the conditions with the mind's perceptions regarding them, the conditions are loosely and improperly said to be the causes instead of the objects of the effort, to which they have no other relation than that which arises from their being the things to be acted on and changed. In these changes, but more especially in the *efforts* for these changes, the conditions are the passive subjects, not the active agents. In the phenomena of effort it is necessary that conditions to be acted upon and changed should exist, but not that these conditions should act, or have any power or force. Effort is itself the exercise of power, and is in no sense the effect or consequence of power exerted. Whatever makes the effort exerts or puts forth the power, and this exercise of power cannot be by one being or thing and the effort by another, for this exercise of power and the effort are one and the same thing.

The conditions external to the mind do not act its will, do not make effort, nor do they act the mind to act the will, nor directly move the mind to will. The direct action of the material external conditions can only be by means of impinging bodies in motion, and neither the mind nor its effort can be the immediate subjects of such action. The mind's effort may be conformed to these external conditions; but such a conforming can only imply that the effort will be such as is required, by the existing conditions, to produce the desired result in the future; and what this result is, the conditions, being unintelligent, cannot know, nor, if knowing, could they devise a mode of action by which to reach it.

Even if there are among the external conditions intelligent agents knowing all the conditions and the result desired by the active being, and also the effort required to produce that result, there is still no known means by which such agent could directly act upon the will of another, or move or act the mind of another to move or act. All such direct action upon the *Will*, by any agency whatever, implies that it is a distinct entity to be acted upon, and not the mere state of something acting; and if an effort could be produced in this way, it would be the effort of the agency producing it. If the effort in my mind is by myself, it is my effort; if it were by some other intelligent agent, it would be his effort, and if by some material thing, it would be its effort. The latter hypothesis needs no comment.

If the effort in my mind is produced by another mind, it must be by the action, *i. e.*, by the effort of this other mind, and the hypothesis involves all the difficulties of self-originating effort (with the alternative of an infinite series of extrinsic efforts); and in addition thereto, the further difficulty of conceiving of some mode in which the effort of one mind can directly produce effort in another, of which mode we have no experience or knowledge, nor do we ever make effort to make the effort of others, or to directly vary the efforts which others will make; but we always do this indirectly, by changing the knowledge of those whose efforts we would influence, and this again we always do by some change in the material conditions of which both parties have a common cognition. This use of material phenomena to change the knowledge upon which the action depends, may be one reason why the action is so generally supposed to be controlled by these phenomena. But, though our knowledge is so dependent upon the extrinsic conditions that change is produced in the former by changing the latter, still, the actual conditions, be they mere change of sensations or otherwise, and the mind's perception of them, are two entirely distinct and different things, and the influence of this perception or knowledge upon the mind's freedom we are to consider hereafter.

It may be said that the present conditions were made as they are by causative powers of change in the past, and action, in conformity to the particular conditions thus created, must also be determined with the conditions. This assumes either that the mere fact of change in the conditions, or the changed conditions themselves, are incompatible with freedom. The former, I presume, will not be asserted, and in regard to the latter, the argument on this point for necessity generally, as drawn from the influence of conditions, has already assumed that the influence attaches alike to all conditions. The nature of these conditions can make no difference to the freedom of the intelligent agent acting upon them, for it is obvious that the mind can act as freely in regard to any one set of them as to any other, or rather in regard to that expectation of the future which it infers from one set of conditions as from that inferred from any other set; and, hence, the power in the past or present to change the conditions to be acted upon, does not imply any power to interfere with the freedom of the actor.

It is of no consequence whether the conditions to be acted upon — things or events — are the creation of the instant, or are in any sense the product of the past. The expectation in regard to the *future*, which arises from the *present* existing conditions, is all that concerns the being in its efforts in relation to them. The events or changes produced by physical agencies (if any such) are of necessity, and must be, if not interfered with, in a certain fixed order of succession, and *this order* may be regarded as a portion of the external conditions to be acted upon, and changed by intelligent causes which alone have power to interfere with and change it.

In reference to action, however, such events and changes differ from those produced by intelligence only in the degree of certainty with which we can anticipate them, and this same difference obtains between the actions of an intelligent being whose character or habit inspires us with confidence as to his action, and one either unknown or known to be erratic. In this respect it, then, makes no difference whether the uniformity of nature arises from the necessitated action of blind forces which cannot change, or from the free action of a supremely wise and powerful intelligence which does not vary its design, nor fail to effect what it designs.

If all the existing conditions external to a conative intelligence are inert and powerless, then there is a positive expectation that the immediate future conditions will be the same as the present, with only such changes as this conative intelligence may itself produce; and in this case there is no extrinsic power to control or direct its effort, which must therefore be self-controlled, self-directed, and free.

If there are other existing powers of change, the conative being still acts upon its perceptions or ex-

CAUSATION AND FREEDOM IN WILLING. 127

pectations of what, with this added element, the future, without, and with its own effort, would become, and in doing this as freely directs his action to produce the result he desires, as when acting upon the more certain expectation which he had when he was himself the only power of change. He acts as freely, though not, perhaps, as confidently, in the one case as in the other.

The whole argument for the controlling power of the conditions is founded upon the assumption that the volition must vary with, and conform to, any changes in them.

That the mind's action, under one set of conditions, is different from what it would be under another set, or that it conforms its action to them, cannot argue any want of self-control or of freedom, for this adaptation of its action to the conditions is just what would be expected of a self-controlled, intelligent being knowing the conditions; and, on the other hand, action without reference to the existing conditions would indicate a necessitated, blind, or unintelligent movement.

The very thing supposed to be freely done, is that the mind determines, in view of the circumstances, of which it is cognizant, and not that it determines in view of any other, or without reference to any circumstances whatever. The object of the conative intelligence being to effect a certain change in the future, the change it wants, and the means of effecting it, will both depend upon what the conditions now are, and hence its efforts, if free, will vary with these conditions, and acting with this reference and consequent conformity to them, would not indicate any want of freedom in the actor. If, then, it were true that the effort is always conformed to the external conditions, it would not prove that the conditions control the effort, but rather that the intelligent being controls and conforms its effort to the conditions.

But the assumption of this conformity, from which the controlling power of the conditions is inferred, is not warranted by the facts.

What is meant by the volition or internal effort being thus conformed to the external conditions? There are no particular internal efforts which can be said to fit certain external conditions. We cannot say that the effort to move the hand up or down, or horizontally, or any other particular effort, especially fits or is adapted to a bonfire, or any other specific external condition, or even to any combination of such conditions. There is no such conformity in fact. The apparent conformity arises from the uniformity of like effort to like conditions.

It would be more nearly true to say that the effort is conformed, not to the conditions, but to the mind's perception or view of them. When the view varies from the actual conditions, the effort is always conformed to the *view*, and not to the conditions. We know this not only by our own experience, but by the narrated experience of others. People often account for their mistakes in action by saying that their view or knowledge of the conditions was erroneous or deficient, — did not conform to the actual conditions. Strictly speaking, however, the conformity is not to the actual conditions, nor to the mind's view of them. but to the mind's perception of the mode of acting upon the existing conditions so as to produce the future effect which it desires. This is the only conformity or fitness in the case; and this, with the same extrinsic conditions, may vary with each individual, and with the same individual at different times. If, then, in the supposed conformity of the effort to the conditions there was any reason for inferring a control of the effort by the conditions, then, upon this altered statement of the facts, this control should now be transferred to the mind's perception or knowledge of a mode of attaining its objects; and this again carries the case to our third category, which we will now examine.

It is urged by the advocates of necessity that the volitions are, and must be, in accordance with the disposition, inclination, desires, and habits, and, being thus necessitated, are not, and cannot be, free. This is substantially your position, except that you disclaim the knowledge of "any must in the case, any necessity other than the unconditional universality of the fact." You say the necessitarians "affirm, as a truth of experience, that volitions do, in point of fact, follow determinate moral antecedents with the same uniformity and (when we have sufficient knowledge of the circumstances) with the same certainty as physical effects follow their physical causes. These moral antecedents are desires, aversions, habits, and dispositions combined with outward circumstances suited to call these internal incentives into action. All these again are the effect of causes, those of them which are mental being consequences of education, and other moral and physical influences. This is what necessitarians affirm."

Upon your statement, that "volitions follow determinate moral antecedents with the same uniformity and . . . with the same certainty as physical effects follow their physical causes," I would remark, in passing, that I have already raised the question as to the existence of any physical causes, and that upon my view the comparison you have here instituted is merely that of the uniformity of the action of the Supreme Intelligence as compared with our own. I have also essayed a demonstration, that the outward circumstances cannot, of themselves, exert any power to control the will; and the same reasoning will serve to show that they acquire no such power by combination with desires, dispositions, or anything else; that it is not in any case the outward circumstances, but the mind's own view of them (its knowledge) which alone has place in the perceptions by which its action is determined. The expression, " moral antecedents combined with outward circumstances," is then equivalent to moral antecedents combined with knowledge. This, I trust, will become obvious as I proceed, as also that the "moral antecedents" you allude to are all either modes of want or of knowledge, reducing all the influence which you attribute to the combination of "moral antecedents" with "outward circumstances," to that of want and knowledge.

These outward circumstances may vary the *effect* of volition, but, of themselves, have no bearing whatever upon what the volition will be, the mind's *knowledge of them*, which has such bearing, being something entirely different and distinct from the outward circumstances. That in the way in which I would walk there is an impassable barrier that I know not of, has no influence upon my willing to walk that way, though it may prevent my walking as I willed. That I know there is an impassable barrier may prevent my willing to walk that way, even though there is in fact no such barrier. It is the *knowledge*, not the outward circum-

CAUSATION AND FREEDOM IN WILLING. 131

stances, which influences the mind in its willing. The moral antecedents mentioned are merely characteristics of intelligent beings, varying more or less in different individuals, but in each making up its character. The character of a being is simply that which constitutes it what it is, and distinguishes it from what it is not. A being or thing with no properties, no character, would be no particular being or thing; matter, with no extension, would be no matter; and being, with no attributes, would be no being; intelligent being, with no knowledge, would not be intelligent being; conative being, without a faculty of effort, would not be conative being; no conception of such existences is possible, and any expression, definition, or description of them must be absurd and contradictory.

The character is thus practically inseparable from the being as it is; and any hypothetical separation of its characteristics, if total, involves the annihilation of the distinctive being, merging its substratum (if any) in the generic existence from which its peculiar characteristics had individuated it, and if partial, its conversion into a different being, with some of the same elements in it. But, in the question of effort, we have to do with the being as *he is* at the time of the effort; and his character constituting him what *he is*, any influence of the character is in fact the influence of the being, thus constituted and thus distinguished, from all other existence.

It may be urged that this character of the being, to which his actions correspond, has been made by the events of the past, including his own efforts, and that this has been the case at every stage of his progress. But it is not the *past*, but the *present* character to which the action is conformed; and how or when this was formed can make no possible difference to the present action : whether it has grown up slowly, under his observation, with or without his agency, or has fallen suddenly upon him from the clouds ready made, is not material ; the action which now conforms to it must still be the same. The doctrine of freedom does not assert that the willing being makes the conditions, external or internal, upon or under which he is to act, but admits that, in determining his own effort, he has reference to these conditions, be they what they may. If his own effort has *heretofore* had anything to do with the formation of his character — has in any way modified it — it may *now* do the same, and he may so change his character at this instant that his action, conforming to the change, will be different from what the previous course of events would have produced.

I have heretofore noted that the process by which we determine our effort is the same as that by which we change our characters. That, in both cases, it is by adding to our knowledge, and, hence, the two may be simultaneous ; and this interference with the chain of causation, reaching from the past (material or spiritual) by a new power thus instantaneously thrown in by a present effort, I hold to be a peculiar characteristic of volition, constituting the intelligent actor an independent, self-active power, or first cause, in creating the future. He might be such a power, though his general character never changed. He might always act in a manner consistent with such fixed character, and yet act freely. Or, yet further, he might still act with perfect freedom, even though his character were changed every instant by some extrinsic power. At each instant he could still direct his own action, and conform it to his own changed condition, and thus continue to be an independent power, varying in some of its characteristics. Through all his mutations he might retain his self-control, and consequent freedom, in effort; such change in the character of another is just what we often seek to effect when we would improve his general modes of acting; and it is in the ability to do this, by imparting new truth, that we can render the most essential aid to each other. In doing this, we act upon the presumption that the being controls its own efforts, and conforms them to its own views; for if its efforts are controlled by some extrinsic power, then, to change its efforts, we should seek to change the extrinsic power which controls them, and not the being in which they are but the manifested effects of this power.

When, to change the action of another, we change the external conditions upon which he is to act, and produce a corresponding change in his knowledge, we do not thereby usually expect to change his general character, but only his view in the particular case as to what action, under the changed conditions, will suit him best, and very often only as to what, being as he is, will appear to him most expedient. But when we inculcate a new truth, touching the relations of action to duty and happiness, we may so change the general character, that the action upon the same conditions will thereafter be improved, or by inculcating selfish and false notions it may be deteriorated. As types of these two modes we might instance, on one hand, the coarse appliances of power by Tamerlane, Charlemagne, or Napoleon; and on the other, the finer influences of Plato, Howard, and Channing; Archimedes, Galileo, Newton, and other scientists, occupying an intermediate ground. But the question, as between us, does not involve these extreme cases of fixedness of character, nor of incessant changes in its elements by extrinsic agencies. Upon the point that we can change our own characters, we do not differ. The admission of my positions, that change of character is always produced by some change in our knowledge, and that we can acquire knowledge by our own primary efforts, would give a broader significance to your felicitous statement that " we are exactly as capable of making our own character, *if we will*, as others are of making it for us."[1] But to get over the answer to this, which you ascribe to the Owenites, that "these words, 'if we will,' surrender the whole point," I think you must go further, and admit that, in virtue of the inherent attributes of our intelligent, feeling, and active nature, we can act without being first acted upon by any extrinsic power; and that our voluntary efforts are not mere terms, in a series of which each is controlled and determined, and made to be what it is by those which precede it; but that, with each new phase of conditions and circumstances, we determine how we will act in reference to them, and may thus, with every such phase, begin a new series, resolving the whole into particular individuated acts, determined in their succession only by our own intelligent perceptions of their fitness to the occasions as they arise. For if, as you hold, our volitions, like other phenomena, are the "necessary and inevitable" result of antecedent " causes which they uniformly and implicitly obey," then, as our efforts to change our character are dependent upon these prior causes or antecedents, the change of our character by such

[1] *Logic*, Book VI. Chap. II.

CAUSATION AND FREEDOM IN WILLING. 135

efforts is also completely, though secondarily, so dependent. We are thus placed in a current of events in which we have no control over our destiny. It is true we do not merely float passively and self-motionless with this current, — we swim ; but the movements of the limbs, which constitute the swimming, are produced or determined by the current, or by sections of it from behind us, as a part of the means by which the current really controls our course among the flowing events, and are not a self-exerted activity, induced by the intelligent perception of a desirable result to be produced in the future, and which as yet, having no actual extrinsic existence, cannot be an extrinsic power. It, as yet, exists only as an intrinsic expectation. As germane to this portion of this subject, I would remark that I fully agree with you as to the legitimate objects of punishment; but I would make some slight alterations in your statement, to show that it is, at least, as properly resorted to upon the hypothesis of freedom as upon that of necessity ; *e. g.*, when you say, " Punishment proceeds upon the assumption that the *will* is governed by motives," I would say, Punishment proceeds on the assumption that the *being in willing* is governed by motives, or that he governs himself with reference to that expectation of the future result of his willing, which I hold constitutes the *only* motive to intelligent effort. Is it not obvious that prevention by motive is more properly applicable to the conditions of freedom than to those of necessity — to those who control their own actions rather than to those whose actions are controlled by something else? Has not the whole world always acted upon this idea? When a man is supposed to be *possessed by devils*, and cannot control himself, physical restraint is at once resorted to. We do not seek to change his willing, but to prevent his doing what he wills. When one is supposed to be *self-possessed*, and to be able to control his own actions, resort is first had to motive, to the threat of future punishment; and if this does not prevent his willing to do wrong, he is forcibly deprived of the power to *do* the wrong by personal restraint, or, in extreme cases, by the death penalty.

I suppose you would consider the provision for punishing crime as among the past antecedents, making one of the prior links in the chain of cause and effect which determines the act. In harmony with this, you say, *if punishment had no power of acting on the will*, it would be illegitimate. I would regard such provision as one of the conditions which changes the view, knowledge, or *expectation* of the mind as to what the effect of action counter to the law will be. The mere existence of the law has, in itself, no power to determine, or to change the determination of the being. If unknown, it might exist forever without any such effect, or tendency to it. But with the knowledge of its existence among the conditions, the being may itself deem best to vary its action from what it otherwise would be. Changing the conditions, by enacting a penal law, no more interferes with free agency than changing the conditions, by a move on the chess-board, interferes with the freedom of one's opponent in making his move to meet it. The agent, in both cases, must himself determine what, in view of the conditions as they now are, with the new law or the recent move, his own action will be; and he does this just as fully, absolutely, and freely, under the existing conditions, as he would have done under any other conceivable conditions; as freely as if no law had been passed, or he had to move with the pieces on the board in the same position as they were before the last move of his opponent was made.

Upon the hypothesis that volition is but an event which is determined by the prior events of the series, extrinsic or intrinsic, or both, the status and condition of every being, whose existence has had a beginning, must be determined by circumstances over which he has no control; for his first action must have been so determined, and this, in connection with other circumstances, all likewise controlled by their antecedents, must successively predetermine each term of the series. The whole character and condition of the being, as before suggested, would thus depend upon the time at which he was thus dropped into the current of flowing events; if at one instant, it may be predestined to unvaried virtue and happiness, and if the next, to eternal degradation and misery. Upon this phase of the necessitarian argument there is no reason to suppose that so long as the spirit exists it can escape this chain of cause and effect, or to expect that even death will break its links; and hence, having once commenced, it matters not whether it here continues to be the subject of it for an hour or a century. Hence, a metaphysical logical basis is made for the doctrine of election and reprobation, including that of infant damnation.

That this necessitarian view, that all events, including volitions, are in a chain of cause and effect, in which each successive link is forged and fashioned by those which precede it, thus logically sustains a doctrine which, however forbidding in its aspect, has been held by good, sincere, and zealous men, including learned divines and intelligent laity, may perhaps be regarded by some as a confirmation of the verity of the position. I confess that, aside from any metaphysical reasoning, I have looked upon this belief as so unnatural and repulsive, so repugnant to all our notions of the goodness, justice, and benevolence which predominate in the universe, that any attempt to reconcile the obvious incompatibility would be hopeless; and, hence, have regarded it as an error, which it was the province of philosophy to expose, and to show how it came to be believed. The specious argument from cause and effect, in some of its aspects, I think, accomplishes this latter object; but I do not see how you can reconcile it with your belief that we can form our own characters, and that the character, or the elements of it, controls our voluntary actions.

In granting this much, it seems to me you surrender the whole ground, for, in making our characters, we virtually, so far, determine all the future volitions which are dependent upon its being what it is, *i. e.*, what we thus make it.

In other places, I have remarked upon our power to change our own characters, and pointed out some of the means which we possess for doing it.[1] I find these in the efforts demanded by the constitutional wants of our spiritual nature, the alternations of its desires for activity and repose, its craving for variety and for progress, and in the fact that our actual physical wants are, in their nature, temporary, leaving intervals demanding no effort for their gratification, in which the mind turns inwardly to itself, and there

[1] *Freedom of Mind in Willing*, Book I. Chap. XIV., and *Language*, p. 95, Houghton, Mifflin & Co.'s edition.

gratifies its desire for activity in the imaginary conception — the ideal creation — of such action as its moral and æsthetic nature require. In this castle-building, the mind may find a pleasurable and improving exercise of its creative powers, in which, freed from the temptations of actual life, from the distractions of sense, and the immediate sway of the bodily appetites and vulgar passions, it decides, disinterestedly, as to what is good, and beautiful, and noble in conduct, and provides itself with ideal cases, to be practically applied as occasions for them arise.

The alternation of desire for repose and activity, and especially as coupled with the want for variety, has a tendency to break in upon the continuity of the succession of events as determined by other causes, and to furnish each mind with occasions for the beginning of new and independent action, and for new series of efforts. But, however important this ability to change one's own character, and its exercise, may be to the happiness of the individual and to the general welfare, it has no bearing upon the freedom of the agent; for, as just stated, he may be just as free if his character is never changed at all, either by himself or by others, though it could hardly so happen that experience in action and in planning it, should not make such addition to his knowledge as would, in fact, change his character.

It may also be observed that, upon the hypothesis of necessity, society loses that incentive to the improvement of its members which arises from the interest it has in their good acting; for if the improved being does not control his own action, there is no ground for supposing that his action will be any better for his improvement.

It might, in such case, even be to the interest of society to deteriorate the character of such of its members as are controlled by extrinsic malignant powers or forces. It is not expedient to give the greatest efficiency to the enemy's weapons.

I have before pointed out, generally, that the regarding every event as the necessary and uniform sequence of its antecedents, acting with the uniformity alleged of cause and effect, necessitates the hypothesis of a multiplicity of causes in the beginning; for if we trace back the various series till we get a starting point which is common to all, then, the antecedents being the same to all, the succession of phenomena in all must be the same. Starting with unity, we could thus never get into diversity of being. This applies to the formation of character, as well as to other events.

If, however, a being has in itself a faculty of activity, and the knowledge to exert and direct its action, it is not material to the question in hand what its other characteristics may be, much less how acquired; for though his being good or bad, wise or foolish, may make a great difference as to the design and nature of the efforts made, it makes none as to the freedom of the being in making them. It is obvious that an effort is neither more nor less constrained for being either good or bad in itself, in its design, or in its consequences, or for being put forth by a good or bad being. However such conative beings may be differentiated from each other, they are equally free. A demon is as free as an angel. What object any one will select, *i. e.*, what effect he will try to produce in the future, may depend upon his character; but this does not affect his freedom in trying to do what he selects as the object of his effort; and that his effort

CAUSATION AND FREEDOM IN WILLING. 141

is in conformity to his character, certainly does not indicate that he is not the author and originator of his effort.

A being, one of whose characteristics is, as in the case you state, "that he dreads a departure from virtue more than any personal consequences," is, in fact, virtuous ; and that in action he manifests such virtue — that his action is in conformity to his character — indicates that he directs his own action rather than the reverse. If the acts of a virtuous person, of one " who dreads a departure from virtue more than any personal consequence," were vicious, the inference then would be that he did not direct his own action. If he acts freely, it is impossible that his character and actions should be in opposition, for the voluntary actions are then but indices of the intentions, and it is in the intentions that the essence of virtue inheres. If the person were vicious, the conformity of his action to his vicious character would equally indicate his freedom. Any necessity that there is that the acts or efforts of a virtuous person must be virtuous, is only that which arises from the impossibility of his being both virtuous and vicious at the same time, or in the same act.

Probably no one will contend that the freedom or non-freedom of effort is affected by the cast of the particular characters of the individual actor in these respects.

The necessitarian argument on this point, like that on the influence of the external conditions, is general, asserting that as the effort must in all cases conform to the character, the effort is determined and controlled by the character, and hence is not free.

Your argument virtually asserts that a man's volitions are not free, because he has a character to which they must or do conform. On this ground it can make no difference what the characteristics are by which the being is distinguished. As before stated, some characteristics are essential to its existence as a distinct being, and the argument for necessity is, that the necessary conformity (not to say identity) of volition and character proves that the mind is not free in its willing; and this, in one of its phases, is to assert that if one of the distinguishing characteristics of the being is that it acts freely, then it cannot act freely, because its action must conform to this characteristic; which, again, is to say that the being is not free, because, as constituted, it cannot be otherwise than free. Again, this argument assumes that the character is something distinct from, and extrinsic to, the willing being which it is supposed to determine and control, for otherwise it would prove the self-control and consequent freedom of the being. But, even admitting the necessary conformity as alleged, and yet further that the being and its character may be regarded as two distinct entities extrinsic to each other, the inference of necessity is not legitimate; for, *prima facie*, as already suggested, it is at least as reasonable to infer that the active being conforms its acts to its character, as that the character (which in itself is passive) conforms the acts to itself.

If the being and the character are regarded as one, or the character as the attribute of the being, then this argument of the necessitarians amounts only to an assertion that the acts must, or always will conform to the character of the agent, and "must," or the uniformity expressed by "always will," implying necessity, and necessity excluding freedom, the agent is not free in such acts.

CAUSATION AND FREEDOM IN WILLING. 143

But this invariable conformity of the acts to the character of the active agent is precisely what we would expect if he controlled his own acts, and indicates that he does so control them, and consequently is free in such acts; while, on the other hand, control of the acts by an extrinsic being, power, or force, with a different character, would furnish no ground of presumption that the acts would be conformed to the character of the actor, if the being in which the action was manifested could then be called *the actor*.

That the observed motion in a body was found to be always in conformity to the inclination, desire, or habit of a certain being, would be strong presumptive proof that this being controlled the motion. So, too, if the effort of a being was found to be always in conformity to the inclination, desires, and habits of some being extrinsic to, and differing in these characteristics from that in which the acts occurred, this fact would indicate that the acts were controlled by this extrinsic intelligence. And this conformity of the acts of will to the inclinations, desires, and habits of the actor, which is on all sides admitted, must be regarded as even more conclusively indicating that in these the active being controls its own actions, and especially as no one contends that the acts thus conform to the character of any other being; in which case the control, as between them, might be in question. Taking intention into account, there can no more be discrepancy between the free volitions and the general character of a being than between the aggregate of four groups of four each, and sixteen; for the sum of such volitions must either make up, or precisely represent and indicate the general character, whether it be what, in comparison with others, we would call an inconsistent or a consistent one. The efforts of a man are the exponents and measures of his character. The summation of his efforts and the resultants of his character are equivalents; and if our idea of character is identical with or involves that of what the man will try to do, — if, for instance, our conception of a just man is identical with that of a man who wills to do justice, then all this reasoning to prove the necessary conformity of the volitions to the character, only affirms the truism that the thing is of necessity equal to and like itself. Any necessity in the case is merely the necessity that the action of a being acting freely will not be in contravention to its character; which is merely to say that the *manifestation* of *the being's character in action* will be a *manifestation of the character of that being*, and not a manifestation of a different character, *i. e.*, what is, is as it is, and not as it is not.

The fact, then, that the effort must be, or always is, in conformity to the character, so far from indicating any want of freedom, indicates that the being controls its own efforts, and hence in willing, acts freely.

The foregoing reasoning deals with the character generally, and may serve to show that conformity of the action to it does not indicate any want of self-control or freedom in the actor, but the contrary; and, if so, it fully meets the argument which necessitarians have founded upon this conformity; but the importance which is attached to the argument by philosophers, and the hold which it has upon the popular mind, claims for it a more detailed examination.

The word " disposition " sometimes means the present inclination in the particular case, and sometimes that fixed general character which is formed or indicated by the general course or habit of action.

I have already treated of the conformity of the volition to the character generally, and have remarked that the character may be changed in and by the process by which we determine our actions. Hence, though the action may always conform to the character as it is at the instant, it cannot be said that there is always a general and habitual disposition to which the volition is invariably conformed. It is the variation in particular cases from the general conduct that makes the inconsistencies of character, good or bad, which are universally admitted to exist in most human natures, and which, perhaps of necessity, pertain to all beings neither perfectly wise, nor yet confined in their actions to the purely instinctive modes, the knowledge of which is innate or intuitive.

As applied to the particular occasions of action, dispositions, in common with inclinations and desires, are but modifications of want. Whatever a man has a disposition, inclination, or desire to possess or enjoy, he wants to possess or enjoy. Whatever he is disposed, inclined, or desirous to do, he *wants* to do; though the use of these terms often implies that the want is not so urgent as to overcome conflicting wants and hinderances. They are often used to signify what a man would try to do if he could separate the effect of his effort from some undesirable consequence of it, or if his trying did not prevent some other desirable effort, or interfere with a desirable ease. They do not exclusively apply to the final decision made in view of all conflicting wants and inducements.

In such cases, the use of these terms suggests the various desirable efforts, or objects of effort, among which, by a preliminary examination, we make a selection, or perhaps reject them all, and make no further effort in regard to them, though it might still be said we had a disposition or an inclination to do so. This preliminary examination is always an effort to increase our knowledge, and the conclusion, when reached, is merely the knowledge that, all things considered, it will suit us best to try to do this rather than that, or not to do either. I have before noted that the general or habitual character is liable to be changed by the additions to our knowledge, obtained in these preliminary examinations which we make for the purpose of determining our actions; and would now remark, that the particular inclination or disposition of the occasion is still more obviously liable to be changed in this process. The object of it often is to test the expediency of such change in the existing inclination. That with every new discovery as to the effects of a contemplated effort, or as to what other desirable results may be reached by effort, our inclination as to what effort we will make may also change, is very apparent.

There may be conflicting inclinations, desires, or aversions, among which we must, by the preliminary examination, make our choice. We may also desire what we know that we cannot attain by effort, or loathe what no effort of ours will prevent; and in such case, even though we may have decided as to the relative desirableness of the various objects compared, we still may not desire or choose to make an effort to attain it, which we know or apprehend would not be successful. It is not, then, till the disposition, inclination, and desires have thus culminated in a preference *or choice* to try to do, that they have any immediate relation to the particular action; and choice being the knowledge (or belief) that one thing suits us better than another,

CAUSATION AND FREEDOM IN WILLING. 147

this relation is that of a form of knowledge to action; and their prior relation to action generally was through the knowledge that effort is the mode of gratifying the disposition, inclination, or desire for some change, either directly or by a preliminary effort to attain the knowledge of the particular mode required to do it. By such knowledge, the effort by which we may best gratify our want is determined, and the question between effort and non-effort decided.

Referring to the position that all these characteristics constitute the being, and make it what it is, there is, perhaps, even less appearance of reason to infer necessity from the conformity of action to the separate elements, than was found in such conformity to the general aggregate character. That the present volition, in each particular case, is as the present inclination, is not only indicative of freedom, but is essential to its manifestation; for any deviation from this would imply restraint or coercion, preventing us from doing (trying being in this case the doing) what of ourselves we would do, or compelling us to do what of ourselves we would not do.

The argument of the necessitarians, which has been applied to the whole character, as applied to the elements of which that character is composed, asserts that, as the volition must be in conformity to the disposition, inclination, and desires of the willing being, it is controlled or constrained by this necessity, and hence is not free. Having shown that the final relation of these affections to action is in the form of choice, I may now urge that this argument virtually asserts that, as the effort of a being must of necessity conform to his choice, he is, therefore, necessitated, and not free in his effort. But this conformity to choice, evincing our self-control, is the especial characteristic of freedom. In doing, we do freely when we do as we choose. If walking is the thing to be done, we walk freely when we walk as we choose ; when willing is the thing to be done, we will freely when we will as we choose.

This is, perhaps, the ultimate analysis of those views which, in looking at the subject, often lead one to regard freedom in willing as a truism ; the fact of willing absolutely implying freedom, the opposite position of willing, and yet not willing freely, involving incompatible ideas, and finding expression only in the contradiction of willing when we are unwilling or not willing, and, in such aspect of the subject, it seems to require some logical entanglement before there can be any question or difficulty to be solved or explained. The argument for necessity, thus drawn from the inevitable conformity of effort to choice, is in the same line, and only one step removed from that in which Edwards argues, that a volition cannot be free, because it is subject to the willing agent ; which is to say, it is not free because it cannot be otherwise than free, or is thus subject to the necessity, or constrained to be free. A sophism arising out of the vague, loose, and contradictory ideas, which, in the absence of any definition of it, have obtained in regard to mental freedom, to which I have already several times alluded.

While disposition and cognate terms are often used as indicating the general or formed character, the term *habit* is exclusively so applied, as when we say a man's habits are good, or are bad ; and for this the tendency to persist in habits once formed, which I have endeavored to account for,[1] furnishes good ground.

[1] *Freedom of Mind in Willing*, Chap. XI.

CAUSATION AND FREEDOM IN WILLING. 149

I have shown that the distinguishing characteristic of habitual actions is, that in them we adopt the modes we have previously discovered, thereby saving ourselves the labor and perplexity of the preliminary examination. We thus work by memory, and use the knowledge before acquired, instead of seeking new. The comparative ease of thus working is an inducement to adopt the habitual mode, and is an economy which greatly facilitates us in action. If we find modes still more easy or more beneficial, we adopt them; or when, in our estimation, the chances of finding such more than compensate for the additional effort of seeking them, we make the effort to find them.

Habit is not, then, as some seem to suppose, a mysterious something, which, getting into the mind, becomes there a distinct power or force, inciting, urging, or compelling it to act in a given certain prescribed way, or restraining it in all others, but is itself only a result of a reason perceived by the mind for adopting a course of action which it has before thought out, and which previous experience has made easy, and shown to be attended with satisfactory results. It is only a name for a particular phase of the general relation of knowledge to action. The mind, in such cases, still directs its effort to the object by means of its knowledge of the mode, which, in such cases, being ready formed through memory, can at once be used, relieving the mind of the labor of working out a mode for the particular occasion. The control of volitions attributed to the force of habitual actions, might with as much reason be predicated of customary or imitative actions, in which we adopt certain plans or modes of action, because we have known other people to do

150   CAUSATION AND FREEDOM IN WILLING.

so in like cases ; the only difference being, that in the habitual, we have, in similar circumstances, known ourselves, and in the customary, have known others adopt the mode or plan with satisfactory results.

That such imitation of the actions of others has not been urged against freedom, as well as imitations of our own, is probably due to the fact that the former have always been well understood, while the latter have been involved in doubt and mystery — a fit covert for the fancied extrinsic causative power which is supposed to produce or control our volitions.

The reasons against making the general character, or the elements of it before mentioned, a distinct entity, with power to control the volition of the being which they characterize, will generally apply also to habit, and with this addition. It is not contended that the influence of habit applies to any other than habitual actions. Habit is the result of repetition. The first action of the kind cannot be habitual, the second may be, and when repeated by memory of the former act it is so ; and to make habit, which is itself formed by this repetition of the actions, the cause of the repeated actions is to make the acts collectively the cause of themselves individually, involving the position that the collective cases existed prior to the individual cases, of which they are themselves composed.

I have heretofore shown the influence of habit in intensifying our wants, and in removing the hinderances to our efforts for their gratification.[1] It appears, then, that this conformity of action to the disposition, inclination, desires, or habits, whether they are regarded separately or as combined in the general

[1] *Freedom of Mind in Willing*, Chap. XI.

character, is, in the last analysis, but the conformity of the action of a being to its own notion of what it wants to do, and the manner of doing it, which argues the self-control and consequent freedom of the willing being; and, on the other hand, that any discrepancy of action with the general character of the actor, or with any of the elements of it, would indicate that he did not control his actions, and was, therefore, not free.

On this point, then, the advocates of necessity seem to have taken a position which is against themselves, and would have better sustained their ground if they could have asserted that the volitions are, or may be, in conflict with our dispositions, inclinations, desires, and habits, or with the general character of the agent willing.

The influence of "motive" is much relied upon by the advocates of necessity. I have heretofore [1] pointed out the vicious circle in which this is applied by Edwards, first asserting that the will is determined by that which influences it; next, that everything which influences the will is a motive; and then, that a motive is anything and everything that influences the will.

The illusion generally seems to be in covertly assuming that the word *motive* is itself, or that it represents, some distinct entity, which has power to influence or to determine the mind in willing, and then, without pointing out any such entity, reasoning upon the assumption that motive is a power distinct from the mind that wills.

Some such definition, and inferences from it, seem to have been in Sir William Hamilton's mind, when,

[1] *Freedom of Mind in Willing*, Book II. Chap. X.

in his reply to Reid's assertion that motives are not cause (which I understand you to quote with approbation,)[1] he says, "Can we conceive any act, of which there was not a sufficient cause or concourse of causes, why the man performed it, and no other? If not, call this cause, or these concauses, the *motive*, and there is no longer any dispute."

A change of name cannot alter the facts, or the proper inferences from them. A asserts that stones will appease hunger. B denies this. A replies, but you admit that bread will; now call the bread stones, and there is no longer any dispute. Suppose Reid should grant all Sir William Hamilton demands — that every act has a cause, and that cause should be called motive — and then assert that the active being is itself cause of its action; would there be "no longer a dispute"? Hamilton seems to think it essential to the freedom of the active being that his action or effort should not be directed or determined, either by the being himself, or by anything else, and in seeking for something which will correspond to this expression, or definition of freedom, is really seeking what is self-contradictory; viz., a being acting freely, and yet not controlling its own action. I do not assert that the mind's effort springs into existence contingently, but admit that it always perceives some inducement to make the effort, and have no objection to calling this inducement a motive. I agree with you and with Hamilton, that a motiveless volition is impossible; but I deem it essential to inquire what this motive is, and what its relations to action, before deciding that it conflicts with freedom. In your enumeration of the various influences to volition, in the passage

[1] *Review of Sir William Hamilton*, Chap. XXVI.

I have quoted, you do not use the word *motives*, but you evidently apply the phrase "moral antecedents" as its equivalent, and regard them as constituting the motives. Among these, "desires and aversions" are made prominent. Conformably to this, in your work on Logic, you speak of a *wish* as a motive. Desires and aversions are not distinct entities, having in themselves power for any purpose, but are merely names, indicating certain states of mind; and, if in these states the mind still controls its action, it is then free. The mind's state of desire is only one of the elements, in a combination of things and circumstances, in the perceptions of which, and of their relations, the mind finds a reason for acting, and for the manner of its acting; but no one of these elements, nor any combination of them, can devise the plan of action to reach the desired result, or can act it out when devised. This must be done by the intelligent active being which perceives the reason, and not by the outward conditions, nor by the *states* of the being, nor by any combination of them. To any and all of these, such perception of the reason for the action, and of its fitness to produce the desired effect, is impossible.

I much doubt, however, if desires or aversions, though closely allied to motives as their necessary prerequisites, can themselves be deemed motives. Used, generally, as implying formed subsisting characteristics of the individual, they cannot be so regarded. They might exist for any time without moving or tending to move to action. That a man's character is such that he uniformly desires justice or abhors injustice, cannot, of itself, induce or produce effort. He may also, in the same general sense, and at the *same time*, desire peace and abhor violence, desire beauty and hate deformity, desire nectar and detest tobacco, but could not make effort in all the directions indicated by these multifarious desires and aversions at the same time. In regard to the particular desire or aversion of the time being, one may desire things to remain as they are, and, seeing no liability to change, make no effort; or, desiring change, and seeing that it will be effected without his agency, still put forth no effort. He may desire an aurora, or have an aversion to thunder; but knowing no mode of procuring the one, or of preventing the other, make no effort for either purpose; and until he perceives that he may attain the one or avert the other, he can hardly be said to have any motive to make an effort to attain or avert. In its relation to action, an aversion is equivalent to a desire to avoid the object of aversion. And desire, which, as before observed, is equivalent to want, does not itself produce action, but is one of the passive conditions to which the mind, by means of its intelligence — its knowledge — accommodates its action in seeking to obtain the end desired; and the motive to effort *is always the mind's expectation of the future effect of its effort*, its *knowledge*, or belief, that by effort it will or may produce the result desired.

If the preceding analysis is correct, all the relations of the affections, including disposition, inclination, desires, habits, and motives to effort, are concentrated in knowledge and want. I have before reached the same result in regard to the influence of the external conditions, and, from the nature of the subjects, having been obliged to so far consider these external and internal influences in connection with each other, no separate examination of them in combination is needed.

This, then, brings us to the position you have taken in the argument which I quoted in my letter on "Causation."[1] In the main I accept your statement of my position. As you say, I do "allow that volition requires the previous existence of two things, which the mind itself did not make; at least, not directly, nor in most cases at all — a knowledge and a want." I also "admit, not only that the knowledge and want are conditions precedent to the will, but that the character of the will invariably corresponds to that of the knowledge and want." Though not, perhaps, important, it may be proper for me to say that I would not admit "that any variation in either of these determines, or, at least, is sure to be followed by, a corresponding variation in the volition." If, for instance, I want a metal, and know that copper for my purpose is worth twice as much as tin, and is just as easily obtained, my volition or action would not be altered by learning that it was really worth four times as much. I agree with you, then, that the volition does invariably correspond to the prerequisite knowledge and want; or, more strictly speaking, to the mind's knowledge of the mode of gratifying its want, but differ with you as to this fact being in any way favorable to the argument for necessity, or against that for freedom. Thus agreeing in facts so nearly ultimate, and adopting the definition I have given of liberty, it would seem that there is little room for us to differ, except in the name of the resultant fact. I contend that it is properly called freedom, for the very essence of freedom in effort must lie in a man's not being restrained or constrained in trying to do what he wants done, or wants to try to do, and in his not being prevented or hindered in thus

[1] Page 1.

trying to do, in conformity to his own notion or perception — to his own knowledge, of the most proper mode of doing it.

It would be a very queer sort of freedom by virtue of which a man would or could do, or try to do, what he did not want to do, or to try to do ; or in the exercise of which he would or could adopt some mode of doing, or of trying to do, which did not conform to his own notion or perception of the proper mode — would actually try a mode which he did not want to try. This would indicate a freedom to be not free.

The invariability, here admitted, between the volition and the mind's antecedent knowledge of what it wants, and the means of attaining its object, only indicates that the conative being invariably conforms its effort to its own notion of the mode of attaining its end ; and if in this there is any necessity, it is not a necessity that implies any restraint or control of the active being, but a necessity growing out of the perfect self-control, which is the essential condition of its own freedom — the necessity that free actions must invariably be free.

The act must be so conformed by some cause or power. The only essential elements in the case are the active being with his knowledge of a mode of gratifying his want, and his effort, and the conditions to be acted upon and changed. The questions as to the control of the conditions, intrinsic or extrinsic, intelligent or unintelligent, have already been disposed of. Effort, as before observed, is a state or condition of the mind, and not a thing or entity, with the attribute of power in any form, or which can itself make effort, or that has the knowledge to direct itself, or to direct effort in anything else, by devising a single

CAUSATION AND FREEDOM IN WILLING. 157

mode, or choosing between different modes of trying to do, or which can know and conform itself to the mind's knowledge of the mode of effort required by the existing conditions. As well say N. 20° E. makes the hurricane, or causes it to blow from that point, when such happens to be its direction or characteristic. So, also, want and knowledge are states and conditions of being, and not entities, which themselves want and know, or which separately or combined can act, devise, or direct action, or know what action will conform to the perceptions of the actor as to the means of gratifying his want, or that can transform themselves into a volition conforming to such perception or otherwise. This invariable conformity of the volition to the infinite variety of the mind's views cannot be the effect of blind, unintelligent force, but must be by something which knows the views of the willing being, to which the volition is to be conformed, and, at the same time, has the power to so conform it. It must be the result of some intelligent, designing action, intrinsic or extrinsic to the being in which the conformity is manifested. To attribute this conformity directly to the active being itself that wants, and that knows the mode of gratifying the want to which its action is to be conformed, is natural and simple. To suppose that the act is thus conformed by an extrinsic intelligence involves all the difficulties of the first position, and others much greater, for this extrinsic intelligence must itself have a separate want of its own — must want to conform the volition of the other to that other's views of the mode of acting — must itself have a view of some mode of producing this conformity, and a faculty of effort by which it can try to produce it. So far, the elements apparently, and in terms, correspond; but, under the latter hypothesis, the causative agent's knowledge must embrace the perceptions of the other being as to the mode of effort, as well as his own, and he must also know some mode of controlling the volition of that other being; and to do this *directly* there is not only no mode experimentally known, but none which is conceivable; and if the only mode of doing it *indirectly* is by first changing the knowledge of the willing being, then, the extrinsic attempt to so conform the volition involves a change in that to which it is to be conformed, which, in this case, defeats that conforming of the volition to the knowledge which was first attempted, that knowledge being changed in the process by which the conforming to it is attempted; and so of any successive attempts. In this process the extrinsic intelligent power will always be one step short of its object, showing that such conforming to the actual existing knowledge, by an extrinsic power, in this indirect manner, is also impossible.

To illustrate this, let C represent the being whose act is to be controlled; E, the extrinsic agent who is to control it; a', the present knowledge of C, to which E is to cause C to conform his action. C, with his present knowledge, either will not act at all, or will not act in conformity to his knowledge a', and to cause him to act or to vary his action, some addition must be made to his knowledge, so that it will become $a' + x$, and to this, and not to the knowledge a', the action must now be conformed. The only way, then, in which this conformity of act to knowledge can be thus brought about, is to conform the act, not to the existing knowledge, but to it plus the addition to it required to cause the being to act, and to direct its action, still further complicating the problem of extrinsic control.

As we never commit the blunder of attempting to make the act of another conform to his knowledge, this difficulty does not practically arise. What we do attempt to do, is to change the knowledge or views of another, so that the act which he himself conforms to it will be as we desire it to be.

Again: the only ground upon which the volition of a being can be supposed to be indirectly affected by change of its knowledge is, that such being will itself conform its action to its changed knowledge, so that this hypothesis of external control, in this mode, still involves the necessity of the intrinsic control which it was intended to discard or deny.

It may be objected that this reasoning assumes that the mind does finally determine its own act of will, and that its determination can only be altered by changing its want and knowledge. But, even if this objection is valid, the reasoning still meets your position, which virtually is, that the mind does determine its volition, but is determined to determine by the pre-existing knowledge and want which cause the mind to vary its determination or volition, as themselves vary.

There is this further radical difference between intrinsic and extrinsic control, that, under the hypothesis of intrinsic control, the conformity is consummated and established by the *effort to do*, whether successful or not; whereas, in the case of extrinsic control, it is only established when the effort to produce the conformity is successful, involving the necessity of actual *power to do*, in addition to the ability and the knowledge before mentioned to *try to do*. If the extrinsic intelligence tried, but failed to do, there would, on the extrinsic hypothesis, be no volition in the mind of the other being corresponding to his want and knowledge. If these views do not go the whole length of proving that the extrinsic hypothesis is absolutely inconceivable or impossible, I think I may still claim that they show that it is absurd to adopt it in preference to the intrinsic, and that we are logically reduced to the necessity of believing that the volition is conformed to the want and knowledge, not by any extrinsic power or force, but by the willing being himself, and such conforming being, in fact, the controlling or directing of his volition or effort, he in such volition or effort acts freely.

Though the foregoing reasoning seems to me to meet your suggestion that the "variation" in the knowledge or want "determines" the volition, and that these are not future, but present, or, rather, past facts, I would further remark that it already appears that it is the intelligent active being that determines, in view of its want and of the other conditions; and that even if want and knowledge, into which, so far as action is concerned, all past existence is now concentrated, are regarded as extrinsic to the willing being, they are then but extrinsic conditions, in which the mind perceives *reasons for its action*, and are not *powers that act;* and further, that the want, thus regarded, like other conditions, is influential only as recognized or embraced in the mind's view; and hence, in the last analysis, volition is dependent only on the mind's knowledge. Knowledge induces effort only when it embraces some desirable change to be effected, and some mode of action which will effect it — a preconception of a desirable future effect of its effort. This preconception, you truly say, is antecedent to the volition. But there is, obviously, no power in this prophetic knowledge to make an effort or to determine its direction. The knowledge or view of the actor as to the future effect, which is to him a reason for his action, and which always constitutes his *sole motive*, is only a passive possession or attribute of the being that exerts power, and not a thing that of itself has power, or that can make or direct effort. The knowledge itself, or the event of knowing, might exist for ages without producing or determining any volition.

It has already appeared that it cannot be the *past events* which conform the action to themselves or to anything else, or in any wise influence it; for if the memory is in fault, or is so perverted that our recollections are directly the reverse of what actually occurred, our effort will be conformed, not to the events which did occur, but to our *recollection* or *impression* — our knowledge of them.

Still, it may be said that this knowledge or belief, right or wrong, is the product of past causes, which thus in advance determine what course of action the mind will adopt in virtue of that knowledge, and of its consequent perception of the relation of the effect of its action to its want. This point I have already discussed, but will here add, that the knowledge being a portion of the characteristics which make the being what it is, and distinguish it from what it is not, the same reasoning which has been applied to the position that the character is formed in the past will apply to this position also, and especially as it is only by change of knowledge that change of character is effected. The knowledge, however acquired, is now that of the being, and not the possession or attribute of the past; and if it were, there is no conceivable way in which the past could use it to control or direct the action of an intelligent being. It is not the facts which have existed in the past, nor the fact that they are now remembered, but the ability which the being now has to anticipate the future, which is an element in the direction of its efforts to the end desired ; and it is of no consequence when or how it acquired the knowledge which is requisite to this ability. The question is not how or when the being came to be as he is, with such attributes as he has, but still is whether, being such a being as he is, he now wills freely. His present perceptions of what now is, his present memories of the past, and his present anticipations of the future, make up the sum of his present knowledge ; and if he now has a knowledge of the future by which he can and does direct his effort wisely and successfully, or otherwise, it is of no consequence to his freedom in directing, what particular things he knows, or how or when his knowledge was acquired. The present relation of his knowledge to the control of his effort, whatever that knowledge may consist of, or when or how acquired, is the same. The fact that, with such knowledge as he has, he can direct his effort, is all that is germain to the question of self-control or freedom. With the changes which are continually taking place, he is, as before observed, at every instant, actually acting with an aggregate of knowledge, and upon an aggregate of conditions, which are the creation of the instant — combinations which, as entireties, have had no past.

As it is the sensuous, knowing, and active *being*, and not the states, conditions, or characteristics, that wills, so it is the *being* that is free in willing. Want, to which the susceptibility to feeling is a prerequisite, is a necessary condition to the being's effort; for without it there would be no occasion, need, or use for effort, and, as the subject of the mind's knowledge of what will gratify its want, it is essential to such knowledge.

A perception or knowledge of some object of effort, and of some mode of attaining it, is also a prerequisite of effort. All the distinguishing characteristics of intelligent active being are thus involved, as essential elements of its free effort; and want and knowledge, instead of hindering or militating against freedom of effort in the being to whom they pertain, are, in fact, the very things which make such freedom possible.

The illusion, that the relation of want and knowledge to effort indicates necessity, seems to arise from attributing the determination or control of the volition itself, or the determination of the being to the volition, to some attributes or conditions of the being, and then reasoning either as though these attributes were powers extrinsic to the being, or as if the being's own control of its efforts were incompatible with its freedom in making them. It is not any one of these attributes or states of being, nor any combination of them, but the conative intelligent being of which they are states or attributes, and of which they are the *distinguishing* characteristics, which feels, knows, and acts.

We know the being only by the characteristics which distinguish it from other existences, as we know matter only by its properties; and to attribute the action of intelligent being to its susceptibility to feeling or its capacity for knowledge, or even to its faculty of effort, is analogous to asserting that it is the mobility, extension, and impenetrability of matter, and not matter itself, that moves.

Whatever theory we adopt as to the substratum of matter or of spirit, it is still the matter that moves and the spirit that acts. If there be no substratum, then matter is only a combination of its sensible properties, and mind a like combination of feeling, knowledge, and will. If the hypothesis of no substratum be admitted, it must also be admitted that it is this combination of sensible properties that moves, and this combination of the attributes of spirit that makes effort. If we adopt my view, that matter, with all extrinsic phenomena, merely indicates that large class of our sensations which we find we cannot change at will,[1] then it is a certain change in these sensations which constitutes its motion; or if, as you say, matter is only a "permanent possibility of sensation," then motion must be a perception of some change in this permanent possibility.

As the combinations are things distinguished from the individual elements of which they are composed, at least by *relations* of the elements which do not pertain to any of them separately, we may denote the different combination of characteristics by distinguishing names; and if, in the ultimate division into only two classes, we call one of them matter, and the other spirit, no logical or practical difficulty arises from the hypothesis that matter and spiritual being are merely combinations of these respective properties and attributes, by which alone we know them, without any separate substratum of existence. This combination of spiritual attributes, without any substratum, would still combine all the essential elements for self-action by effort, and for the direction of the effort. Indeed, my argument, asserting that the sway or control of

[1] *Freedom of Mind in Willing*, Chap. II.

CAUSATION AND FREEDOM IN WILLING. 165

the will, which is imputed to the influence of the characteristics, is really the influence of the being characterized, would be strongest upon the hypothesis that these characteristics or attributes in fact constitute the being, without any substratum whatever. If we suppose a substratum which is not itself a characteristic, or even a substratum whose only characteristic or property is that of a nucleus in which the attributes of being may inhere, which enters into no influential relations with the inhering attributes, the case would not be materially altered; and if this substratum is itself a characteristic, then the being is still wholly made up of its characteristics, and exists as it is only as a combination of its characteristics: thus, upon either hypothesis, equally sustaining and supporting my position, that the determination of a volition by the character is, in fact, the determination by the willing being. Is it conceivable that a substratum can be anything more than a *characteristic*, which pertains in many individuals otherwise distinguished from each other? However this may be, it is evident that we know nothing of such substratum, and can only reason upon the properties which we do know; and no argument can go back of that which rests on those properties.

In some respects, Extension, in its relation to matter, seems most nearly to fulfil the conditions of our notions of a substratum. It is that which universally and inevitably remains when all its other properties — we might perhaps say when *all* its properties — are annihilated. But the void space — the extended vacuum — cannot be the essence of matter, nor, except by contrast with its negation, aid us to any conception of what it is *in* itself.

It is in the distinction that knowledge is not an active power that wills or that controls the will, but only a passive possession or attribute of a conative being, by which it directs its power in effort, and in a similar distinction touching the other elements of character, that my views diverge from yours; yours leading to the conclusion that our efforts are links in a uniform chain of events, each of which is successively determined to be as it is by some causative power in those which precede it, and mine to the very different result, that only the circumstances, intrinsic and extrinsic, under or upon, or in view of which, the being acts, are thus determined by prior causes (including its own prior action), but that the being, with its knowledge and characteristics, in view of the circumstances including its own preconception of the effect, must of itself make and determine its own effort, without being first acted upon by any extrinsic power or force, and hence that such being, in virtue of its knowledge and inherent activity, is an independent, self-active power in the universe, freely putting forth its own isolated power to coöperate with or to counteract any or all other powers, and thus to vary the combined effects of all causes extrinsic to himself, and of himself, without the prior action of any extrinsic compelling power upon him, beginning and directing his efforts to create the future, and make it different from what, but for his individual effort, it would have been. And this result, that every being that wills is of itself, in virtue of its inherent characteristics, an independent power — a Creative First Cause — in its sphere, however limited, as individually and as freely doing its part to create the future as superior intelligences in their larger sphere, or as God in the infinite, I deem in itself and in its consequences the most important involved in the discussion.[1] In this view, every intelligent being, in its own sphere of knowledge, is elevated to the position of an independent sovereign power in the universe, with all its prerogatives and duties, all its powers, and all its responsibilities.

The argument from the "possibility of prediction" remains to be considered. In replying to the reasoning of Edwards upon the foreknowledge of God, I

[1] In speaking of "moral antecedents" and "outward circumstances" in the passage I have quoted at page 129, I supposed you intended to include all the prerequisite conditions to volition. In the same sentence, you speak of the former as "internal." This gave me the impression that you also classified all the elements either as "internal" or "outward." In such classification it seemed to me so clear that our knowledge must be classed with the internal, that I regarded your omission to include it in the enumeration of them as unintentional. But in the following passage you distinctly assert that our knowledge is *external*, and place it, in this respect, in direct antithesis to our desires and aversions. " When we think of ourselves hypothetically as having acted otherwise than we did, we always suppose a difference in the antecedents; we picture ourselves as having known something that we did not know, or not known something that we did know, *which is a difference in the external motives;* or as having desired something, or disliked something, more or less than we did; *which is a difference in the internal motives.*" (Review of Sir William Hamilton, Chapter XXVI.) The Italics are mine. Though I had read this passage, 1 did not observe that it thus classed our knowledge till after I had concluded the whole argument. The question whether our knowledge is, in fact, internal or external to us, seems to me so far ultimate as to admit of no argument. Each one must determine it for himself, as each one must determine for himself what is sweet and what bitter. However little reason your general accuracy leaves for such assumption, I cannot but think that in this case you have inadvertently applied expressions to our knowledge, when you had the *objects* of knowledge in mind, and that these happened to be external and not internal phenomena. Be this as it may, it seems useless to offer any proof upon this fundamental point, and I therefore leave my argument as it is, interpolating this explanation here, and remarking that the same point arises in the reasoning upon prescience which follows.

sought to meet him upon his own ground, and show that if there was any necessary incompatibility of Divine prescience with man's freedom in willing, he had, of these two alternatives, elected not to foreknow our volitions, and that the position taken by Edwards that such foreknowledge is essential to the Supreme governing power is not tenable. In opposition to his views, I then urged that a Being of infinite wisdom does not require time to prepare in advance for what may arise, but can perceive at the instant what action is best; and further, that, if this preparation were necessary, such a Being could anticipate every possible combination of conditions, and determine in advance what his action in each should be. I then reserved the question as to whether a free volition could not be foretold as well as one not free, and also as to God's power, or the power of any intelligent being, to influence a future free volition, thus making it more or less certain that it would take place, and of course subject to be foreknown with a corresponding degree of certainty.

I propose now to include these questions in the discussion. The phrase "possibility of prediction," of itself might be taken to mean that the prediction of a future event may *possibly* turn out to be true, or, that things might possibly be so constituted that future events could be predicted; for instance, a being with power to produce a future event could predict such event, provided he decided to exert his power to produce it. If he never exerted such power, this ability to predict would never actually exist; but as he could exert it, such ability would still, to him, be possible. I, however, understand you to mean that, as things now are, the elements essential to such prediction exist, and that it is, therefore, always within the bounds of possibility. I have already urged that our voluntary actions, at least in most cases, are predicated upon our prophetic anticipations, expectations, or conjectures of what other causative agents will do, or tend to do, including the action of other intelligent beings by Will. This involves the necessity of prescience more or less reaching and reliable, as a prerequisite of such voluntary actions. So far, then, we agree that we have sufficient confidence in our predictions or expectations of the future volitions of others to make them the foundation of action; and I hope to show that this, or even any degree of certainty in such predictions, is consistent with the hypothesis of freedom in willing. If I understand your argument, it is that the possibility of predicting a volition proves that volition is subject to the same law of uniformity of cause and effect as physical events, which are compelled by their causes, and hence not free. Admitting this, how does it conflict with my position that the volition or effort is itself the causal action of an intelligent being? The "law of cause and effect," at best, only asserts that the *effect* of the action of its cause is necessitated, not that the *causal action* is constrained. Or if any one insists that volition or effort is not merely the action of cause, but is itself an effect of such action, then, in reference to the freedom of the being in which it is manifested, the question still arises, does this being, as a cause, control its own volition? The analogy to the action of any mechanical causes and their effects might indicate that the volition itself, as a distinct entity or a mere effect, is not free, but not that the action of its cause is not free, and merely carries us back to the questions as to whether the intelligent being is the cause of its own volitions, and is a cause which can act without being first acted upon and determined in its action or volition by some extrinsic power or cause. These questions I have already considered. In regard to material phenomena, we count upon their uniformity, in most cases, with great confidence. If we see two solid bodies approaching each other from opposite directions, we know that *some change* must take place when they meet. This is a necessity which might be anticipated without experience; for without it we should know that both cannot occupy the same space; that two extensions cannot be one extension; that two cannot be one. If every material phenomenon were *individually* of this character, we could predict it from its antecedents without any knowledge of actual occurrences of the same kind. But however true the general proposition that, in the case stated, *some change* must take place, the necessity does not, even in it, apply to any particular change embraced in the phrase " some change."

Experience teaches us that one or both the bodies are uniformly arrested in their course; but there is no reason to suppose that this is from an absolute necessity. It is not a result which we could have reached *a priori*, for it is quite conceivable that the effect of the collision might uniformly be, that the particles of each would spread and pass through among those of the other, each resuming its original form and motion on the opposite side; or that each should revolve around the other, and so continue, as some twin stars do, or each resume its original track when it reached it; or that greater or less portions, or all of one or both, might be scattered in any of the infinite number of directions in space.

If these various modes are in themselves equally conceivable and possible, then, admitting that some change must of necessity occur, we still want some directing power to determine among these possible changes, and by its own unvaried action produce the observed uniformity. The actual uniformity, in such cases, of itself indicates either that the particular uniform result must be attributed to blind force, which, acting of necessity, cannot vary its action or its consequences; or to an intelligent percipient power acting either with design to produce such uniformity, or for the reason that it deems such particular action in itself always better than any other, or than inaction.[1]

In seeking to look into the future, we do not usually even attempt to determine the primary cause of the order of succession. It is not, then, from any perceived inherent necessity in the case, but from the uniformity of our experience, that we anticipate that one or both of the solid bodies moving directly towards each other will be arrested in its course; and the same in other like cases of material phenomena. The cause of this uniformity is not essential to our foreknowledge and prediction of the event; nor do we usually seek the cause for this object.

[1] The argument for design derives no preponderance from the uniform repetition of any one set of events, however often they may occur in the same order. That the sun rises every morning no more proves design as against the hypothesis of blind mechanical force or movement than its first rising did, for each successive rising may be attributed to such force or movement as well as the first. Such preponderance is only acquired when the design is manifested in various cases, not in themselves connected with each other, indicating an agency of more extended presence, both in time and space, than the blind forces, acting only on the occasion of the moment, and at the particular points of pressure or collision, in which these only can act, without reference to future or to distant events.

If, as I have contended,[1] this uniformity of the changes in matter is not from an inherent necessity, but results from the uniform mode of the acting of an Intelligent Being upon it, then the problem of the prediction of these changes becomes the same in kind as that of predicting the sequences of the volitions or efforts of other intelligent beings.

If the Being, whose power is thus manifested in the material phenomena of the universe, is in fact Omniscient, then his action is not liable to be varied by any change in his knowledge. He will have no occasion to try experiments, or to adopt any other than those best modes of action which he knows in the first as well as in subsequent cases.

Freely conforming his action to his perfect knowledge of the circumstances, and what they require, — *i. e.*, himself so conforming, — his action is always the most wise. If some other being with less knowledge, or some force with no knowledge at all, controlled his action, there would be no reason to presume that it would be uniformly consistent with perfect wisdom, and this ground of prediction is availing only in case the actor controls his own act of will, *i. e.*, acts freely. We have here, then, two means of predicting the action of an omniscient being. 1. If we know in advance what action will be most wise, we can foreknow that this will be his action, and, without any experience, predict it. 2. If we do not know in advance what action will be most wise, then our observation in a single case reveals it to us, and we can thence predict what this action will be in all like cases. This conformity of action to the knowledge of an omniscient

[1] *Freedom of Mind in Willing*, Book I. Chap. XII., and Book II. Chap. XII. and XIII.

being, in whom knowledge admits of no change, and action of no deviation from the wisest mode, by necessary consequence, produces the most perfect uniformity; and as this uniformity is a consequence only of the self-controlled or free volition and corresponding action of such a being, and would not be a necessary result of its unfree volitions, or of volitions controlled by some less perfect extrinsic intelligence, the uniformity in the volitions or actions of such being, and the consequent possibility of predicting them, argues freedom, and not necessity.

In regard to the first of these two means of foreknowing the action of omniscience, it is obvious that there may be cases in which two or more modes are equally wise; and I have suggested that there may also be other cases in which the advantages of variety may more than compensate for a departure from that mode which, in itself, is best, and further, that such might more especially, or more frequently, be the case, but that uniformity in the action of the Infinite is essential to free agency in finite being; and hence, from this uniformity, which, in the form of the doctrine that the same causes of necessity produce the same effects, has been much relied upon to prove necessity, I have drawn an argument from final causes in favor of the existence of the free agency, for which such provision is thus made.[1]

Both these means rest upon the assumption that the Being is in fact omniscient, and that he wills freely, the first more especially on the premise that such a Being will always do what is most wise, while the second is founded on the immutability of that knowledge which admits of no addition or diminution. As bear-

[1] *Freedom of Mind in Willing*, pp. 131 and 379.

ing upon this I have suggested that God, even if he could foreknow the volitions of finite conative beings, may have chosen to limit his own knowledge, and not to foreknow them; and hence, such volitions, as they actually occur, may become additions to his knowledge, and the occasions of corresponding variations in his action. I have, however, also endeavored to show that all these variations may still be embraced in general rules of action in a more extended and complex uniformity,[1] and that our efforts to ascertain the laws of nature, by which we are enabled to predict the recurrence of physical events, are only efforts to learn the uniform modes of God's action in reference to them. Even though there is a sphere in which his actions may be varied by that of other free agents, still there is a large material domain, in which he may act as a sole first cause, and in which his action is not liable to be varied by increase of knowledge. For predicting the volitions of finite intelligences, we can neither count in advance upon their being perfectly wise, nor upon invariability in their knowledge, and hence the difficulties in predicting the volitions of such which do not pertain to the Infinite. Their knowledge being always liable to change, the action in conformity to it may also change when all other conditions are the same; and hence no uniformity with these other conditions can be relied upon. At the lower end of the scale of conate intelligence there may be beings with so little ability to add to that innate knowledge, which is the basis of their instinctive action, that there is little chance of its varying; and in these we may count with great, yet not with entire, certainty upon the uniformity of their efforts, for though the

[1] *Freedom of Mind in Willing*, Book II. Chap. XI.

CAUSATION AND FREEDOM IN WILLING. 175

change of knowledge in such may be both slow and infrequent, so long as the little sphere of what they know is bounded by what they do not know, the extension of it is possible. To some extent, then, the difficulty of predicting the volition of a being increases with the ability of that being to acquire knowledge.

It may also increase with this actual deficiency in wisdom; and it not unfrequently happens, when *new conditions require new plans* by the actor, that the greater his ignorance, the greater the difficulty of predicting what he will do. Any superior knowledge as to what is most wise does not help one to predict what the unwise will do. So far, then, as relates to knowledge alone, as an element of prediction, there is no reason to suppose that Omniscience can foreknow the volitions of finite beings more certainly than beings of finite knowledge can, and it seems, at least in some respects, true that the greater the difference between two beings, the greater will be the difficulty of either predicting the course of the other.

In regard to many future events, we may have the power directly to bring them to pass, and hence may be able to predict them; but if I succeed in showing that a volition in one being directly produced by another, involves a contradiction in idea, and is impossible in fact, then even Omniscience could not thus foreknow a volition. Our power indirectly to influence the volitions of others, I will consider hereafter.

There are many cases in which one being acting as a sole cause on the existing conditions, without interference from other conative being, can predict the events which he has the power to produce; but this can never occur in regard to the volition of another, for the action of this other is necessarily involved in the premises, as otherwise no such volition could even be conceived of, much less predicted, and the case does not admit of the action of a sole cause. The nearest conceivable approach to it is that of one cause producing the action of the other cause; and this in the case of volition, it has been shown, can only be done through change in the knowledge of this other, which again is effective only through his freely conforming his action to his changed knowledge.

I introduce these considerations to bring into view some of the difficulties which are peculiar to the prediction of a volition, and am aware I do not thus meet your argument, which rests not on any degree of ease or difficulty in actually predicting, but on the "possibility of prediction;" and I admit that an argument founded on an ascertained possibility of evolving the knowledge of a future volition from what is known in the present, or even on what now exists or is known to have existed, would be as availing as if founded on actual predictions ever so easily and universally made.

In any plane triangle, two sides and their included angle being given, the third side is thereby determined, and may be known without a resort to its actual measurement. It, in fact, is of necessity made to be one certain length and no other, whether we are able to ascertain that length from the data or not. The diameter of a circle determines the length of the circumference, and it is not the less thereby determined, and made to be exactly what it is, because no one can actually tell or express in terms the exact length; the actual controlling dependence of the one upon the other is not changed by this incidental practical difficulty.

No human being might be able to tell on what spot a ball, thrown from the hand upon a tract covered with small hillocks, would eventually rest; but still the force and direction of the throw, and the shape and nature of the surface over which it subsequently passes, do determine it, of necessity, to one particular spot, and to no other, and thus in some sense involve the possibility of the foreknowledge of that spot, though we may be unable actually to work out the problem.

I understand your ground to be that prediction of volition is possible, and that this, even without actual experience of the fact, proves that a future volition is dependent upon something now or previously existing as its cause, and that, as the same cause produces the same effect, the effect of this preëxisting cause must be one certain future volition, which being probably this, and no other, the necessary effect or consequence of the action of this cause must exclude subsequent freedom in the willing being.

I say, "without actual experience," because I think, upon your own statements, as well as in point of fact, the exceptions to our actual ability to predict the volition of another are so numerous, — I might, perhaps, say the cases in which we can do it are comparatively so few, — that experience does not prove that such prediction is always "possible."

The argument in this view seems to be open to the objection that the necessary dependence of the volition upon its antecedents is assumed to prove the "possibility of prediction," and then the "possibility of prediction" is taken to prove the necessary dependence upon which its own proof is rested. Though the positions I have asserted make it, at least in most cases, essential to the proper design and efficacy of our own efforts, that in determining them we should have preconceptions of the future volitions of some others acting in the same sphere, and effecting changes in the same conditions upon which we are about to act, and which will be simultaneous with our own contemplated effects, and in many cases also of those still subsequent volitions of others which are relied upon to extend or otherwise vary the sequences of our own action, I have not held that these preconceptions or prophetic anticipations of these volitions, or of the sequences of them, are, or can be, infallible. If they were, and all changes in matter are the result of intelligent efforts, — infinite or finite, — we should only have to add certain knowledge of the relation of our own efforts to that of these others to make us capable of acting with perfect wisdom. The fact, I think, is, that we oftener err in our own efforts from being mistaken as to what others will do, than from any other or all other causes. I think you will agree with me that experience does not warrant any certain reliance upon such anticipations of the volitions of others. I understand you to assign as a reason for this our imperfect knowledge of the antecedents, and virtually to assert that we can attain certainty in the prediction of volitions "when we have sufficient knowledge of the circumstances." This may be true if we know all the antecedents up to the *moment* of volition, including the determination of the willing being as to what effect he will seek to produce, and by what effort he will try to produce it:[1] that, at this point, we can always predict the volition, is because the volition must or does always conform to the determination, *i. e.*, if the being has itself determined, because the being has itself determined its own volition. Such predic-

---

[1] For the proof that such final decision is not itself the volition, see *Freedom of Mind*, etc., p. 60.

CAUSATION AND FREEDOM IN WILLING. 179

tion is really founded upon and proves the freedom of the agent in willing, and of course furnishes no ground for inferring a want of freedom, but the contrary.

Those who use this argument from the "possibility of prediction" cannot intend to assert that the future volition as an *isolated* fact, which as yet is not, can be *directly* known, as a present existing thing, which already is, and which may have always existed, and had no antecedents, may be. No such prescience is experimentally known to us, and perhaps none is conceivable; and if a future volition could be thus known, this fact would ignore its necessary connection with its antecedents, which is inferred from the possibility of prediction, and urged as proof of the necessity of the predicted volition; and besides, such foreknowledge would obviously apply to one event as well as to another — to a free volition, or even to a volition springing into existence of itself, without any connection with any antecedent, or with any being, power, or force whatever, as well as to a volition necessitated by its connection with its antecedents. No such connection could be necessary to such prescience, and no such could therefore be inferred from it, or even from the prediction which, if possible, would prove the existence of such prescience. In such case the prescience would obviously have no other relation to the future volition than that of knowledge to the thing immediately known, which does not indicate how such thing came to be. It could not indicate whether the volition was, or would be, caused by the being in which it was manifested, or by something extrinsic to that being, nor even whether the volition produced itself. The argument, to avail, then, must assert that the "possibility of prediction" is proof of such an invariable connection of the future event, volition, with the antecedent conditions now present, or now known, that it may be presumed to be dependent upon these as its cause. If this connection is broken, there is no ground for such presumption. But the mind's final determination as to its effort, above alluded to, must be one of the links in this connection; and that we can predict the act of will from knowing this last link connecting with it, as above stated, can be only because the mind, by this decision, does inevitably control its own volition, and hence is free in such volition; and if, on the other hand, we can predict it without knowing this link, then its connection with antecedent causes, which was inferred from the possibility of prediction, because such connection was supposed to be essential to such possibility, can no longer be so inferred, for the prediction is made without reference to it, and the argument for necessity, founded upon that dependence of the volition upon its antecedents, which was inferred from the possibility of prediction, wholly fails.

It appears, then, that if the prediction is a direct prescience of a future volition as an isolated fact in time, it does not indicate necessity; and that when it becomes possible only by its connection with the present, as the last link in this connection is the mind's own determination as to its effort, the fact of such possibility, then, depends upon the mind's self-control, and favors freedom. In view of these positions, the argument for necessity must recede a step, and show that the *determination* of the mind to a certain effort or volition is controlled by those antecedent conditions or circumstances, the knowledge of which is supposed to afford the means for predicting the determination,

CAUSATION AND FREEDOM IN WILLING. 181

and through it the volition — that the mind, as you and Sir William Hamilton seem to agree, is thus "determined to determine."

There seems to me good reason for at least a doubt as to whether the foreknowledge of the future determination of an intelligent being is always possible — whether, as in the case of the plane triangle, in which only two sides, without the included angle, are given, there are not cases in which the data are insufficient, and from the nature of the case necessarily so. I have already remarked that in regard to Omniscience there may be two or more modes of action just equally wise; so, in regard to finite agents, there may be two or more modes which to them, with their limited knowledge, appear in all respects to suit them equally well. In such cases there can be no connection of the final determination with any antecedents by which it could be foreknown, for there is none with which the decision or determination is connected as a consequence; and even if there is usually a chain of events firmly linked with each other, the recurrence of these cases, which must be arbitrarily decided, breaks the chain, and a new series is begun. It is not essential to this result that the two or more cases should, in fact, be exactly equal, nor yet that the active agent should be absolutely unable to discover any ground of choice between them, but only that, during the time he allots to the preliminary examination, he does not, in fact, discover any such ground, and determines without doing so.

Looking at the phenomena more generally, and excluding those vague notions of the direct perception of a future event as an isolated fact, which, for reasons before stated, may now be eliminated from the argument touching freedom or necessity, the only mode in which any future event may be known is by means of its ascertained connection of dependence with something which now is. The future determination of a being cannot be thus directly dependent upon things and events extrinsic to it, for, as before observed, whenever the view of the mind differs from the existing facts, the determination conforms to the view, and not to the facts. Hence it is only as these extrinsic things and events affect the knowledge of the agent that his determination is affected, and this knowledge, of necessity, becomes a channel through which the prediction of the final determination must be sought. If we know the views or knowledge of the actor, including that of his own wants, and the relations of his knowledge to them, and know this up to the instant of determining, so that there can be no change, we should have the data essential to predict his determination. But is such knowledge in advance possible in the case? If not, then we must be deficient in an essential element of prediction. The final determination itself is not yet fixed by the conditions, and no prediction from the antecedents is yet possible. With this deficiency in the data the problem is analogous to that of knowing only two sides of a triangle without the included angle, in which case no amount or perfection of intelligence could ascertain the third side; it is not fixed nor determined by the data, and the variety of lengths which will fulfil the conditions is infinite.

That a volition is always a new power thrown in to break any connection there may be between the past or present causative agencies and their future effect, and make the future different from what this connection undisturbed would make it, and also that volition,

CAUSATION AND FREEDOM IN WILLING. 183

is the beginning of action, or of a new series of action, requiring no past, but only present conditions to be changed, and future object to be attained, both indicate that there is no such necessary connection of the volition with the past, nor of its dependence upon it, as can afford a ground for predicting it, or the determination of the mind of which it is the immediate consequence. The peculiar difficulty of predicting the future event, volition, or determination of the mind to it, arises from its being dependent upon the knowledge of the agent, which is a variable element, liable to be changed in the very process of determining what the volition shall be. In the instinctive and habitual actions, as also in the customary or imitative, in which, following modes already known and with which we are satisfied, we do not seek any new knowledge to guide or determine our efforts, prediction is most reliable; but even in these cases, as already suggested, the additions to our knowledge by mere passive observation and perception may at any time, as experience shows, change our views, and induce a departure from the accustomed modes of action.

In all other cases we seek by a preliminary effort to find the proper mode of acting; *i. e.*, we seek more knowledge for the purpose of determining our volition; which is to say, that in the very act of determining we change the knowledge upon which the prediction of this determination, and of the consequent volition, is based, and the changes which may thus take place in this element, in and by the very process of determining, are infinite.

The case in this aspect seems to be analogous to what we would witness, if, instead of the results which uniformly attend the collision of two solid bodies, a variety of effects, such as those before mentioned as conceivable in the case, with others which might be added without limit, sometimes one and sometimes others, should follow without any uniformity, the collision itself in each individual case determining the sequence, without any reference or relation to other like cases; under these circumstances, prediction of the sequence of collision would be impossible, the data being insufficient. Again, in these cases of rational actions — actions in which we devise a mode and make preliminary effort to obtain the knowledge to do it — this preliminary effort is a connecting link between the present conditions and our final determination, which will depend upon the result of this preliminary effort or volition; and to assume that we can foreknow this result again begs the question as to prescience of the determination of that volition, and something more, viz., the *result* of that volition, *i. e.*, the failure or success of the effort for change, thus involving another very uncertain element. Again, what knowledge he will acquire by his own preliminary effort must often depend upon the results of the volitions of others, as it also does when one is passively waiting to see what others will do before he determines what to do himself, in both cases making the foreknowledge of these volitions of others and of their sequences an essential element of the prediction of this final determination of his own volition; and to assert the possibility of such prediction, by himself or by others as before, assumes that a volition and its sequences may be foreknown. Further, to illustrate the necessary deficiency of the data for predicting the future determination of a volition, suppose A seeks to foreknow the future volition of B. It is admitted that A will determine that volition, and this determination B now seeks to foreknow. It is also admitted that this determination of A will conform to his own knowledge or notion of what at the time of his determining will suit him best, and it is through the present knowledge of A that B seeks to foreknow A's future determination. But A cannot possibly know more of the present knowledge of B than B himself knows, and B is yet undetermined, and of course does not know what his own determination will be ; the chain does not reach to the end desired. A may be more able to infer from all the facts what B, with his knowledge, *should* determine ; but it is not the inference of A with his superior ability, but that of B with his less ability, that is to decide the matter. To say that A may be more able to infer what B's determination *will* be than B himself is, and hence can infer or know it sooner than B does, begs the question, asserting that B's determination may be foreknown, and further, that it may be so foreknown before the connection between it and the present known is completed — before B has himself determined or knows that upon which his determination depends. These considerations point to the conclusion that the difficulties which arise from a volition being dependent upon our knowledge, which, up to the very instant of determining the volition, is liable to change and to be changed by the very process of determining, are insuperable, and could not be overcome by any amount or perfection of intelligence. But, be this as it may, every attempt of A to reach the determination of B by its connection with the present must be through the knowledge of B to which it is conformed, and must assume that the last step in the process will be the so conforming it by B ; and whether always this conforming by B is an indispensable condition or consequence of his acting freely, or is a result of extrinsic coercion, makes no difference to the susceptibility or possibility of predicting the consequent act, and, hence, does not touch the question of freedom or necessity in this act.

In another view we reach a similar result. I have before remarked that the interference of any causative power with our freedom in willing is in no wise affected by the uniformity of its action; that it is just as perfect in the first instance as at any subsequent time, and would be just as much an interference if it varied its action at each recurrence.

The coercive element of such cause, if any, which alone interferes with our freedom, does not aid us in foreknowing the coerced volition, and a subsequently ascertained uniformity is the sole ground of the prediction. Hence, conversely, the prediction can only indicate uniformity in this causative action, and not its interference with our freedom.

The foregoing reasoning goes to prove that necessity is not an element in the prediction of a future volition, and hence that such necessity is not to be inferred from the "possibility of prediction," or even from actual prediction. I may perhaps go farther than this, and assert that freedom is an element of those anticipations, expectations, and conjectures of the volitions of others, which we more or less rely upon in determining our own actions.

The main peculiar difficulty in predicting a volition increases with a liability to change in the knowledge of the active agent.

We place implicit reliance upon the uniformity of God's action; and in the case of an inferior animal, with little or no ability to add to its innate knowledge, if we know its wants and its opportunities for gratifying them, we count with great certainty upon its *instinctive* effort. The difficulty lessens at either extreme of intelligence, because in these the liability to change of knowledge is less.

It is greater in man than in the inferior animals; but much of our knowledge is derived from the great reservoir of absolute truth which is common to us all, and our wants and the consequent knowledge of what we want are more or less similar; hence there is a degree of similarity in our knowledge, and in the actions which conform to it. There is, also, more or less persistence in the knowledge even of the most mercurial. In no one does it all change at once, and in most persons its mutations are very slow. There is always, then, an element of steadfastness upon which we can count in our expectations of the volitions of others, though, being in its nature more or less variable, we can never predict the result with entire certainty. We however do, in fact, act upon these expectations, though with more or less uncertainty as to their being realized.

I have already argued that the volition of A is not such an event as B may ever absolutely foreknow as an event which, acting as a sole cause in the premises, B may by his own power bring about; still, any power one may have to influence the volition of another furnishes him with a ground for probable, though not for certain prediction. This is a consequence of the mutual dependence of the volitions of each active agent upon those of others, and upon the changes which the others produce. I may, for instance, not doubt that if I make a particular move on the chess-board, my antagonist will meet it by a certain move; and the ground of my faith may be that I perceive, and do not doubt that he also will perceive, that this is the only move by which he can avoid checkmate. I have changed the conditions to be acted upon, and thus indirectly changed his knowledge and influenced his action.

If I inform a man who is going in a certain path, and cause him to believe that enemies are upon it, in wait to kill him, I can be pretty certain that he will not proceed in it. I have, here, more directly changed his knowledge, and thus influenced his action. In neither of these cases, however, is the prediction infallible, and the whole ground of its probability lies in the presumption that the person thus influenced will perceive, or will believe, certain things, that, so perceiving and believing, he will deem best to make a certain effort, and will conform his action to what, in his view of the changed conditions, or the new knowledge which I have imparted, he thus deems best; *i. e.*, as before shown, that he will act freely. If God can impart knowledge or vary our views without limit, He may thus present to us a sufficient reason for any specific action, which, being freely adopted upon our own perception of a reason, is a free action, and which, if it depended wholly upon the knowledge thus imparted, would be a free action which He could foreknow. Undoubtedly some actions, thus influenced by knowledge imparted either by the Infinite or by finite beings, could be counted upon as morally certain to take place; but there is still this difficulty: that, so long as we are such beings as we are, we have a capacity for knowing, independent of the action of any other being whatever, and there never can be any previous certainty that one will not thus have additions to his knowledge which will vary his action from what the imparted knowledge alone would lead to. In view of this fact, men often conceal, or by some device prevent those whose action they would influence from knowing, some things which they suppose would incline them to a different action; but knowledge and its sources are infinite, and the finite mind cannot guard it at all points, or foreknow what may flow into the mind of another. We may suppose the Supreme Intelligence to thus shut out all adverse knowledge; but even in this extreme case it would still be only the Infinite adopting means to influence that knowledge to which the finite being still of itself conforms its action, and in so doing acts freely. If He does this by changing the conditions, He succeeds only because the finite being freely conforms its action to the changed conditions. If He does it by changing the knowledge, He succeeds by changing the characteristics of the being, and making it a somewhat different being from what it was; but such as it is, it still freely conforms its action to its own character — to its own views of what it would do, and of the manner of doing it.

I may be ever so confident that the conditions to be acted upon being as they are, and the conative intelligence being as he is, he will act in one particular way, and no other. I may believe that a man standing on a railway track will make an effort to step off to avoid an approaching train; but the ground of my belief is, not that the train will produce in him a volition, but that he will himself perceive in the conditions, or rather in the comparison of his primary and secondary expectations, a reason for the effort, and that he is *free* to make it. If he were not free to make it — if the effort is made or controlled by some extrinsic power, the fact that *he* perceives a reason for making it, would furnish no ground for supposing that he would make it or that it would be made at all, and none for predicting it.

So, too, if we look to the internal conditions: knowing the man, we may know how he will probably be affected by certain circumstances; and hence, if he controls his own volitions — wills freely — what, under such circumstances, his action or volition will be; but, if he does not determine his own volitions, no such inference can be drawn from our knowledge of his character, and of the circumstances in *view* of which he acts, or in connection with which the volition occurred. In all these cases it is because of the freedom of the volition that we are able to anticipate it with more or less of probability; and in this prescience of free actions there is obviously nothing which is inconceivable or contradictory in thought or impossible in fact. It appears already that a free volition, at least in some cases, is in fact more susceptible, or more "possible of prediction" than a necessitated one would be; and I shall have occasion presently more generally and broadly to assert this position.

The whole argument for necessity from the "possibility of prediction" rests upon the assumption that what may certainly be predicted must of necessity come to pass in the future; and this must be admitted; but, admitting such predictions in any degree of certainty whatever, freedom in action, as already shown, may still be one of the known elements upon which the prediction is founded. The problem in this view, under my definition of freedom, resolves itself into this question: Is a volition which is controlled by the willing agent himself less "possible of prediction" than a volition which is controlled by some power or force extrinsic to the willing agent? Or, which comes to the same thing, is a volition which a being produces or controls in itself less " possible of prediction " than one which it produces or controls in another being? From what has been already said, it appears, and is perhaps obvious in itself, that to predict the volition which is caused or directed by an extrinsic power or force involves all the difficulties which arise in regard to predicting a volition which is caused and directed by the willing agent, and some additional ones. In both cases it is admitted that the action conforms to the views of the willing agent, and the extrinsic power or cause must act in reference to these views, and at the same time conform the action by which it so conforms them to its own views of the conditions; and further, not only be able to make the effort to do this, but actually to accomplish it, thus complicating the problem of its action : this addition to the process may obviously make prediction more difficult, and certainly cannot make it less so.

In your view, the " possibility of prediction " must be based on the uniformity of the succession — on the law that the same causes of necessity produce the same effects; or on the observed fact that the same antecedents are always succeeded by the same consequents. The prediction of a future volition as an isolated fact, as before shown, would not avail; it is essential to the argument for necessity to show that the possibility of prediction is proof that the volition has a connection of dependence with some antecedents which are now known. It cannot, however, on this ground, be argued that this possibility indicates that volition is an effect of some extrinsic power, or cause, or antecedent, whose action or sequent is more uniform than that of the being within which it is manifested, and hence more easy of prediction than the volitions of this being; for, under the very law which is thus made the ground of the prediction, volition, admitting it to be such a necessary or uniform effect or consequent, and not, as I hold, a beginning of action, must be just as uniform as the action of the power or cause which produces it; and if the action of the being is any less uniform than that of the extrinsic powers to which it would thus be attributed, this fact would prove that it was not caused by the action of such extrinsic powers.

It is obvious, then, that if this "possibility of prediction," admitted in its fullest extent, has any bearing whatever upon the question, it does not argue any want of freedom, but rather the contrary.

In stating the proofs adduced by the necessitarians, after mentioning "the power which every one has of foreseeing actions," which I have just considered, you say, "They test it further by the statistical results of the observation of human beings, in numbers sufficient to eliminate the influences which operate only on a few, and which, on a large scale, neutralize one another, leaving the total result about the same as if the volitions of the whole mass had been affected by such only of the determining causes as are common to them all. In cases of this description, the results are as uniform, and may be as accurately foretold, as in any physical inquiries in which the effect depends upon a multiplicity of causes."[1] The uniformity of results in the aggregate of human actions, like that of the similarity of acts in individuals, grows out of the facts that our primary wants are similar; that all derive

[1] Examination of Sir William Hamilton's Philosophy, Chap. XXVI.

knowledge from the same common reservoir of truth; that the action of the Supreme Intelligence, to which each must in some degree adapt his action, is uniform and common to all, and that the aggregate of events and conditions brought about by the prior action of all causative agencies, is at each instant the same to all. With such causes tending to produce uniformity, we seem to need some element of diversity to account for the individual variations; and this may be found in the independent action of each individual Will, and especially when exerted in those cases in which there are two or more modes really, or to the actor apparently, just equal, furnishing no ground for preferring one to any other of them. After having shown that any degree of uniformity in the actions of individuals does not conflict with freedom, it seems hardly necessary to-contend that a uniformity in the aggregate of these actions would not, and even though such uniformity were more perfect than it is asserted to be. The chances are, that the number of individual variations from uniformity will be just in proportion to the number of cases; but if the number of variations on the one hand are taken to " neutralize " those on the other, the chances of the average variations in the aggregate will, of course, be much diminished, and such average uniformity of the aggregate is consistent with the greatest possible diversity in the individual actions. The average uniformity of aggregates is a uniformity of the second, or still higher order, and may be designated as the uniformity of diversity. If there were no diversity of particulars, there would be no *average species* of uniformity. The laws applied to such averages assume that there is a tendency to the greatest possible diversity, in the particulars of which the aggregates are composed. The calculation that in shuffling and cutting a pack of fifty-two cards fifty-two times, the chance is that any one of them, e. g., the ace of spades, will turn up once, and only once, is founded on the assumption, not that there will be uniformity, or any tendency to it, but that the results will tend to spread themselves over all the possibilities, and be as diverse as possible. That the chance of each one to be turned up once in fifty-two trials will be realized in practice, is infinitesimally small; and hence no reliable prediction can be made in regard to any one of them, and no such prediction as to the average uniformity of a large number of human actions has any application to any one particular volition. That a very large proportion of men, when hungry, will eat bread, and not hay, or that a large proportion of those who commit suicide will resort to drowning or poisoning, rather than to burning, is as readily explained by the free will as by the necessitarian hypothesis.

At the moment I am inclined to doubt whether the fundamental idea upon which the calculation is based admits of any reasonable expectation that it will be experimentally confirmed. Suppose the only distinction in the cards to be that one half are black and the other half red. The rule properly assumes that the chances of black and red are exactly equal; and hence it is inferred that if the trials be extended to a sufficient number of cases, the cuts of black and red will become equal. But suppose one cut has been made resulting in black, which is thus one ahead. Now, the future equality of the chances of black and red has not been affected by this first trial; and if the rule can be relied upon for this future, black will remain one ahead, proving that the rule was not reliable at the start, and if red requires this one, then on commencing with the second it was not reliable. In Rouge et Noir, the chances of black and red are just equal, but I am told that at Baden-Baden, black once won seventeen times in succession.

Perhaps nothing but the volitions of finite free agents, varying the results of the action of the Infinite, and acting upon and breaking up the uniformity which must obtain in the necessitated results of any blind mechanical causes, can produce the variety which is the basis of the peculiar uniformity found in aggregates. The Intelligence, thus interfering with such uniformity, by acting through matter in motion, might construct a machine which would shuffle and cut cards, and vary the process in conformity to any preconceived design; but in this there would be no room for any variation from the design, and it would furnish no occasion for the calculation of chances and of averages. Even such variations as might result from the wearing of the parts of such a machine, would be determined by the conditions, and be the subjects of calculations in which chance and averages would be excluded.

If one could *design* a machine which should continually vary its action, and yet in its variations be subject to no *particular design*, or rule, it might produce this diversity. I apprehend, however, that that which itself designs, and can form or change its designs at each step, that Intelligence, acting by Will, is the only conceivable contrivance capable of doing this; and if its action, as you assert, is so subject to an inevitable law of cause and effect, as to be certainly calculable from *existing data*, though these data may not be always at our command, it can make no basis for the existence of chance, and the only foundation for it would thus appear to be an intelligent being, acting independently of this law of cause and effect, and at each step capable of beginning and of varying its action independently of all other causative agencies. This only could produce that variation from the uniformity in the particulars which makes room or occasion for the calculation of chances and averages, and, if so, then, that there is a doctrine of chances and averages, attests the existence of an intelligent power in Will, which is not controlled by the uniformity of "cause and effect," but acts independently of, and interferes with, any such uniformity in other causative agencies.

The hypothesis that every being freely determines not only between any one act and its opposite, but between it and the whole circle of possible acts, accounts for the observed diversity better than that of necessity.

I am not, however, disposed to give much weight to arguments drawn by either side, from uniformity in the results of aggregates neutralized by opposing diversities; but I think this much must be admitted, that for reasons analogous to those before applied to individual cases (and because the aggregates of action are made up of the particular cases of it), the average of the aggregate uniformity of free actions may be as nearly perfect as that of coerced or unfree actions, and, hence, such uniformity or any prediction based upon it has no bearing whatever upon the question of freedom in willing.

If, as I believe, the views I have now advanced in connection with those heretofore presented, make a complete map of the whole subject, in which there is no unexplored region, the question may arise, and it may be profitable to inquire, why this exploration has not heretofore been successfully made. The answer, I think, must rest mainly in the fact that former explorers, with reverential feeling, perhaps I might say with superstitious reverence and awe, have shrunk from intruding upon ground which they have regarded as a hallowed domain concentrated to the Infinite. They have at least hesitated to ascribe to humanity the attributes of a *Creative First Cause* — of a Cause which in virtue of its intelligence can perceive among the existing conditions a reason for acting, and a mode of acting to attain the object, and which *of itself* can act — can make effort in conformity to these perceptions without being first acted upon by any other power or Cause ; and upon any position short of this, Freedom cannot logically be maintained. Once admit that we can act only as a consequence of the prior action of some other power or cause, and the element of freedom in our action is virtually excluded. The examination not only has not advanced far enough, but it has also been too narrow. It has lacked scope. It has sought to account for the phenomena of *human* volitions only. The views I have presented apply to all voluntary actions of all intelligent beings, from that which acts only instinctively, or from its innate knowledge of a mode of gratifying its want, to that which, with limitless capacity for knowing, with perfect wisdom devises modes of action and conforms its efforts to the most complicated and varying conditions. While some, on the one hand, may deem it too presumptuous to claim a freedom which in the sphere of our knowledge is as perfect as that of Omnipotence, many, on the other hand, recoil from the humiliation of accepting a freedom in which the worm and the oyster, to the extent of their knowledge, may participate. The element of freedom is alike perfect in all intelligent being, but the sphere in which the being freely acts is limited by its knowledge. It must perceive an object, and have some idea, right or wrong, of a mode in which, by action, it can attain that object.

Among the secondary causes of the failure, the absence of any definition of freedom which applies to the act of willing stands conspicuous. In my very limited reading on the subject, I have nowhere met with such a definition, or even any indication that any such existed. The popular idea of freedom is, that it consists in our not being restrained from doing what we will to do; but this comes after the act of willing, and cannot apply to it. This deficiency has led some investigators to seek the impossible conditions of a freedom which at the same time may not be freedom, *i. e.*, which is not restrained from being unfree, and which might, at the same time, be both free and unfree — be free to be unfree. The definition I have proposed, and from which as yet I know of no dissent, clears up this confusion.

Another difficulty has been the confounding of Choice with act of Will or Effort, and regarding them either as identical or as modifications of the same element, when they are, in fact, entirely distinct and different. Choice belongs to the domain of knowledge, and not to that of the Will. The effort to choose is only an effort to obtain the *knowledge* of what will suit us best; all effort, preliminary to acting, is to obtain knowledge by which to select the object, or the mode of action to attain it. On the false assumption that choice and volition are the same, the argument for necessity runs thus : the facts we know, not being within our control, the knowledge of what will suit us best, or choice, is not; and if our choice and our volition are the same, then it follows that volition is not controlled by us, and hence, in it, we are not free. This sophism falls with the correction of the error upon which it is founded.

Inquirers have also been misled by supposing that knowledge and other characteristics by which the being is distinguished, including the faculty of Willing, are extrinsic powers controlling his volition. I trust I have shown the fallacy of this position, against which it would perhaps be sufficient to say, that we know nothing of any being except its characteristics : if we eliminate these, and regard them as a distinct extrinsic power, there is no known being, to be free or otherwise. Closely allied to this is the argument from motives, which are also supposed to be powers extrinsic to the being and controlling its volitions or efforts, whereas a motive is always but the being's knowledge — his perception or expectation of the future effect of his effort, and his desire or choice as to such future effect.

Again, Instinct and Habit have been regarded as extrinsic powers controlling our actions. If my analysis of these traits is correct, Instinct is only a voluntary action, conformed by the being to a mode or plan the knowledge of which is innate, requiring no effort to devise a plan; and Habit is a voluntary action in conformity to a mode or plan which the being has itself *previously* discovered and acted upon till it can repeat it by memory without reëxamination of its fitness. Such actions, in both cases, differ from others only in the fact that for them we have the knowledge of the mode or plan ready formed in the mind, enabling us to dispense with the preliminary effort to attain it which is requisite in rational actions : after the knowledge is attained, there is no difference in the subsequent volition based upon it. The difference is neither in the knowledge, nor in the volition, nor in the relation of the two to each other, but only in the mode in which the related knowledge was attained, or came to be in the mind. If, in each or in any particular case of instinctive action, we suppose the knowledge to be *immediately* imparted to the actor by a superior intelligence, it would still be but a case of the common mode by which we influence and change the action of another by changing his knowledge, and thus influence and change because this other freely conforms his action to his knowledge without reference to the manner in which he became possessed of it.

In regard to prescience, it seems to have been overlooked that the cause with which the volition is supposed to be connected and controlled as the ground of prediction may be the being that wills as well as any other cause, and in this case, his effort, caused and controlled by himself, is free. If I have succeeded in showing that a volition which is controlled by the being itself is quite as easily predicted as that which is controlled by causal power extrinsic to it, then this argument, so much relied upon by philosophers and theologians, and which is so puzzling to people generally, is thrown entirely out of the question.

Yours very truly,
R. G. HAZARD.

JOHN STUART MILL, ESQ.

APPENDIX.

EXISTENCE OF MATTER.

I HAVE heretofore alluded to the embarrassment which arises, in the question of our Freedom in Willing, from the hypotheses of the existence of matter as a distinct entity, and further from its being regarded, when in motion, as an independent cause. I have also confessed my inability to prove or disprove either of these positions, though the argument seems to me to favor the negative in both. That you recognize in matter nothing but a "permanent possibility of sensation," indicates that, in this, so far, I am in accord with you. This expression for your view seems, however, to go farther, and to imply not only a doubt as to the existence of matter as an entity distinct from intelligent being, but raises the further doubt as to the existence of anything extrinsic to the being that is conscious of the varying sensations, for his sensation, actual or potential, cannot inhere in what is extrinsic to him, or be directly and of itself the evidence of any such extrinsic existence, material or spiritual.

The idea of such extrinsic existence is only an inference from the changes in our sensations, growing out of our notions that every change — every effect — requires a cause. With Comte, extrude this idea of cause, and we could not, from any change in our sensations, infer the existence of anything extrinsic, nor even of any power, or anything else in ourselves, beyond the cognized sensations. Unless power be postulated, as necessary to change, we cannot predicate the existence of anything, except our own sensations, the changes in which may, in such case, spring up spontaneously, without any agency whatever within or without us; for our own efforts in such case may be only the spontaneous change in our sensations, without any *real* activity on our part, but only the *feeling* of action. We should have no reason whatever to infer the existence of anything else. No exercise of power, no internal effort on our part being essential to any of the changes of which we are conscious, we cannot infer the existence of any external power or force as a cause for such of these changes as are not attended by a consciousness of effort in ourselves, or which we believe to be beyond our ability to produce. If the changes in my own mind are but sequences of previous states, requiring no action of my own, or of other causative agencies, then I have no evidence that anything exists but myself, whose sensations are changed or intermitted; and these changes may have been going on through all past eternity, and constitute the whole universal history, of which only so much is known as I remember. If we neither postulate power as essential to change, nor get the knowledge of it from consciousness, no one can infer the existence of anything outside of his own sentient being, with its mutable states of sensation. If each successive state is but a sequence of a previous state, without any intervening cause or power, then nothing but a constant succession of states and the order of their succession can be known; and from these nothing can be inferred. Our sensations, as you say, would then be only a string of feelings. Against this I attach great weight to your suggestion, that, in the absence of any sensations, there is a consciousness that we have been, and may again be, the subject of them. It is not easy to conceive that it is the present sensation which knows itself, or that remembers that there were other and very different sensations in the past, and that expects them to recur in the future; *e. g.*, that the sensation of red now existing remembers that a twinge of the gout was felt, and expects that the sound of a bugle will be heard, and that this twinge was felt by itself, or that the sound will be heard or cognized by the fleeting auricular sensation. Equally difficult

EXISTENCE OF MATTER. 203

is it to think that this knowledge pertains to any combination of sensations, of which there may be now only one existing. We cannot divest ourselves of the idea, that *knowing* all the various sensations with those memories and expectations is distinct from the variety which is known, and from any portion of it, and that there is something permanent that knows, and that this something is distinct from the fleeting sensations known, and has a relation common to them all. Admitting, then, the idea of cause as essential to any investigation of the questions involved in the inquiry as to external existence, it is still conceivable that the whole substratum of intelligent being — of spirit — might be only a combination of the attributes of feeling and knowing, it being impossible that the former should exist independently of the latter. Such a being would be a mere passive recipient of sensations and emotions, with no active power in itself. But as, under our admission, we must still further admit cause or power in something, it is most reasonable to conform this necessity to our consciousness. We are conscious, at least, of effort in ourselves to produce change. This is the only power or cause of which we are directly conscious; and hence, rationally and logically, to the two attributes just mentioned we must add that of Will. Whether this *combination* of the attributes of feeling, knowing, and willing constitutes the ultimate substratum of intelligent being, is a very different question from that as to the changing sensations alone being such ultimatum. That the capacity for knowledge — the ability to know — is an original attribute of intelligent being, and that the knowledge of our sensations is intuitive, no one will question. That the ability to produce change is inherent, is generally admitted, and I have endeavored to show that there is no possible way in which we ever could have acquired the knowledge that effort is the means by which we move our muscles; and hence, as we now have this knowledge, it must be innate.[1]

[1] *Freedom of Mind in Willing*, Chap. XI.

This combination of the attributes of feeling, knowing, and willing, embracing all that is essential to spirit, and it being impossible for us to know anything except by its properties or attributes, any further inquiry as to its substratum must be merely to ascertain whether it has other properties or attributes. The only other properties, of which we have any idea, are those which we predicate of matter; and hence such inquiry would be, Has spirit extension, resistance, or color, etc.? Is it hard or soft, rough or smooth, etc.? Any one of these inquiries is, perhaps, as pertinent and important as any other of them. The inquiry in all of them virtually is, has mind a material substratum? or do these attributes of feeling, knowing, and willing pertain to some form of material substance? To the idealist, this is to inquire, whether these attributes have a substratum of sensations, or are the co-effects of whatever produces sensation; and if these sensations are known only as changes in our feelings, then the inquiry becomes, have the spiritual attributes, by which we recognize the changing conditions of existence, a substratum of change? But the idea of mere effect, or of change, is contradictory and destructive to that idea of permanency which is the essence of what we are seeking in a substratum — a something which, though it may be the subject of change, may be affected — still retains its distinctive characteristics, as wax, which, however much it may be moulded or impressed, still retains its property of being moulded and impressed, consequently, its property of still being thus affected, and, so far, is still wax. A feeling not felt by that which feels is a most complete absurdity. In feeling we must, at least, know our own passive existence as a combination of the attributes of feeling and knowing — mere feeling reveals nothing beyond this. It is only through the idea of cause that we reach farther. The innate knowledge that effort is the mode by which to produce change, involves the essential idea of cause, and through it we know ourselves as cause, or, at least, may do so as soon as, by experiment, we find that by effort in conformity to this innate

EXISTENCE OF MATTER. 205

knowledge, we really do produce or change our own sensations. But we also find that some of our sensations occur or change without any effort or exercise of causative power by ourselves, and this leads us to attribute these to other like causative power not in ourselves; and if they exceed our own power, to like but superior power — to a power able to make the changes in our sensations which are made — of doing what we see is done.

In our known sensations, and the knowledge that by effort we can produce or change our sensations, we have a rational ground for believing that there is a combination of the attributes of feeling, knowing, and willing, which constitutes our identity, and distinguishes us from any other forms of existence, and that each of such combinations is distinguished from other like combinations, not only by the difference in the combination of sensations, knowledge, and efforts (which, admitting of a variety absolutely infinite, probably is in no two alike), but by the distinct consciousness existing in each of its known sensations. Whether there is any common substratum to these combined properties, as before observed, is, so far as we can know, simply a question as to whether the combination embraces still other properties, and, if this were decided affirmatively, the only further question would be, are these other properties the same as those now recognized in matter, as resistance, extension, mobility, etc., or are they properties of which we have now no conception? It would be only a short step farther to inquire whether this substratum of mind is marble or metal, mist or moonshine, magnetism or music. Such questions, in any view, have as yet little practical importance. But though, from the peculiar relations of knowledge to sensation, we infer a combination of the two, we cannot, from these, further infer the existence of matter as a cause of the sensations. We cannot thus know matter, for all the phenomena of sensation can be as fully accounted for without it. We can, in fact, produce many sensations in ourselves, in the absence of any external materiality.

This is especially the case with the sensations of sight, by which we most readily comprehend an external variety. In doing this, as, for instance, in imagining a landscape, we are conscious of *effort ;* but we find that similar landscapes arise in our minds without any effort of our own. Having found that by our efforts we can create such sensations or images in our minds, the natural inference would be, that any such which we find existing without our own effort are created by a like effort, but one which is not ours. If the creations of our own efforts preceded those which we find existing in our mind, without our efforts, we probably would thus reason. But the probability is, that the sensations which are independent of us exist in our consciousness before those which we perceive to follow as a consequence of our efforts, and we then have no reason, from experience or otherwise, to refer them to effort. The idea of cause is, in itself, a negation of the notion that the thing can produce itself, and, when this idea is attained, we must refer our sensations to something. In regard to some of these, we can find no reason to believe that we have ourselves created them. We cannot attribute their existence to their own agency, and we know nothing beyond. Hence, we merely substitute a representation of each sensation as a thing distinct from the sensation itself with which it may be associated as its cause. This is, perhaps, the earliest of those philosophical fictions or hypotheses which have been made to stand for an unknown cause, and which, getting firmly rooted in the mind before there is any competing growth, it is very difficult thereafter to eradicate. Very few people, though they correct the belief of childhood, ever come habitually to conceive of the sun as relatively at rest, and its apparent diurnal motion as caused by the earth's revolution on its axis. And so, from the effects of early impression and association, we come to regard the internal sensations, which we do know, as merely images or representations of something external, which we do not know. Our belief that in sleep our sensations are changed without the agency either of our own efforts or the presence of matter, favors the belief that such changes are by other intelligent agencies. Mr. Herbert Spencer, in " Mill *versus* Hamilton — The Test of Truth," attempts to show that the reasoning by which the idealists defend their position is vitiated by a " covert *petitio principii*," tacitly assuming the existence of matter as a basis of the proof " that Mind and Ideas are the only existences." Assuming the existence of a thing to prove that *it is not* is very different from assuming its existence to prove that *it is*; the former may, in some cases, be legitimate. I cannot find, however, that, as against the ideal hypothesis, he makes out either case. Of the argument of the idealist he says: " Though the conclusion reached is, that Mind and Ideas are the only existences, yet the steps by which the conclusion is reached, take for granted that external objects have just the kind of independent existence which is eventually denied. . . . The resolution of all knowledge into ' impressions ' and ' ideas ' is effected by an analysis which assumes, at every step, an objective reality, producing the impressions, and the subjective reality receiving them. . . . Now, assume that object and subject do not exist. He cannot stir a step towards his conclusion; nay, he cannot even state his conclusion, for the word ' impression ' cannot be translated into thought, without assuming a thing impressing and a thing impressed."

But if this " objective reality," this " thing impressing," is only another active intelligent spirit, it still meets all the demands of the argument of the idealist, and is no less an objective reality than that which is associated with our idea of marble or music. Mr. Spencer further says: " Empiricism . . . is open to an analogous criticism on its method, similarly telling against the validity of its inferences. . . . Evidently there is tacitly assumed something beyond the mind by which its experiences are produced — something in which exist the objective relations to which the subjective relations correspond — an external world." The empirical " method," however, applies no more to the materialistic than to the ideal hypothesis, under which the "something beyond the mind, by which the experiences are produced," etc., would be only other intelligent agencies.

The question, then, really is, not as to whether there is or is not to each intelligence an objective reality, but whether this reality is material or wholly spiritual. As already suggested, if we extrude the idea of cause, there would be no reason to refer those sensations, which arise without any conscious agency of our own, to anything within or without us, for the phenomenon of a cognized sensation might arise of itself, as well as anything else. We cannot, then, advance a single step in the investigation of the question on hand, without recognizing that every change, of necessity, requires the action of a cause. But this fact of itself gives not the slightest indication as to the nature of the cause, and of course cannot indicate whether it is material or spiritual. Coupled with the consciousness that some changes in our sensations are produced by our own mental efforts, and that our knowledge of the connection between our effort and these changes is innate, it would seem that we should refer similar changes, not by ourself, to a like cause which is not ourself — to the mental effort of another intelligent being — to a spiritual cause; and in such case, the existence of matter becomes a gratuitous and needless assumption.

There is still this further question : Is there any such difference between the sensations or imagery (the landscape, for instance) which I create in my own mind, and the sensations or imagery of a landscape which I find in my mind, without any such effort of my own as to justify the reference of the former to a mental effort, or active spiritual cause, and the latter to a passive material cause ?

I have suggested [1] that the only difference between the phenomena, in the two cases, is that the landscape, which is our own creation, is subject to our will — that it can be changed as we choose — while that which is not our own creation cannot be thus changed at will, and that if, from

[1] *Freedom of Mind in Willing.* Chap. II.

any cause, our own imaginary creations should become fixed, and not changeable by our act of will, they would at once become to us external realities.[1]

If I am right in asserting that this is the only subsequent difference in the phenomena of the two modes of sensation, which are distinguished in their inception, the one as associated with our own effort, the other as not so associated, there seems to be no such difference in their subsequent actual existence as will justify referring one of them to a spiritual, and the other to a material, cause.

In any view which recognizes the external universe as created, or even moulded, by an intelligent being, a *thing* created, or the *form* into which a coexisting material entity is moulded, must have existed as a thought or conception of that being before he gave actual objective existence to such thing or form ; and, as I have before suggested, it can make no difference to us whether this thought or conception — this imagery — of the creative intelligence is transferred immediately to our minds, or mediately by first writing, picturing, carving, or moulding them in matter. Nor is it of any consequence to us whether our sensations are produced by a material or a spiritual cause. I have also remarked that the ideal hypothesis makes creative agency conceivable to us.[1] We can all create in our own minds imaginary scenes, and can, to some extent, impress these creations upon others. That, on the ideal hypothesis, these powers make up in ourselves the complement of all the powers which we attribute to the Supreme Intelligence, or infer from the existence of the universe, adds to the reasons for adopting it.

To most persons, the existence of matter as a distinct objective entity, no doubt, seems to be a necessary belief. Mr. Spencer intimates that such necessity is a test of truth, alleging that " the fallacious result of the test of necessity, which Mr. Mill instances, is due to a misapplication of the test." He before contends that " if a particular proposition is, by some, accepted as a necessary belief, but by one or more

[1] *Freedom of Mind in Willing*, Chap. II.

denied to be a necessary belief, the validity of the test of necessity *is not* thereby disproved in respect to that particular proposition."

But his very first statement seems conclusive against his position; viz., "In alleging that a belief is said by some to be necessary, but by others to be not necessary, the test of necessity is thereby shown to be no test. Mr. Mill tacitly assumes that all men have powers of introspection, enabling them in all cases to say what consciousness testifies; whereas a great proportion of men are incapable of correctly interpreting consciousness in any but its simplest modes, and even the remainder are liable to mistake for dicta of consciousness what prove, on closer examination, not to be its dicta." Now, if most men are incapable of correctly interpreting consciousness, and the remainder are liable to be mistaken as to its dicta, there would seem to be no reliance upon the test, except in those cases in which there is no denial by others; and even in these, error may subsequently be discovered, and contrariety of opinion arise, showing, as Mr. Spencer himself observes, "that there is a liability to error as to what are indissoluble connections." If it be admitted that the dictum of consciousness is, in itself, infallible, we still, on Mr. Spencer's statement, need some means of ascertaining what the dictum is; and again, if we admit that *some* "men have powers of introspection, enabling them, in all cases, to say what consciousness testifies," we still need a test by which to distinguish those who have these powers from those who have not. In the absence of any absolute test of this, each one would accredit those whose testimony coincided with his own belief. Any attempt of an idealist to convince a London newsboy that he was not conscious of the distinct existence of brick walls, as an external entity, would probably result in the idealist's believing that the newsboy was ignorant, and the newsboy being quite sure that the idealist was crazy. Who shall decide? The majority would be with the newsboy.

The illustrations of errors in consciousness, which Mr.

EXISTENCE OF MATTER. 211

Spencer adduces, indicate that he uses this term as coextensive with knowledge; and confirmatory of this, the cases in which he says, "an appeal to the direct verdict of consciousness is illegitimate," are cases in which we are in doubt, and do not know. From this, as I hold that the acquisition of *all* knowledge is a passive perception — an effortless assimilation — by the mind, it might seem that I ought not to dissent. I admit that identity in this important feature of passive perception is a sufficient reason for including all we thus perceive under one name, and for this we have the term knowledge. But this passive perception seems often to be regarded as the peculiar and distinguishing characteristic of the knowledge which we attribute directly to consciousness, when, being the characteristic of all, it can thus distinguish no particular portion of our knowledge. The term consciousness seems to be frequently used, and advantageously so used, to distinguish some mode or modes by which these passive perceptions were obtained, or the circumstances in which they had their origin, and which made their acquisition possible. Our cognitions may be thus classified: 1. Those of which we have an immediate perception without any preliminary effort, including those which reveal our innate knowledge, and also those which arise from simple observation or experience. We see these as we see objects before our eyes. 2. Those in which we make effort to so arrange things or ideas, that the truth will become apparent, as we remove obstacles to see what is behind them, or bring material objects or extensions near to each other to compare their relations. 3. Those in which we substitute signs (as words) for the things, or for the mental imagery, and then observe the relations among these signs. 4. Those cases in which we accept the facts upon the testimony of others, without empirical or logical proof. In all these cases, however, the resulting knowledge is itself a simple passive perception of some real or supposed truth, which may have been brought within the limits of our vision by effort. but the view or knowledge of it is still the same as if it had been in sight, and cognized without any preliminary effort. From the assertions of others, however infallible we deem them, we acquire no knowledge, unless we get such perceptions of what they describe or assert; and the same in the other cases. I have heretofore given my reasons for applying the term knowledge to any and all of those perceptions, of the verity of which the percipient has no doubt.[1] The cognitions included in the first of the above classes seem to me properly, and in accordance with the common use of the term, to be regarded as dicta of consciousness. We thus directly know that effort is the mode of moving our muscles; we cannot account for this knowing; we can give no reason for the belief; we are simply conscious of a perception of the fact without any knowledge of its having been preceded by any effort of our own, or that there has been any other cause of its existence in us. The term, however, as already intimated, has a wider range and we are also said to be conscious of those intuitions of which our sensations are the occasion. We are conscious of the pain which we feel, and of the sights, sounds, tastes, and odors which we experience. It will, perhaps, be generally admitted that we are also conscious of such general truths as that, what is, is, and that a thing is equal to itself; but as to how far in this direction simple consciousness goes, there may be much diversity of opinion. Some persons perceive relations at once which others learn only by slow and careful ratiocination. Truths flash upon the poet which the logician reaches through repeated syllogisms.

I have heretofore pointed out that the difference between the second mode, in which we deal directly with the imagery in the mind, excluding terms, and the third mode, in which we use substituted terms to the exclusion of the imagery, constitutes the generic distinction between poetry and prose, and that, in the graphic delineation of the processes of the former mode lies the poetic art, of which the most perfect type is in the representation and communication of the

[1] *Freedom of Mind in Willing*, Chap. III.

thought and imagery of the mind of God in the material universe, without intermediate signs or words; while the most perfect type of the latter, or prosaic mode, is in mathematical reasoning, and especially in the algebraic formulas, in which, for the time being, we know nothing but the substituted terms, and their quantitative relations.[1] In geometry we really deal as exclusively with the terms in which the definitions are stated; but this fact is obscured by the use of diagrams to aid our conceptions of the things defined, or rather the things created by the definitions, and of the relations among them. This makes a very slight deviation from the purely prosaic method of terms, and in the direction of the poetic method of imagery. That the poetic processes are carried on without the use of conventional signs or words, makes it difficult to communicate its results to others. For this, the additional process of translating the imagery into language, is a prerequisite. The logical or prosaic process, being carried on, from premises to conclusion, in terms, are already in the state admitting of easy communication to others; but here, in a large proportion of cases, before they admit of practical application, the reverse process of translating the term into imagery, which can be perceived and apprehended by the mind, is necessary. We may more clearly recognize this necessity in the fact that the perceived relations among the terms sometimes force us to a conclusion, which we, at the time, not only do not perceive to be true, but do not believe, and which may or may not stand the test of further examination in this reverse process. In both modes we really reason. In one, directly with the imagery of the mind; in the other, with the terms put in its stead. But from the superior quickness of the poetic processes, and the fact that its results are in a form which admit of immediate assimilation and application, these results are more likely to be accepted as dicta of consciousness than those of the slower abstract prosaic mode.[2]

[1] *Language*, p. 5, Houghton, Mifflin & Co.'s edition.
[2] For the same reasons poetry is the nearest approach which lan-

These views show that it is not without reason that the term consciousness is used as coextensive with knowledge, all of which, in its acquisition, has the common characteristic of simple passive perception, and is not distinguishable in the manner of its immediate inception, but only by the difference in the antecedent processes by which these ultimate perceptions were obtained. The similarity in the processes two and three, and the manner in which the boundary between one and two varies in different individuals, indicate the difficulty of making any general rule of division founded on the difference in the processes. Some persons would see that all the angles of a triangle must be equal to two right angles, as quickly, and with as little intellectual effort, as others would see that things which are equal to the same thing must be equal to one another.

But, wherever the division be made, or if not made at all, it is evident that the whole effect and influence of consciousness upon our knowledge lies in the fundamental and common element of simple perception, and that this, while it is the sole foundation of knowledge and belief to the percipient individual, is not proof, and as a rational argument avails nothing with one whose perception is *different*, nor even with one who does not himself have the same perception. Our perceptions are not alike; we see things differently, with different eyes, or in different aspects or circumstances, but each must believe in conformity to those perceptions of his own which constitute his whole knowledge.

If any of these perceptions classified as those of consciousness, or not, are in themselves really tests of truth, or if any such perceptions of any individuals having " powers of in-

---

guage can make to reality, and the poetic power is the most important element in common sense and business ability. It is that which enables one most quickly to perceive the actual relations and significance of circumstances in the common affairs of life, and most readily to adapt his action to them. Those in whom the poetic element prevails may give bungling reasons for logical action, while those wholly prosaic will give logical reasons for bungling action.

trospection, enabling them, in all cases, to say what consciousness testifies," are to be received as infallible, we still, in the first case, need some means of ascertaining which of such perceptions constitute such test of truth; and in the second, of knowing whose individual cognitions are to be accepted as authority. That the perceptions of some men of clear and profound thought, and especially of such men upon the subjects to which they have given special attention, will be regarded as more reliable than those of other men, will be generally admitted. But this superior knowledge of a leading mind will be of no avail to others, until they get the same perceptions that he has.

Even those most impressed with their own comparative ignorance will cling to the conviction that they know something, and that what they do know they know as well as anybody else does. Without such faith in their own perceptions, their knowledge, if they could be said to have any, would be comparatively useless to them.

Mr. Spencer asserts that in Necessity we have a test of the authority of the dicta of consciousness. That among our passive perceptions we recognize various degrees of reliability, from the absolutely certain, to the probable, or the merely possible, will also be admitted. The absolutely certain propositions are those of which we not only have a clear perception, but also clearly perceive that it is impossible that they should be otherwise; and if to any, it is to these that the test of necessity must apply. This, however, is a different test of necessity from that adopted by Mr. Spencer, in which "there remains in the inquirer the consciousness that certain states of his consciousness are so welded together, that all other links in the chain of consciousness yield before these give way." These "indissoluble connections," which, for the time being, " he is compelled to accept," may be only the indissoluble associations of repeated experience; of simple passive observation of the coincidences in time or place, without any perception of the impossibility of their negation or dissolution by other experience or by abstract reasoning.

All mathematicians agree that numerical and mathematical truths are necessary in the sense I have stated. We can perceive not only that they are true in the particular cases before us, but that it is impossible that there can be other cases in which they are not true. But, admitting that these perceptions of numerical and mathematical truths are dicta of consciousness, and that, in fact, there is this certainty of *necessity* in regard to them, it avails nothing with the man who does not perceive this necessity. He would be very apt to doubt that in all the variations of which a triangle admits, there can be no variation in the aggregate of its angles. And in the case taken by Mr. Spencer, though, in fact, thirty-five and nine of necessity make forty-four, the ignorant may as readily believe that they make forty-five.

In some cases it is difficult to determine whether the idea of necessity has its origin in experience or in reasoning. Most persons will assert that a body cannot move one way, and then directly back, without stopping at the extreme point of its advance. This can hardly be a result of observation, for even if uniformly true in fact, the time of rest is generally imperceptible. I am inclined to think that it is believed to be necessarily involved in the ideas as a necessity of thought, and that this belief has been wholly or in part generated by the terms used in describing the phenomena. We begin the assertion by saying the body *stops*, and add, going in that direction.

Be this as it may, the assertion is generally made with great confidence. This confidence may be somewhat shaken by the inquiry, how much must the body be deflected from its original course to make its stopping a necessity? If a very small change from directly forward will not, will a very small variation from directly back, suffice? and if so, what is the precise degree of deflection at which the body will actually stop at the angular point? If we now present the case of the direct collision of two bodies, perfectly hard, and moving in opposite directions, one weighing four pounds and the other only two pounds, with the suggestion that, if the small body stops at the moment of collision, the larger one must also stop, and that there would then be no power to move either, it will appear that the assertion as to the stopping is in direct conflict with other admitted facts, and, on further examination, may be found not to be a necessity of thought, but that a body may really be conceived of as moving to and fro with the same uniform velocity at every point, including the extreme points, as well as when it is moving steadily and directly forward. He who thought otherwise has been deceived by experience, or by the apparent or real testimony of consciousness; but still, so long as he has the uncorrected perceptions, however acquired, his knowledge must be identical with them.

In further illustration of his idea of the necessity of thinking "an objective existence," Mr. Spencer says of this inquirer: "When grasping a fork, and putting food into his mouth, he is wholly unable to expel from his mind the notion of something which resists the force he is conscious of using; and he cannot suppress the nascent thought of an independent existence, keeping apart his tongue and palate, and giving him that sensation of taste which he is unable to generate in consciousness by his own activity." The cases here presented are as good as any which could be selected, but I think they do not reach the point he aims at. They do not show that " an objective existence " is an immediate revelation of consciousness. It is true that one cannot, by a direct single effort, produce the sensation of the " something which resists his force; " nor can he thus directly produce " the sensation of taste," nor even the sensation of touch in any form, but the immediate antecedents, in both cases, generally are our own efforts, often made with design to produce the resulting sensations; and hence the effects may reasonably be referred to these efforts. In pressing one hand against the other, we would refer the sensation of touch to our own effort; and the difference between this and producing the sensation of taste is merely in the degree of directness, or the greater or less complexity of the series of efforts by which the effect is reached.

If one, without prior effort of his own, should have the notion of "something which resists the force he is conscious of using," or should thus become suddenly conscious of the "sensation of taste," he would (if he recognized the necessity of cause or power for every change) attribute this change to some power other than himself, and with the knowledge that he does himself, by his own efforts, sometimes produce such changes, he would logically refer those changes of which he is conscious, and which are attended with no conscious effort of his own, to like efforts not his own.

I do not find that Mr. Spencer's arguments or illustrations touch the question of the existence of matter as a distinct, independent entity; or that they tend to prove or elucidate anything beyond the point that there is "an objective existence" of some kind, though, from the current associations with the terms necessarily used in the discussion, and the difficulty of finding language free from these associations, one might at first be led to think otherwise. I see no reason to suppose that he intended to do more than assert such "objective existence," without asserting the verity of that of the materialists; and upon this point, in view of the statements I have just made, I cannot agree with him, that, in the immediate revelations or dicta of consciousness, or in their relatively strong cohesions, "the inquirer discovers a warrant higher than any argument can give for asserting an objective existence," but must adhere to my previous notion that, as by consciousness we can only directly know our subjective sensations, our belief in an objective existence is only an inference, founded on our idea of the necessity of a cause for those changes in our sensations which occur without our own agency, and that it is more rational to regard this objective cause as similar to the subjective cause which produces similar effects than as something wholly different; in other words, that, as we know that we produce changes in our sensations by an internal effort, we should logically impute like changes, which are not the result of efforts within us, to *efforts* without us, and, consequently, to intelligent power, and not to material force, and that this cognition of "objective existence," though in the last analysis, like all our cognitions, an immediate perception, so far from revealing a " warrant higher than that which any argument can give," really has its foundation and warrant in an argument which, put into words, runs thus : Every change must be effected by some power — by some cause — this cause must either be ourself, or something which is not ourself ; some changes occur of which ourself is not the cause, and, hence, must be effected by a cause which is not ourself. As the existence of this extrinsic agency is a mere inference from the difference in the phenomena of the change, it would be unphilosophical and irrational to infer any greater difference in the cause than is required by the differences in the phenomena or effect; and, hence, we must suppose that these causes are in all respects alike, except that one is intrinsic and the other extrinsic, and that the changes in our sensations are, in all cases, caused by intelligent effort within or without us, in neither case requiring the existence of matter as a distinct entity to account for the phenomena, nor furnishing any proof or indication of such existence.

OUR NOTION OF INFINITE SPACE.

MR. HERBERT SPENCER, in the article referred to in the preceding paper,[1] says : " Here, then, is the flaw in Sir William Hamilton's proposition : that space must be infinite or finite, are alternatives of which we are not obliged to regard one as necessary, seeing that we have no state of consciousness answering to either of these words, as applied to the totality of space, and therefore no exclusion of two antagonistic states of consciousness by one another." But the obvious truth of the general proposition, that everything " must

[1] *Mill* versus *Hamilton — The Test of Truth.*

be infinite or finite," does not depend upon our having a state of consciousness answering to the particular thing to which it is applied. We assert that all the angles of *every plane triangle* are equal to two right angles; but we have no state of consciousness corresponding to triangles in general, or to *every plane triangle*, and hence, if such consciousness of the thing to which the general proposition is applied is necessary, we would only assert this of the *particular* triangle in the mind's view at the time. But in demonstrating this geometrical theorem, we perceive that we use no elements which do not pertain to every plane triangle, whatever its form or size, and hence assert its truth of every plane triangle. The only condition essential to the demonstration is, that the figure shall be bounded by three right lines. So, too, when we assert that a thing is infinite or finite — is or is not bounded — we perceive that the truth of this proposition does not depend upon any peculiar property whatever of the thing to which it is applied, but is as true of a thing with one property, or one combination of properties, as of a thing with other property, or other combination of properties; and hence, whether we do or do not know or conceive of the properties of the particular thing to which we apply the proposition is not material to our faith in its universal application to all things whatever. The only ground upon which space could be excluded from its application would be to assert that space, in itself, is no thing — that it is but our conception of nothingness; but it has the property of, or is in itself, extension — the very property or conception to which the idea of being bounded or not bounded most palpably applies.

If I see only a portion of anything, I know that it either *is* or is *not* bounded. A telegraph wire, of which I cannot see any end, I know either has or has not an end in each direction. It may be infinite, and every portion of it present the same appearance as that which I now see. It may make an entire circle, and thus, though finite, in a common sense of the word, have no end. Even in this sense, to deny one

INFINITE SPACE.   221

of the positions asserts the other, both in terms and in thought. In regard to space, it is asserted that, in its entirety, we can neither comprehend nor conceive it as bounded, nor yet as not bounded. The first seems to me certain, but I am by no means sure that we cannot and do not conceive of space as boundless. That we know it must be either bounded or not bounded, taken in connection with our inability to conceive of it as not bounded, seems to indicate that we do, in thought, regard and conceive it as boundless.

The mental process by which we attempt to grasp the idea of infinite space is peculiar. We begin with the admitted fact that it can have no bound or limit, and yet the next thing we attempt is to find its bound or limit, and then, because we cannot find in it that which we know does not belong to it, and cannot possibly pertain to it, we conclude that we do not comprehend it. This is as if one who had never before seen any shot, except those made of lead, should, on looking at some made of silver, say these are pure silver shot; I cannot find any lead in them; therefore I do not comprehend them. That our conception of anything does not embrace in it a property or quality which does not, or cannot, pertain to it, is so far proof that our conception of it is not incorrect. As the fact that one does not and cannot find any lead in pure silver shot, is so far evidence that he has a correct conception of silver shot; so, too, that we do not and cannot find any limit or bound to infinite space, so far indicates that in this respect we properly conceive it. The knowledge or conception of a thing in *itself* is impossible to us. We can only know it by its properties of producing change in ourselves, and, if an outward object, the only way in which this can be done is through our sensations. The same object may have the property of effecting a variety of sensations, and we have not a full conception of it till we know all these properties, or, rather, all the effects attributed to them, for the properties, as distinct from the effects, like the things in themselves, are unknowable, and are recognized only by their effects upon us. When we name these properties, we only name a cause, the existence of which is inferred from the effect. This object may also have the property of changing itself, or of changing other objects, and, maybe, of being changed by them. The knowledge of all these elements is necessary to that full comprehension which *is* possible.

We comprehend a thing in itself when we know all its component parts and properties, and all the relations of these parts and properties to each other. As an entirety, we comprehend a circle whose radius reaches to the remotest star. We know that all its properties are the same as those of any other circle. We cannot readily divide it into, and particularly notice each of such magnitudes as we have been accustomed to move over, or even to clearly apprehend by the eye, for to fix the attention on each of such portions would require centuries. These cannot all be the objects of real or imaginary sensations. We cannot thus make it up or construct a conception of it by the addition of the minor perceptions which our senses have supplied. But this does not imply that mentally we do not comprehend this vast circle, with all its intrinsic properties and conditions. One must at least have a clear conception of those parts, properties, and relations, which he can fully and accurately present, on a smaller scale, to the senses. Now, the idea or conception of infinite space, in itself, is the simplest which is possible. Its only property by which it is related to, or distinguished from, anything else, is its capacity to contain extension, or admit other existences into itself; and for these it is equally essential, whether we regard it, with these other existences, as distinct, self-subsisting entities, or as mere ideal creations, or imagery of the mind. Strictly speaking, perhaps, this capacity of space to be a receptacle for *things* or for certain *mental imagery*, is rather a use than a property. Its component parts are perfectly homogeneous — nothing but space — and the relations of *each portion* to *all the rest* are the same, and there is nothing external to it to which different portions of it might have different relations.

INFINITE SPACE. 223

The idea of a periphery of a circle, considered merely as an isolated line, has this same homogeneity: every portion of it is precisely like every other equal portion, and has the same geometrical relation to every other portion. So, too, of the surface of a sphere: every portion is like every other portion of like dimensions, and each of such portions has the same relation to all the rest of the surface. But in the cases of the circle's periphery and the sphere's surface, we always have a difference in the relations of the different parts to what is extrinsic to them, as that one part is farther from the earth than another, or one part is farther to our right than another, which cannot occur in regard to infinite space, to which there is nothing without to compare.

Intelligent being, intrinsic to space, may regard one portion of it as to his right, and another as to his left; but change in his position does not change his relation to all the rest of space in this respect.

If, instead of periphery and surface, we consider the enclosed area of the circle, and the enclosed quantity or space in the sphere, then the portions in each vary in their intrinsic relations to each other; some are nearer the periphery or the surface than others, or some are nearer to the centre than others; but make this sphere infinite, and this variety in the intrinsic relations of its parts disappears, for there is then no circumference, consequently no centre, but every point in it is as much a centre, and as much on or near the circumference, as any other point.

The homogeneity of the isolated periphery of the circle, or of the surface of the sphere, is again attained, and the conception is not embarrassed or complicated by any difference in the relations of its component parts, and has the additional exemption from such embarrassment and complication that there is nothing without it with which it can have any relations whatever. The idea of infinite space is thus simpler than that of a finite homogeneous sphere in which the different parts stand in different relations to each other, and also to surrounding objects. No conception of anything can be

224   APPENDIX.

simpler than of that which is perfectly homogeneous in all its parts, and in which every part has the same relation to every other part, and nothing outside with which to have varying relations, and in which, having only one property, this can of course have no relations whatever, and, therefore, no diversity of relation to any other of its properties. In regard to the surface of the finite sphere, we cannot in our conception of it take in separately each point, and observe its relations to every other point, for the number of these points is infinite; but knowing that each of these points has the same relation to every other point, we are justified, after ascertaining this fact, and having observed the relation of one point to the rest of the surface, which includes all other points, in saying that we comprehend this relation of every point to the whole surface.

So, too, in the case of infinite space, though we cannot consider each of the infinity of like finite spaces, of which it is composed, yet, knowing that the relation of each one to the whole is the same as that of every other, we may in like manner assert that we conceive and know that every point or portion has the same relation to the whole which every other point or like portion has. It seems, then, that our conception of infinite space which properly extrudes the element of limit or bound, which does not belong to it, and which embraces a knowledge of all its component parts, and of all the relations of those parts to each other, and of all its properties and their relations to each other, and of all its uses, is as full and perfect a conception as we have of anything whatever.

The idea of what is thus homogeneous in all its parts, and in their relations to each other, which has but one property or use, and nothing without it to which it can have varying relations, is the simplest possible conception of existence, having indeed so few elements of thought in it as, in the last analysis, to raise a doubt as to whether the conception is that of existence or of its absence.

Perhaps the principal difficulty in the case is that of believing that an idea so simple and so limited in its conditions, really fits an object which, in its vastness, is illimitable. Hence we seek to add to our conception of it, and find that in so doing we immediately come in contact with ideas that do not belong to it, showing that on all sides we have reached the limit of the conception we are exploring, and have already embraced in our survey all that pertains to it. If extension is regarded as its property, this does not generically distinguish it from other *things ;* for all have this property, and the consideration that this is the only real property of space, and that space is necessary to all material existences, strengthens my previous suggestion that extension is the nearest approach to our notion of a substratum. Mere extension is unoccupied space, and is that which always remains when all the other properties of that which occupied it are abstracted ; but the extension, in itself, is then reduced to a vacuum or nonentity.

The reduction of our notion of tangible space to an idea of the simplest character, and eventually to a mere extended vacuum, is not wholly an isolated fact, without parallel in other objects of thought. As the tangible quantities of an algebraic formula may sometimes be reduced in the aggregate to zero, and more especially as the combination of such formulas in an equation, sometimes, when reduced to their lowest terms, results only in $0 = 0$, so, too, in subjecting some of our abstract ideas to that last analysis, in which they elude further reduction, analysis, or comparison, we get glimpses of relations by which they seem to be neutralizing each other, and in the aggregate resolving into nothingness, suggesting as a corollary the converse possibility that from nothingness they may have been evolved, and brought into existence by the creative plastic power of an Intelligence of a higher order than that which thus by its action resolves them again into their original nonentity.

If, by a fuller knowledge — a clearer perception — of this resolving process, or otherwise, we shall ever come to be able to reverse it, then, in connection with the ideal philosophy, the creative power of the finite, as well as of the Infinite Intelligence, will no longer be veiled in a mystery which has thus far been impenetrable to mortal vision, and the origin of all existence, except that which creates, would be revealed to us.

We may, perhaps, even now anticipate, or venture the prediction, that the creative power of mind will be found to reside mainly in its poetic modes of thought, and its annihilative, mainly in its logical prosaic modes.

This would be in harmony with the suggestions I have heretofore made, that the representation of the thought and imagery of the mind of God in the creations of the material universe, is the purest type we know of poetry; that the province of the poet is to create, and to make his creations palpable and tangible to others, and that the appliance of the logical modes to his productions immediately reduces his creations to mere abstractions, with a cessation or revulsion of all the poetic vision and emotion which they were fitted to produce. We may thus, by a resort to the logical modes, annihilate the creations of the most gifted in our own sphere of intelligence, or at least reduce them to intangible abstractions. We may further note in this connection, that mathematics, the purest type of the logical processes which thus dissolve or reduce the creations of the poet, is only the science of quantity, or simple extension, or mere space; our idea of which, involving the fewest properties and relations, is the nearest approach to nothingness of which we have any conception.

But this power of annihilating is by no means the only characteristic of the logical faculty. It is not creative, but it discovers and analyzes what already exists, and in its ability to reduce, to disintegrate, and to abstract, it is an important agent in the advancement of our knowledge of what already is, often harmoniously coöperating with the poetic modes to this end.

ANIMALS NOT AUTOMATA.

THE doctrine of necessity has been ably advocated by many acute philosophers, and is to-day, in various forms, including fatalism, the accepted creed of a large portion of mankind. A doctrine thus supported, and so immediately bearing upon our actions and our powers, cannot but be worthy of serious attention.

Professor Huxley, approaching it on the material side, in the true spirit of philosophical inquiry, trustingly following wherever truth seemed to him to lead, and regardless of the apprehended consequences of attacking dominant creeds and opinions, has pushed this doctrine to its legitimate logical consequences, in the conclusion that all animals, man included, are but "conscious automata," moved and directed in their movements by extrinsic forces.

With him, I believe that all progress in knowledge is beneficial; I deprecate no enterprise in experiment nor any boldness in speculation, if we are duly cautious in accepting and applying its results. The revelations of intelligent and honest inquiry always merit respectful and careful consideration, but are not properly exempt from scrutiny.

Although I have perhaps deviated as far on one side of the current opinions as Professor Huxley has on the other, I cannot claim any credit for fearlessness of the consequences — my only apprehension in that respect being, that any arguments I may present, unrelieved by interesting experiments, will not excite sufficient interest to provoke either commendation or censure.

I think, however, I may properly say that, viewing the problem on the spiritual side, and carefully excluding popular prepossessions and theological dogmas, I have carried the opposite doctrine of "freedom" to its legitimate logical consequences in the conclusion that every being that wills is a creative first cause, having, in virtue of its attributes of knowledge, feeling, and volition, a power of itself to begin action. That the object of every volition or effort is to make the future different from what it otherwise would be, and hence. that every such being is an independent, self-active power in the universe, freely doing its part and coöperating with all other active intelligences in creating the future, which is always the composite result of the action of all such intelligences; that even an oyster, though it have no other power than that of moving its shell, may, so far, create the future and make it different from what it otherwise would be; and further, that as every intelligent being will conform its actions to the conditions under, or upon, which it is to act, the action of each, in changing the conditions, may affect the action of any or of all others, and the action of the lowest may, in this way, influence that of the highest.

We both, however, admit knowledge and feeling, and recognize consciousness, or the phenomena of knowing, in man and other animals. In discussing questions so fundamental, this must be largely relied upon for the foundation and support of the argument on either side, and I will briefly state my views in regard to its authority.

Mind, as manifested in man and in brutes, I regard as entirely made up of a *capacity* for knowledge, a *susceptibility* to feeling, and a *faculty* of effort (will); this last being the only *power* we possess; and if it — the effort of intelligent being — is not the only power *known* to us, it is at least that power of the existence of which we have the most direct and reliable evidence. The recipient and receptacle of all our knowledge, whatever its source, is consciousness. Our conscious perceptions and feelings (including emotions) are the foundation of all knowledge, and all belief; but the consciousness of one man, of itself, avails nothing against another having a different consciousness and a different belief. Belief is not a matter of will or of choice, but each must believe in conformity to his own consciousness, and retain his existing belief till his consciousness is in some way changed. The denial of this involves a contradiction, and we may assume, as a corollary to it, that it is not only reasonable, but a necessity, that we believe things to be as they appear to be, till we recognize a sufficient reason for believing that the appearances are deceptive. The testimony of consciousness is not equally reliable as to all subjects. In some cases it is conclusive, in others far from it. In regard to our internal perceptions, sensations, and emotions, our consciousness is conclusive evidence that we have them, and that they are what consciousness represents them to be. The consciousness of the sensation of pain is the pain itself; and the consciousness of perceiving that the whole is greater than its part is, itself, the perception of that fact, and there can be no question as to my actually having the sensation of pain, or as to my having the perception of the inequality. But the consciousness is not conclusive as to the conformity of the perception with the existing fact, nor as to any inference which I may draw from the sensation. One may have as full and decided perception of what is not, as of what is; and the liability to erroneous inferences from our sensations is a matter of daily experience.

Even a universal belief, founded on entire uniformity in the perceptions, or in the inferences from our sensations, is not conclusive. If it were, no error in such belief could ever be corrected. If, for instance, the belief that the sun daily revolved around the earth was once universal — and universal belief is regarded as conclusive — the present belief never could have been substituted. Still, to assume things to be as they appear to be, till a sufficient reason is given to the contrary, is a necessary condition to our progress in science and philosophy. If this proposition is denied, then all Professor Huxley's array of facts and arguments may be fairly met by saying, "True, these things appear to be as you say, but, then, this appearing is no reason for supposing that they really are so." There would be an end to at least all physical investigations.

Instinct is, perhaps, a more important element in this discussion than Professor Huxley has suggested; the various and vague notions in regard to it which obtain both in the popular and philosophical mind do much to confuse the consideration of voluntary and mechanical action.

Professor Huxley assumes that instinctive action is mechanical. He says: " When we talk of the lower animals being provided with instinct, and not with reason, what we really mean is, that, although they are sensitive, and although they are conscious, yet they act mechanically, and that their different states of consciousness, their sensations, their thoughts (if they have any), their volitions (if they have any), are the products and consequences of their mechanical arrangements. I must confess that this popular view is, to my mind, the only one which can be scientifically adopted."

There is much and high authority for the doctrine that instinctive actions are mechanical, but I believe it is very generally rejected by those who have observed the actions of animals without any knowledge of subtile theories to account for them. " What," incredulously exclaimed one of my grandchildren, on hearing of " Professor Huxley's statement," " what sort of a mechanism is it that carries the wild-geese from Canada to the Gulf of Mexico every fall, and brings them back every spring?" This seems to me a fair illustration of the prevailing notions, indicating that Professor Huxley is mistaken in assuming that the " popular view " favors the mechanical theory. I am aware that the " popular view " cannot be urged against special inquirers, whose object often is to correct prevailing errors, as well as to extend the limits of our knowledge ; but misapprehension of the popular view may give a wrong direction to their efforts and make them unavailing.

No mechanical contrivance, no mechanism furnishes any *power*, but is only a means of applying power; and, even if the term mechanical embraces all the phenomena of matter in motion, we still have the question as to whether the mechanism or the matter moves by its own power, or is moved by the effort of some intelligent being.

He who views the perfect crystal as the direct creation of an intelligent designing power, and he who sees in it only the orderly effect of natural forces, will alike class it with the mechanical; so, too, both would speak of the celestial mechanism.

In investigating the *laws of Nature*, the one is observing and generalizing the uniform mode of God's voluntary action, the other is finding the necessary consequences of the action of material forces. Each attributes any phenomena which he cannot class with any of his generalizations to some inscrutable exercise of power — the one to intelligent effort, the other to unintelligent material movements; so that, in the mechanical, we have still the question as to the two forms of power — intelligence in effort, and matter in motion; and, as between these, admitting the existence of both, it seems most reasonable to attribute instinctive action, the action of a conscious and hence intelligent being, to the former, rather than to the latter. Instinctive action is not mechanical, even in the most extended sense of the term, but must be referred to the power of the being itself, and not to extrinsic power of any kind. Every voluntary effort is put forth to gratify a want, to make the future in some respect different from what, but for the effort, it would be. To do this, always requires that the effort, or series of efforts, should be adapted to the specific object, and that, in any series of them, each one should be in the appropriate consecutive order. There must be a mode or plan of action. This plan is either a part of our knowledge, or is formed by means of it.

In all our actions, whether instinctive, rational, or habitual, we thus apply our knowledge to direct our efforts to the end desired, and there is not in the actions themselves, nor in their immediate antecedents, any difference whatever. In all of them it is but an effort suggested by the want, and directed to a given end by means of our knowledge. The difference is not in the action, nor in the knowledge, nor in the application of the knowledge, but one step farther back — in the manner in which we became possessed of the knowledge we apply. In a rational action we, by a preliminary effort, obtain this knowledge — we make the requisite plan. In the instinctive action this knowledge is innate; the plan is ready formed in the mind, requiring no premeditation, no deliberation to determine the mode of action. In the rational actions we acquire the knowledge of these plans for ourselves, and it is the preliminary effort to determine what to do, and how to do it — to find the mode of action — that tasks our intellectual abilities. But, when we have once formed the plan, and acted upon it often enough to remember its successive steps, so that we can repeat them in action by rote without any reference to the *rationale*, it becomes a plan ready formed in the mind, and the acting upon it becomes habitual. The instinctive and habitual actions, then, are precisely alike in this, that both are in conformity to a plan ready formed in the mind, requiring no effort to form them for the occasion, and differ only in this, that in the instinctive we found the plan ready formed, while in the habitual we *originally* formed it by our own effort. If, after the latter plans had become fixed in our memory, we should forget that we had originally acquired them by our own effort, we would know no difference between the instinctive and habitual action.

The popular consciousness of this similarity is expressed in the common adage that habit is second nature. If this view, which seems to me to account for all the peculiarities of instinctive action, is correct, instinct is not a distinct faculty, capacity, property, or quality, of being, which may be compared with or substituted for reason, but has relation only to the mode in which the knowledge by which we determine some of our actions was originally obtained. Whether the innate knowledge of modes and plans is by transmission, or otherwise, does not affect the theory. It is sufficient that they are thus ready formed in the being without effort of its own.

All intelligent actions, except perhaps those which are merely imitative, must in the first instance be either instinctive or rational, the habitual coming later through the transformation of the others by repetition and memory; the instinctive, however, not being materially changed thereby.

But the foundation of all our actions must be instinctive, there being no possible way in which we could ever learn that effort is the means of using either our muscular or mental powers.

In regard to the rational actions, I see no distinction in kind, but only in degree, between those of man and the lower animals. Descending in the scale of intelligence, we may, and probably will, reach a grade of beings which do not invent or form plans to meet new occasions for action, and the efforts of such must be wholly instinctive; but I have seen both dogs and horses draw inferences, and work out ingenious plans of action, adapted to conditions so unusual and so improbable to them, as to preclude the assumption that they had been specially provided by Nature, through hereditary transmission or otherwise, with the knowledge of the plan suited to the occasion.

Professor Huxley asserts that matter is a cause, a power not only in what is generally regaarded as its own sphere, but that it also produces all mental phenomena. At the same time, while admitting the consciousness — the intelligence — of man and brutes, he denies to them the faculty of will, thus virtually denying to them any power.

He thus raises the question as to the power of matter, and also as to that of intelligent beings; at least of beings of no higher grade than man. It is not very clear whether or not he denies *all* intelligent power. In saying he has with him " Père Malebranche, who saw all things in God," he seems to recognize a supreme power; but then this power in his system might logically be but a deification of material forces, ignoring intelligent activity.

Against attributing power to matter, we may urge that its existence as a distinct entity has never been proved, and is seriously questioned. To assume that so important a quality inheres, and especially to assume that it inheres only in something the existence of which is doubtful, when it may, with equal reason, be attributed to something, the existence of which is admitted, would be a grave philosophical and logical mistake.

Professor Huxley admits the existence of intelligent (conscious) beings, but perhaps does not admit that power may, with equal reason, be attributed to them, nor perhaps that there is any reasonable doubt as to the existence of matter as a distinct entity; leaving these two questions open to discussion. In regard to the latter, he will probably admit that there is no decisive proof, and that the existence of matter is only an inference from the sensations which we attribute to its agency. But all the phenomena of these sensations are as well accounted for on the hypothesis that they are directly produced in our minds by some intelligent power as that they are the effects of matter.

If the material universe is regarded as the work of an intelligent Creator, working with design to produce a certain effect, then, upon either hypothesis, it is the expression of a conception of this Creator, existing as thought and imagery in his mind before he gave it palpable, tangible existence in ours, and the only question between the two modes is, whether, in making it palpable to us, he transfers this thought and imagery directly to our minds, or first paints, moulds, or carves them in a distinct material substance. The external universe would not, in the first of these modes, be any the less real. The sensations, which are all that under either hypothesis concern us, or that we know anything about, would be the same in both cases. But we can no more impute power to such imagery than to an image in a mirror, and under this hypothesis material causation would have no existence.

One consideration favoring the ideal theory is, that, under it, creation becomes more conceivable to us. We can, any of us, conceive or imagine a landscape, and vary its features at will. This is an incipient creation, which, if we could impress it upon the mind of another, would be to him an external creation — to his vision as thoroughly material as the fields, and streams, and trees, he now looks out upon; and, if from any cause it should become fixed in the mind of him that conceived it, so that he could not change it at will, it would become to him an external reality. And this sometimes happens in abnormal conditions of the mind. In order to thus create what, at least to the visual sense, would be an external material creation, the only addition, then, which is required to the powers which we habitually exercise, is that of impressing our conceptions upon others. With this addition we could create and give palpable existence to a universe, varying more or less from that now palpable to us. And this power of impressing our conceptions on others we are none of us wholly devoid of. Sculptors, painters, architects, and more especially poets, have it in marked degree.

We, however, find no rudiment of force in these incipient creations of our own, and, hence, they furnish us with no logical ground for attributing it to similar and more perfect creations of a Superior Intelligence. That these creations of our own are mostly evanescent, and those to which, with great labor, we give a persistent reality are very limited and imperfect, does not disprove the position that creation is more conceivable to us upon the ideal hypothesis than upon the material. The ideal hypothesis is also commended by the consideration that man, having, in a finite degree, all the other powers usually attributed to the Supreme Intelligence, lacks, under the material theory, the power of creating matter. Corresponding to His omnipotence, omniscience, and omnipresence, man has finite power and finite knowledge, and can make all the objects of his knowledge present, which is equivalent to a finite presence, limited, like our other attributes, to the sphere of our knowledge. This hypothesis, then, rounds out our ideas of creative intelligence, relieving us of the anomaly of the creation of matter as a distinct entity, for which, having in ourselves no conscious rudiment of a power to accomplish, we cannot conceive the possibility.

I may further observe that, if I am right in supposing that the only difference between our own incipient creations, of a landscape for instance, and the external scenery which we perceive, is that we can change the former at will, while the latter is fixed, it shows how narrow is the space that divides the creative powers of man from those of the Supreme Intelligence, and that the difference is mainly, if not entirely, in degree, and not in kind. This gives warrant to the logic, and shows how short the steps by which we attribute all creations and all changes, which we regard as beyond our own power and beyond that of other embodied intelligences known to us, to a superior intelligence, with the same powers which we possess and use to create and change, increased, I will not say infinitely, but to a degree corresponding to the effects which we see and ascribe to them.

If the existence of matter be admitted, it may still be urged that, being unintelligent, it can have no causative power, and can produce no change, for all changes in matter must be, by its motion, massive or atomic, and matter cannot move itself.

Even if it could be imbued with motive power, it could have no inducement, no tendency, to move in one direction rather than another ; and a tendency which is equal in all directions is no tendency in any direction. If all matter were at this moment quiescent, even the materialists will not assert that it could of itself begin to move.

It may, however, be urged that both the arguments thus drawn from the difficulty of conceiving the creation of matter, and the necessity of motion to its causal power, may be met by the hypothesis that matter was not created, but has existed through a past eternity, and that its original condition was that of motion, and that there is no more difficulty in conceiving this than in conceiving that intelligence, with its activities, has had no beginning.

But, granting that matter has always existed, and originally had motion, and consequent power, still, if the tendency is to expend and exhaust this power in producing effects, by collision or otherwise, or, admitting the conservation of force, if its tendency is to become merely potential, then the force which it originally had, in virtue of being in motion, must, in the infinite period of its existence, have been either wholly exhausted or reduced to an infinitesimal, requiring the intervention of some active power to again give it any practical force.

But whether matter, supposing it to exist, can of itself, by means of its motion, be an independent power or force, still depends on another question, viz., Is the tendency of a body in motion, when the power which put it in motion is withdrawn, to continue to move, or to stop? In other words, is the application of extrinsic power required to keep it in motion, or is such application required to stop it? Having no power to move itself when once at rest, it could have no power to act, but could only be acted upon, and, if it has inertia, it would be a means of exhausting other force.

If when once in motion its tendency is to continue in motion, then it could be used as an instrument by which intelligent power, putting it in motion, could extend the effects of its own action in time and space.

If the tendency is to stop, then it could have no power or force, in virtue of being in motion, and could not even be a means of extending the effects of the action of other powers.

I have heretofore confessed my inability to solve this question as to the tendency of a moving body to continue its motion, or to stop when the motive power is withdrawn. I have not, perhaps, been able even to disentangle it from the empirical meshes in which it has become involved, and which, in my view, do not and cannot furnish any clew to its solution; but, until this point is settled, I do not see how matter, though in motion, can properly be regarded as a force, or even as a conserver of force, imparted to it by some other power.

If matter in motion is power, then all its effects must be such as take place of necessity, it having no power to select or vary them, and, whatever the course of such effects, it cannot change. If, for instance, the moving body is approaching another body, then, as two bodies cannot occupy the same space, some effect must of necessity result from the collision; and all the effects of unintelligent cause or force must be from some like necessity. In this case the material hypothesis has an advantage, there being no apparent connection of *necessity* between an intelligent effort and its sequences. This, however, as matter cannot put itself in motion, nor, perhaps, even continue any motion imparted to it, may only make it an instrument of other power, and not a power itself.

Some of the considerations in favor of the existence of intelligent power have already incidentally arisen in connection with the question of the existence of material force, and others pertain to that of the will, to which we will now turn.

The question which Professor Huxley raises is not merely, Does man will *freely?* but, Does he will *at all?* If he recognizes any volition in us, it is a volition in which we have no agency, but of which we are only conscious.

Between the two questions, of not willing freely or

not willing at all, there is perhaps little of practical importance; for, if our actions are controlled by some extrinsic power or force, it is not important whether this control is exerted directly on or in the action, or indirectly through controlled will. It might, perhaps, even be properly urged that, philosophically as well as popularly, a willing which is not free is a willing which is not willing, and this would identify the two questions.

Professor Huxley, from divers physical experiments, comes to the conclusion that animals, including man, do not will, but that the effort-phenomena, of which we are conscious, are only a series, or the effect of a series, of mechanical changes of matter, over which we have no control. He admits that we have knowledge and feeling, and there is no difficulty in conceiving that these may exist without will, though the existence of either feeling or will without knowledge is impossible.

To most persons the actual making of an effort, or willing, seems to be as fully attested by their consciousness as a sensation is; and there is high philosophical authority for putting it in that category, in regard to which the consciousness is positively and of necessity conclusive. It seems to me, however, that there is room for a distinction between the consciousness of effort and the effort itself. If the changes, which seem to us to be the consequences of our effort put forth with a preconception of these changes, and for the purpose of producing them, are really caused by some extrinsic power or force acting through us, it is quite conceivable that such a power, especially if intelligent, may impress us with the emotion of making an effort when we make none, though I see no reason why such a circuitous mode of action should be adopted. But, though the consciousness of making an effort is not conclusive as to the *actual* making, still, as it is of internal phenomena, it is evidence of a higher order than that which consciousness of a sensation gives as to the existence or character of the external phenomena.

The senses through which the external is presented may not act perfectly; and this, as compared with the consciousness of internal phenomena, makes an additional risk of error similar to that which arises from seeing an object through glass or in the reflection of a mirror, instead of directly without any intervening medium.

Those, then, who set up physical phenomena against our consciousness of effort, labor under the disadvantage of impeaching the accuracy of the testimony by other testimony which is less reliable than that which they impeach.

Professor Huxley admits that men and other animals know and feel. The existence, then, of that for which *power by effort* is claimed as an attribute, with these prerequisites to its exercise, is admitted.

On the other hand, any belief in matter or in its motion is but an inference from our sensations, which, as we have seen, is not a necessary or conclusive inference; and hence we have no reliable evidence of the existence of matter, nor of the attributes which, if it exists, are essential to its having power.

In the first case, we know the existence of the active agent; its feeling, subjecting it to want; and its knowledge, enabling it to adopt a mode of gratifying its want; which are all the elements which are requisite to the exercise of a power by effort; and though we have no conclusive proof that it actually makes the effort, the testimony in regard to this, for reasons already stated, is more reliable than the inferences from our sensations, that matter exists, and that it moves, and that one portion impinges on another portion: all of which are essential to material causation. In the first case, the existence of the agent, with all the prerequisites to the exercise of power, is known. In the latter, not a single one of them is known. This shows that the material phenomena which Professor Huxley presents are not, in this case, sufficient to rebut the testimony of consciousness that we do will — do make effort, and thereby produce change.

The further question, Do we ourselves determine our efforts? is identical with that of our freedom in willing, which I do not propose here to discuss; but will remark that it is not probable, perhaps it is not conceivable, that any unintelligent agent should create the whole system of wants, knowledge, and the application of knowledge involved in an effort, as just stated, and impress the *whole* as illusions on the mind of the actor; nor yet, that any blind force should direct the effort in exact conformity to the wishes and the preconceptions of the manner and the effect which are in the thoughts of him who has the emotion of making an effort, and which the unintelligent power, or agent, of course cannot know. Only an intelligent agent could know this; and, if the conforming of the effort to this want, knowledge, and preconception of the effect, must be referred to some intelligent being, it seems most reasonable to refer it to that which directly feels its own want, knows its own perceptions of the mode of gratifying the want, and its preconceptions of the effect to be produced, to which all the effort is to be conformed, and which, at the same time, is conscious of making the effort, and of thus conforming and directing it by its own knowledge. Between the sensation of making the effort, and the antecedent and subsequent knowledge of the subject of this sensation, there is a harmony which it seems hardly conceivable should be produced by any power not having this particular knowledge, and much less by a power incapable of knowing anything.

As germane to the whole question of intelligent and material power, I will suggest that it would be unphilosophical to assume the existence of two primary powers, when one is sufficient to account for all the phenomena, and that as it seems hardly conceivable that matter should create intelligence with its phenomena — that what does not know should create a power to know — while, as already shown, it is quite conceivable that intelligence should create all that we know of matter and its phenomena, the hypothesis of power in matter should, on this ground, be discarded.

Let us now look at the very curious and interesting experiments upon which Professor Huxley relies for his conclusion that animals, including man, are "conscious automata." He says that, if, when a man is so paralyzed that he is wholly unable to move his limbs, and has no sensation in them, "you tickle the soles of his feet with a feather, the limbs will be drawn up just as vigorously, perhaps a little more vigorously, than when he was in full possession of the consciousness of what happened to him." He also states that, in the case of a frog similarly paralyzed, the result of irritating the skin of the foot is the same: in both cases the foot being drawn *from* the source of irritation. This certainly bears a very close resemblance to the voluntary action of an intelligent being, conscious of the irritation, and seeking relief from it by its own efforts. Professor Huxley, however, positively asserts that the animal could not feel or will, and this being so, he seems to be justified, by common usage, in calling the action "mechanical." But, as I have already suggested, this term is applied to material phenomena, whether they are results of matter in motion, or of the uniform modes of God's action.

Other experiments still more remarkable are presented. He says: "Take this creature (the same frog), which certainly cannot feel, and touch the skin of the side of its body with a little acetic acid, which in a frog that could feel would give rise to great pain. In this case there can be no pain. . . . Nevertheless, the frog lifts up the limb on the same side, and applies the foot to rubbing off the acetic acid; and what is still more remarkable, if you hold down the limb, so that the frog cannot use it, he will, by-and-by, take the limb of the other side and turn it across the body, and use it for the same rubbing process."

This goes a step further, requiring a more complicated mechanism to direct the force, when it fails to move one foot, to the movement of the other. In still another case, he says: "Suppose the foremost two thirds of the brain taken away, the frog is then absolutely devoid of any spontaneity; it will remain forever where you leave it; it will not stir, unless it is touched; . . . but, . . . if you throw it in the water, it begins to swim — swims just as well as the perfect frog does; . . . and the only way we can account for this is, that the impression made on the sensory nerves of the skin of the frog by the contact of the water conveys to the central nervous apparatus a *stimulus* which sets *going a certain machinery* by which all the muscles of swimming are brought into play in due order of succession. Moreover, if the frog be stimulated, be touched by some irritating body, although we are quite certain it cannot feel, it jumps or walks as well as the complete frog can do."

Most persons, I presume, have seen men and other animals made so torpid by injury or disease, that they would show little sign of vitality, and great indisposition to make any effort, but that they still moved when pricked with a pin has been generally regarded as evidence that they still felt; and the movements they would make to avoid danger, or escape pain, have been thought to be conclusive that they were *not* " absolutely devoid of any spontaneity."

It is not uncommon for a man, who, in ordinary circumstances, seemed wholly unable to move his limbs, under great or sudden excitement, as the approach of fire or sudden apprehension of drowning, to make vigorous and successful muscular efforts.

The common observer, then, would infer from the foregoing experiments that Professor Huxley was not justified in inferring, from the fact of mutilation, that the frog was "absolutely devoid of any spontaneity," and that " we are quite certain it cannot feel." If the facts stated do not prove that the frog still feels, still wills, and still has knowledge to direct its efforts to get rid of the irritation, it seems difficult to devise any mode of proof that a being ever feels, knows, or wills. Professor Huxley admits that we do feel and know, but infers from these experiments that we do not will. If his theory of them is correct, they seem to afford little ground for this distinction.

Professor Huxley, in still another case, says of a frog deprived of the most anterior portion of the brain, that "it will sit forever in the same spot. It sees nothing, it hears nothing," yet placed on the hand would, on the turning of the hand, make all the movements necessary to prevent its falling off, and that "these movements are performed with the utmost steadiness and precision, and you may vary the position of your hand, and the frog, so long as you are reasonably slow in your movements, will work backward and forward *like a clock*." Referring to this experiment, Professor Huxley afterward says: "If the frog were a philosopher, he might reason thus: 'I feel myself uncomfortable and slipping, and, feeling myself uncomfortable, I put my legs out to save myself, knowing that I shall tumble if I do not put them farther. I put them farther still, and my volition brings about all these beautiful adjustments which result in my sitting safely!' But if the frog so reasoned, he would be entirely mistaken, for the frog does the thing just as well when he has no reason, no sensation, no possibility of thought of any kind. The only conclusion, then, at which there seems any good ground for arriving is, that animals are machines, but that they are conscious machines." And he afterward says: "Undoubtedly, I do hold that the view I have taken of the relations between the physical and mental faculties of brutes applies in its fullness and entirety to man." Of this last experiment Professor Huxley further says: "And what is still more wonderful is, that if you put the frog on a table, and put a book between him and the light, and give him a little jog behind, he will jump (take a long jump, very possibly), but he won't jump against this book, he will jump to the right or to the left, but he will get out of the way, showing that, although he is absolutely insensible to ordinary impressions of light, there is still something which passes through the sensory nerve, acts upon the machinery of his nervous system, and causes it to adapt itself to the proper action." This is certainly very wonderful, and becomes even more so when taken in connection with the next case — that of a man who had been shot in the head, and who, Professor Huxley says, " is in a condition absolutely parallel to that of the frog," but afterward says, " very nearly " in the same condition ; and also says, " he has only one sense organ in a state of activity, namely, that of touch, which is exceedingly delicate." Yet of this man, thus described as virtually in the same condition as the frog, except that he has a very delicate sense of touch, we are told that, " if an obstacle is put in his way, he knocks against it, feels it, and goes to one side; if you push him in any direction, he goes straight on until something stops him."

It is certainly very remarkable that the frog, with no sense at all, avoids leaping against the obstruction, while the man, with a delicate sense of touch, and other conditions parallel or very nearly the same as the frog, knocks against it. It must be a very curious mechanism which can make such discrimination in the effects of his action.

Let us examine the case of the frog a little further. Professor Huxley ascribes its leaping obliquely and not directly forward to " a something which passes through the sensory nerve, *acts upon the machinery* of his nervous system, and causes it to adapt itself to the proper action," and this " although he is absolutely insensible to ordinary impressions of light."

Does Professor Huxley mean that this "something" passes through the book, and thus reaches the sensory nerve, and that, but for the intervening book, it would not pass that way? Under some circumstances, it might be that a conductor would facilitate the passage of a "something" which would not pass through the air, but in this case there is the difficulty of getting this "something" to the book, and then of sending it forward through the air. The only alternative seems to be to suppose that when there was no intervening book, a "something" passed to the frog which was necessary to cause it to jump directly forward, the passage of which the book prevented. Neither of these hypotheses seems satisfactory, even if no objection is made to the unknown "something."

To those skilled in scientific investigation it may not appear important, but I apprehend that many, like myself, not familiar with its modes, will regret that the experiment in this case was not pushed somewhat further. To find, for instance, what would be the effect when the obstruction extended equally to the right and to the left? What if it extended indefinitely both ways? And what, when it made an entire circle around the frog in the centre; and what if in different positions other than the centre.

But, even admitting, in all the cases, all that Professor Huxley claims as ascertained facts, what does it all amount to further than that he has brought to light some additional phenomena which, like the movements of the material universe and the pulsations of the heart, must be referred to some inscrutable agency? He who believes only in intelligent powers refers them, with all else that he does not effect by his own efforts, and which he regards as beyond the power of any known embodied intelligence, to a Superior Intelligence, acting through the instrumentality of matter or otherwise; while he who believes only in material causation attributes them to the influence of matter, in some form or some mode of its movement differing from those forms and modes which are familiar to him. Nor is it material how many steps there may be between the power applied and the effect. If there are three or thirty ivory balls in a right line, and the first of them is put in motion causing each one successively to impinge on the next, the final effect of motion in the last is caused by the power applied to the first. We may by our own efforts put the alleged power of matter in action, or may thus act through the uniform modes of God's action.

In voluntary muscular movement the intermediate effect of a flow of blood to the contracting muscle has long been known; now, the propagation of molecular movement is ascertained. That we are not conscious of the movement of the molecules indicates (though far from conclusively) that we do not ourselves move them, but this does not indicate that the muscular movement is not the result of our own effort working through other agencies. That he who throws the stone which kills a bird does not know what curve the stone will describe, nor by what power its motion is continued after it leaves his hand, does not show that he is not the cause of the killing.

If the knowledge of the intermediate changes is a necessary condition to the exercise of the power which produces the final result, what becomes of the hypothesis of causation by material movements, or forces, which know nothing? In regard to the special phenomena in hand, it would seem that no power less facile, or less variable and adjustable in its application than that of intelligent effort, could be adequate ; and that no blind power or force, the effects of which must of necessity be uniform, could, from the same conditions, produce such diverse effects as those attributed to the man and the frog.

Considering the clear line of demarcation which there is between those cases of change for which we are conscious of making effort and those for which we are not, I do not see how the discovery of any number of cases of the latter discredits the testimony of consciousness as to the former. All this exhibition of material phenomena, then, really weighs very little on either side of the question as to the existence of intelligent or material causality ; and this little, I think, may be fairly claimed on the side of the intelligent.

There is another criterion which, as Professor Huxley, in applying a somewhat analogous test, has very appropriately said, " though it could not be used in dealing with questions which are susceptible of demonstration, is well worthy of consideration in a case like the present." I cannot demonstrate, but I have great faith in the proposition that all progress in truth will increase the happiness and conduce to the elevation of man. I also have some faith in the converse of this proposition — that whatever tends to diminish our happiness and degrade our position will be found to be not true.

In this case, by adopting Professor Huxley's views, we should be deprived of all the dignity of conscious power, and with it of all the cheering and elevating influences of the performance of duty ; for that which has no power can have no duties. Instead of companionship with a Superior Intelligence, communicating his thoughts to us in the grandeur and beauty of the material universe — the poetic imagery, the poetic language, of which it is the pure and perfect type — and in his yet higher and more immediate manifestations in the soul, we should be doomed to an inglorious fellowship with insensate matter, and subjected to its blind forces. That sublime power — that grandeur of effort by which the gifted logician, with resistless demonstration, permeates and illuminates realms which it tasks the imagination to traverse; and that yet more God-like power by which the poet commands light to be, and light breaks through chaos upon his beautiful creations, would no more awaken our admiration, or incite us to lofty effort. We should be degraded from the high and responsible position of independent powers in the universe — co-workers with God in creating the future — to a condition of mere machines and instruments operated by "stimuli" and "molecules"; and, though still with knowledge and sensibility to know and feel our degraded position — "so abject, yet alive!" — with no power to apply our knowledge in effort to extricate, and to elevate ourselves. We might still have the knowledge of good and evil; but, having no power to foster the one, or to resist the other, this knowledge, with all its inestimable consequences — all the aspirations which it awakens, and all the incentives to noble deeds which it, in combination with effort, alone makes possible — would be lost. And with it, we might almost say, there would again be no death, for all mutation now being but changes in the indestructible atoms of matter, by means of its motion, also indestructible and eternal, there would be little left to die, as there would again be little left to live for. For all this, I see no compensation in the doctrines now so clearly and frankly presented.

LETTER ON CAUSATION.

PEACE DALE, RHODE ISLAND, *July* 19, 1877.

MY DEAR SIR: I have read with interest your pamphlet " On Liability," etc., and am much impressed with the importance of the questions therein discussed. In compliance with your request I submit the following synopsis of such of my views on " causation " as seem to me most germane to the particular phase of the subject you are examining:

Cause is that which produces change.

An act of will is simply an *effort*. All effort is of the mind, and is the only causation of which we are directly conscious. As we know nothing of its *nexus* with the immediate effect, it is, so far as we know, our ultimate agency in producing the effect.

The object and intent of an effort is always to make the future different from what it otherwise would be. This is the only conceivable motive.

Freedom, as applied to willing, does not imply *no* control, but *self*-control.

A being with a desire or want for some change, a faculty of will or effort, and knowledge to direct its effort to the gratification of its want, is a self-active cause, which can act (*i. e.* make effort, which is the only causative act known to us) without being first acted upon — could act if there were no other power, and nothing but passive, inert conditions to be acted upon and changed. Hence such a being may determine its own effort — may will freely.

The only other *conceivable* cause is matter in motion; but, as matter cannot move itself, it cannot, like intelligent will, be an originating cause. As its conditions of motion are as fixed and as unchangeable, by itself, as its conditions of rest, matter, even in motion, may still be properly regarded as but one of the passive conditions to be acted upon and changed by intelligent effort, which can increase, retard, arrest, or change the direction of a moving body, as it can impart motion and give direction to one at rest.

As matter cannot move itself, its causative power in motion (if it have any) is due to the efficient cause which put it in motion, and matter is thus rather an *instrument* by which intelligent cause extends the effects of its own action than a cause itself, and for these effects the intelligent being that put it in motion is responsible.

A being thus constituted with want, intelligence, and a faculty of effort, being self-active, self-controlling, is an independent power, freely doing a part in creating or moulding the future, which is thus the composite result of all such active agencies. All change being, in our conception, identified with time, this creating of the future is the only creating which is conceivable to us ; and in this we each perform a part.

There is no conceivable mode of constraining or compelling the will. A coerced willing is an absurdity in idea and a contradiction in terms. It is willing when we are not willing. Every being that wills, by means of its knowledge, freely determines what change in the existing or expected conditions it will seek to produce ; and, by means of its knowledge, it also directs its effort to produce this change. This indicates that the only mode by which the will can be changed or influenced is by changing — i. e. adding to — the knowledge of the willing agent. New knowledge as to the existing or expected conditions may be directly imparted; or, the existing conditions may be so changed that the knowledge, conformed to them by the perceptions of the active agent, will be different. The restraining influence of statute-laws is wholly in such change of knowledge.

Every intelligent being will, with more or less of wisdom, conform his action to existing conditions, and, hence, one of the most common modes of influencing his willing is to change the conditions; but no change in the conditions impairs his freedom in acting upon them. He freely conforms his effort to any change in the circumstances, and acts just as freely upon one set of them as upon any other set. It is because he freely determines his own action by means of his own knowledge, that his action may thus be influenced by the change in his knowledge, affected by change in the circumstances, or otherwise. His knowledge, not being subject to his will, may be changed whether he will it or not. Hence he who changes the knowledge of another is often justly responsible for the action of this other, though there was no interference with his freedom.

Nor does the greater or less extent of his knowledge or intelligence vary his freedom in willing. To make effort for any desired effect he must know some mode of action by which it shall at least seem to him possible that the result sought may be reached; and ignorance of modes may thus lessen his sphere of action, but in that sphere, thus always coextensive with his knowledge, he is as free as though he were omniscient.

Nor does the moral debasement or elevation of a man's character affect his freedom in willing. A demon is as free as an angel.

In these views, which present man as an independent power in the universe, whose *freedom in effort* cannot be infringed by any other power, nor restricted by circumstances, nor diminished by moral debasement, and which even his own ignorance, though it lessens his power and limits his sphere of action, does not impair, we have a broad and firm foundation for holding him responsible for the results of his efforts in that future the creation and moulding of which is always the object and effect of his effort.

In opposition to these views the advocates of necessity, and the materialistic philosophers generally, hold that the existing phenomena, including the volitions of intelligent beings, are always the *necessary* sequences of their antecedents, determining a certain flow of events in which the volitions of intelligent beings are *necessary effects* of the *past*, and not *free*, originating *causes* of the *future*. For such necessitated action, or its results, the being in which it is manifested can no more be accountable than for the destruction of a building to which his body had served as a conductor of the lightning which consumed it.

One form of this theory is thus stated by Mill: "The real cause is the whole of the antecedents." This does not discriminate between the passive conditions which by their inertia resist change, and the active agency which changes them. As uniform antecedents it makes life the cause of death; day and night reciprocally the causes of each other; and the increasing light of dawn the cause of the sun's rising. An essential adjunct to this theory is that *the same causes necessarily produce the same effect.* Without this there is not even the semblance of anything to give a direction to the alleged force (whatever it may be) of the blind antecedents which, under this theory, are the creative cause of the future; and any force exerted equally in all directions neutralizes itself. This law of necessary uniformity seems to be applied to blind forces as a substitute for the discretion of free intelligent causes. With this adjunct of necessary uniformity it is obvious that, if the "cause is the whole of the antecedents," then, as at each instant the whole antecedents are everywhere the same, the effect would everywhere be the same. Throughout the universe there could be only one and the same effect at the same time.

But it is also obvious that in this theory of the "whole antecedents" there can be no possible application of the law " that the same causes produce the same effects;" for the moment the cause — the whole of the antecedents — has once acted, its action and its effect are added to, and change, the cause, so that the same cause can never act a second time, and this law of uniformity cannot, under this theory, determine the direction of the future events, or even indicate what it will be. There are various phases of the theory that make the whole existing conditions the cause of the changes in themselves, which I have elsewhere considered; but it will, perhaps, be sufficient for our present purpose to say that all of material causation and effects must be from matter in motion; that matter cannot move itself; and, if it could so move, could not determine its direction; and any self-moving power in it would be equal in all directions, and neutralize itself. And to say that the " whole antecedents" include intelligent action, which may move inert matter and direct its blind force, would be to yield the whole position, and admit that intelligence in effect is the only real cause; for that which directs and determines a force to a particular result is the cause of that result, and is certainly that which is accountable for it. In these positions, which I have heretofore more fully discussed, we have eliminated material causation, the influence of circumstances, or the conditions to be acted upon, as also the moral and intellectual characteristics of the active agent, and, so far, much simplified the problem of responsibility for action and its results. It must rest on some intelligent being that wills.

On the other hand, in regarding the future as the composite result of all such intelligent activity, we encounter the difficulties of a causal responsibility, divided as to the aggregate, and often also as to the particular results. In distributing this responsibility we must often consider the right or wrong of the divers acts leading to the result.

The elements of action in each individual are the same — a want, ability for effort, and knowledge to direct his effort to the gratification of his want. The want is always, in the last analysis, to make the future different from what it otherwise would be; and, hence, to determine in what he will try to make the future different, or whether to make any effort at all, he must have some notion of what the future will be without his agency, and in this notion his prescience, more or less reliable, as to what others will do, is a very important factor. I have heretofore argued that the postulate "that the same causes *necessarily* produce the same effect," so much relied upon for this prescience, has no sufficient foundation in fact or logic, but that, in the action of intelligent agents (the real causes), there is only a *voluntary* uniformity which furnishes a ground for probable prediction. This is especially the case in regard to the action of the Supreme Intelligence — perhaps because He would, in the first instance, without experiment, know the wisest and best mode, and then and after adopt it; or, perhaps because such uniformity is essential to the existence of finite free agents. We act in reference to, or through, His uniform modes — the laws of Nature — and would make no effort if in these there was no reliable uniformity, and the result would as probably be the reverse of what we desired as otherwise. This would bar all finite effort, and human labor would cease.

So far as these uniform modes are known — and science is continually extending our knowledge of them — we are bound to recognize them and govern our own actions with reasonable reference to them — *e. g.*, it may now, in some cases, be a man's duty to erect a lightning-rod.

The same rule applies to those rightful actions of other persons which are so far uniform, or within the range of probability, that they may reasonably be expected. And we must thus regard even these uniform modes of the lower order of intelligence, to whose acts the laws of moral right and wrong are not applied, but whose efforts, directed by their knowledge to the gratification of their wants, still make the future different from what it otherwise would be. But brutes are restrained from harmful efforts to gratify their wants, not by written laws, but by physical obstruction, as are idiots and lunatics who cannot comprehend laws, and as criminals who in act have refused to conform to them. This brings into view the difference between the rational actions and the instinctive, which, though in a less ratio, obtain in man as well as in the lower animals.

In regard to this difference I believe there is much popular error, and even so advanced a thinker as Professor Huxley has recently stated, as his settled conviction, that instinctive actions are wholly mechanical, and that such is the common belief. Many other eminent philosophers have held, and still hold, this view. The problem has very direct relations to our ability to control such actions, and on our responsibility for them and their consequences. If they are the result of a mechanism not subject to intelligent will, restraining laws in regard to them will be of no avail, and the only protection is in physical restraint or obstruction.

In reply to Huxley I have urged that no mechanical contrivance has any power in itself, but is only a means which intelligent power uses, or through which it acts — that our every act, whether instinctive, rational, or habitual, is always an effort inspired by a want and directed by means of our knowledge. The difference between any two of these kinds of action is not in the want, the effort, or the creative knowledge, nor yet in the application of the knowledge, but one step further back — in the manner in which we became possessed of the knowledge we apply. In each case this knowledge must be of a mode or plan of action. In a rational action we, by a preliminary effort, obtain this knowledge — we make the requisite plan. In the instinctive action this knowledge is innate; the plan is ready formed in the mind, requiring no premeditation, no deliberation, to determine the mode of action. In the rational actions we acquire the knowledge of these plans for ourselves, and it is the preliminary effort to determine what to do, and how to do it — to find the mode of action — that tasks our intellectual abilities. But, when we have once formed the plan and acted upon it often enough to remember its successive steps, so that we can repeat them in action by rote without any reference to the *rationale*, it becomes a plan ready formed in the mind, and the acting upon it becomes *habitual*. The instinctive and habitual actions, then, are precisely alike in this : that both are in conformity to a plan ready formed in the mind, requiring no effort to form them for the occasion ; and differ only in this: that in the instinctive we found the plan ready formed, while in the habitual we *originally* formed it by our own effort. If, after the latter plans had become fixed in our memory, we should forget that we had originally acquired them by our own effort, we would know no difference between the instinctive and habitual action.

The popular consciousness of this similarity is expressed in the common adage that habit is second nature. If this view, which seems to me to account for all the peculiarities of instinctive action, is correct, instinct is not a distinct faculty, capacity, property, or quality of being, which may be compared with, or substituted for, reason, but has relation only to the *mode* in which the knowledge by which we determine some of our actions was originally obtained. Whether the innate knowledge of modes and plans is by transmission or otherwise, does not affect the theory. It is sufficient that they are thus ready formed in the being without effort of its own. The phenomenal difference between rational and instinctive actions has, usually and very naturally, been sought in the actions themselves, in which, if these views I have just stated are correct, it would not be found, for the reason that there is really no difference in them.

These acts, then, are all equally free acts of the intelligent actor, and equally subject to his control. The instinctive and habitual, however, require no preliminary effort to form the plan, and, hence, involve less deliberation; but this facility, though it may mitigate blame, makes them more, rather than less, properly the subjects of legal restraint.

I do not propose to follow these views in their application to practical affairs, but a few simple cases may illustrate what I have so crudely stated: Suppose A, in his field, throws a stone towards a quagmire, and B, by a blow, so changes its direction that it breaks his neighbor's window; the action of A, being in itself rightful, and having no tendency to cause the damage, is strictly chargeable to B, as really the sole cause of it. Again, suppose a man throws a stone directly into his neighbor's window; he may say, "I exerted no influence upon that stone after it left my hand. Its movement thereafter was either by the direct action or the pre-contrivance of some other intelligence beyond my control; it was the act of God." Still it was a uniform mode of His action, which, however inscrutable in its mode, was empirically well known. The rightfulness of the act cannot be questioned; and but for such uniformity there would be no incentive to human effort. We are bound, in deciding our own actions, to regard those uniform modes, and the whole blame is upon him who, with such prevision, has done the act which, thus supplemented by the uniform action of the Supreme Intelligence, has done the damage.

So, too, a railroad company *uniformly* and *rightfully* running its trains is performing a beneficial service to the public, in which its uniformity is very important. The farmers remote from consumers would make no effort to produce surplus food if they could not depend on the road to get it to market. There would be a loss of labor. In the daily running of its trains the public good requires uniformity, which could not be attained if it were necessary every trip to ascertain if some one had left combustible matter near the track, and, if so, to delay the trains till it could be removed. In the in itself rightful and useful act of procuring hemlock timber, the refuse branches left on the ground may have made a long train of very combustible material, which a spark may ignite and occasion damage to a ruinous amount. The analogy I have presented suggests that the person cutting the timber should so direct his action that no such risk of damage should attend the uniform running of the trains. But I am aware that such analogies are often fallacious, and I do not propose to attempt the solution of questions new to me, and requiring, even from those familiar with such subjects, much laborious and patient investigation.

I will be glad if this statement of my views shall aid you in the work, or in any way interest you.

       Yours very truly,
         R. G. HAZARD.
TO FRANCIS WHARTON, LL. D.

MAN A CREATIVE FIRST CAUSE.

TWO DISCOURSES DELIVERED AT CONCORD, MASS.,
JULY, 1882.

DISCOURSE I.

MAN A CREATIVE FIRST CAUSE.[1]

§ 1. In the preface to "Freedom of Mind in Willing" I have spoken of the general indifference to metaphysical pursuits; attributing it, in part, to the more easily appreciated discoveries in physical science, and their immediate contributions to our material com-

PREFACE TO FIRST EDITION. — In these discourses I have intended briefly to present the leading results of the previous investigations, most of which had already been published; but more especially to vindicate metaphysical science from the charge of being unfruitful, by showing that in its proper application to the subject of its investigation, it is susceptible of the highest practical utility.

I have endeavored to show that, to say nothing of the invigorating exercise of such study, it may be a means of making the same amount of intellectual power more effective, by the invention or discovery of better methods in its application; and further, that in this its own proper realm — the realm of the spirit — it may achieve a yet higher utility, a utility transcending all other, in creating, moulding, and elevating the moral character. I have also pointed out some modes in which the creative powers of mind may be successfully exerted for these objects.

PEACE DALE, RHODE ISLAND,
   September, 1883.

[1] See Note I. p. 337.

forts. The inventions, by means of which these comforts have been so largely increased, are the result of the application of the intellect to the study of matter. But if, as I have suggested, the study of the mind may elicit practical modes of increasing the efficiency of the intellect, then this study, which thus improves that which achieves all other improvement — which invents inventive power — may, even in its relation to the most materialistic utility, become the first and most important factor.

This, however, is merely incidental to the higher purpose of increasing the mind's power for the discovery of truth generally, to which it should be subordinated and made subservient.

But beyond and above all such comparatively grovelling application to our bodily wants, which philosophy once disdained, — beyond and above even the increase of intellectual power, — I hope, in furtherance of what I have heretofore suggested, to show more fully that the special field of *metaphysical utility* is in our moral nature ; that every one has within himself a domain, as illimitable as that of the external, in which to exert his energies in the construction of a moral universe ; and that within this domain, the finite intelligence is not only a creative, but a *supreme* creative power, and that therein, by the exercise of its faculties upon itself, it may devise or discover and impart new modes of forming and moulding the moral character, and thus supply a demand which, always important, has now, by our progress in other directions, become the prominent and urgent necessity of our time.

§ 2. The mind, like all other objects of its knowledge, is itself known only by its properties. These, as directly revealed in consciousness, are Knowledge,

Feeling, and Volition. It knows, feels, and wills. In knowing or in feeling it is not active, but passively perceives and feels. The will is its *only real faculty*. By this alone it acts. An act of will is simply an effort of the mind — an effort of the intelligent being — to do.

When we speak of an effort of memory, or imagination, or judgment, we only mean that we make effort to remember, to imagine, or to judge. We distinguish the particular effort by its object or design. But the effort is *by* the intelligent being, and the whole intelligent being acting as a unit; and when we speak of bodily effort we do not mean an effort made by the body, but the mind's effort to move the body; and by mental effort the mind's effort as to its own movement or action. The characteristics, then, of which we are conscious in our own minds, are a *capacity for knowledge*, a *susceptibility to feeling*, and a *faculty of effort or will*. And such seems to be the constitution of every intelligent being of which we are cognizant. They all know, feel, and make effort.

To these attributes there is, as to each in itself, no conceivable limit. Having the want, and the knowledge or idea of a possible mode, the effort — the *trying to do* — is always possible. Nor can we conceive of there being in the nature of the phenomena any limit to our susceptibility to an additional sensation or emotion, or that our capacity for knowledge should be so filled that there would be no room for more. The internal capacity is as unlimited as external space.

§ 3. It is conceivable that a being might have knowledge only; but it could not have feeling without knowing it. It might with knowledge have feeling, and enjoy or suffer without will — without any faculty or power by which it could change, or even try to change, its states of enjoyment or suffering, however well it might know that such change would be beneficial, or however decidedly it might *choose* or ardently *desire* such change.

It may seem to be conceivable that a being might have will without knowledge or feeling, that it might have the faculty and ability to try to do, and even the power to do; but such faculty would be dormant, and such power would be merely potential. Without feeling there would be no occasion, no inducement, no purpose, or motive for its exercise, and without knowledge no means of knowing or of directing its effort to an object.

If it be conceivable that such being could have a potential faculty of action, its tendency to act must be equal in all directions, and all tendency to action would be neutralized. An unintelligent being cannot be *self-active*.

Our sensations and emotions are not dependent upon our will. We can neither hear nor avoid hearing the sound of cannon by an act of will. By effort, we may bring about the conditions precedent to a particular sensation or emotion; but whether they are brought about by our own act or by other cause makes no difference to the effect.

Nor is our knowledge subject to our will. We may, by effort, bring about the conditions essential to our knowing. We can remove an external obstruction to sight, so as to see what was hidden by it. And we can also by effort call up and arrange our ideas so that some new truth will become apparent; but in neither case can we will *what* we shall perceive.

But the truth may be, and often is, apparent without any prior effort, by merely observing things as they happen to be. But whatever preliminary efforts we may make to bring about the prerequisite conditions to our knowing, the additions to our knowledge are always *simple immediate mental perceptions*, separable from the effort, and in its essence as independent of it as the smell of musk or brimstone is of the movement of the hand which brings it to the nose.

Feeling (*i. e.*, sensation and emotion) is an incentive to action, but is not itself active.

Knowledge enables us to direct our efforts, but is itself passive.

Through its only active faculty of will — its effort — the intelligent being strives to produce *change*, of which, when effected, it is the *cause*.[1]

Our own individual effort is the only cause of which we are directly conscious, but we are directly conscious of changes in our own sensations, for some of which we have and others we have not made effort. From some of these sensations we infer objective material changes, some of which we have and others we have not caused. From some of these we also infer the existence of other intelligent beings, like ourselves, to whose action we attribute many of these changes in our sensational or in objective phenomena, which we have not ourselves produced. But as some of these changes require a power beyond any indicated in ourselves or in our fellow-beings, we infer the existence of a superior intelligent power adequate to their production. We thus come to know ourselves, our fellow-beings, and God as cause.

§ 4. Of the existence of matter or of its properties we are not directly conscious. We know nothing of

[1] See Note II. p. 337.

it except by the sensations which we impute to its agency, and as these sensations can exist in the mind in the absence of the external material forms or forces to which we impute them, e. g., in dreams, the sensations are not conclusive evidence of any such external existence. All our sensations which we attribute to matter are as fully accounted for by the hypothesis that they are the thought, the imagery of the mind of God directly imparted or made palpable to our finite minds, as by that of a distinct external substance in which He has embodied this thought and imagery.

In either case matter is but the expression of his thoughts and conceptions. In either case, too, it is to us equally *real*, the sensations by which alone we apprehend these to us external phenomena being the same.

In either case, too, spirit and matter are still antithetically distinguished, as that which sees and that which is seen: the one having the properties of knowledge, feeling, and volition, while the other is unintelligent, senseless, and inert.

The hypothesis that the material phenomena are but the thoughts and imagery of the mind of God *immediately* impressed upon us is the more simple of the two, and makes creative attributes more nearly accord with powers which we are ourselves conscious of exercising.

We can ourselves by effort create such imagery, and to some extent make it durable and palpable to others.

We, however, find no rudiment of force or causative energy in these creations of our own. We can no more attribute inherent power to them than we can to an image in a mirror, and there seems no reason to suppose that any increase of power in the creator of such imagery could imbue it with causative energy.

On the other hand, if the existence of matter as a distinct, independent, objective entity is conceded, it may still be urged that it can, within itself, have no causative power. If wholly quiescent, it could exert no power to change itself, for all change in matter is by its motion in masses or in atoms; and matter cannot move itself.

But it does not appear to be claimed that matter except when in motion can be regarded as a power. It is inert and has no self-active power by which it can begin motion in itself without being first acted upon, nor can it determine the direction of its own motion. This beginning and determination must therefore be by the only other possible cause — by intelligent being — and that which thus begins and directs the motion is properly the cause of all the effects which follow, and matter is only an inert instrument which intelligence uses to produce these effects.

Even if it could be endowed with power to move, it could have no inducement, no tendency, or means to determine its motion in one direction rather than another; and a tendency or power of self-movement which is equal in all directions is a nullity.

Its quiescent existence might be a fact perceived by intelligent beings as among the conditions for them to act upon, but any change thus wrought in such being is the result of its own perception, or its own action on the quiescent matter. Clay may be moulded; it cannot mould.

It may, however, be urged that both the arguments thus drawn from the difficulty of conceiving of the creation of matter as a distinct entity, and from the necessity of motion, which it cannot begin, to its causal power, may be met by the hypothesis that matter never was created, but has always existed, and that its condition has ever been that of motion; and that this involves no more difficulty than the hypothesis that intelligence with *its* activity has had no beginning.

On this we would observe, as germane to the whole question of intelligent or material causation, that to assume the existence of both when one is sufficient is unphilosophical; and that as we are *directly* conscious of the spiritual phenomena, and only *infer* the material from our sensations, those who set up the material against or to the exclusion of the spiritual are impeaching testimony by testimony less reliable than that which they impeach. And further, it seems inconceivable that matter should be the cause of intelligence and its phenomena — that what does not itself know should create a power to know — while, as already shown, it is quite conceivable that intelligence may create all that we know of matter and its phenomena. These considerations seem to furnish sufficient reason for discarding the hypothesis of causal power in matter.

But whether matter, if it exist, can, even if in motion, be a force, power, or cause, still depends on another question, namely, Is the tendency of a body in motion to continue to move, or to stop when the moving power ceases to act upon it? In other words, is the application of extrinsic power required to keep it in motion, or is such application required to stop it? The problem may be thus stated. Suppose all existence were comprised in one power and one ball, and that this power was directly moving that ball. If this power were instantaneously annihilated, would the ball continue to move or would it stop?

If in virtue of being in motion it has power, it still could not select or vary its action or its consequences, and all its effects must be of necessity. For instance, in the collision of one body with another, as both cannot occupy the same space, some effect must result. All the effects of unintelligent cause must be from some like necessity. In this respect the material hypothesis would have the advantage, there being no apparent connection of *necessity* between intelligent effort and its objective sequences. If matter has such tendency to continue its motion, then it could be used by intelligent power as an instrument to extend the effects of its own action in time and space. But if its tendency is to stop, then it can have in itself no power or force whatever, and could not even be an instrument for thus extending the effects of the power that put it in motion. I confess myself unable to make or find any solution to this radical question, but until it is settled I do not see how matter, though in motion, can properly be regarded as a force, or even as a conserver of force imparted to it by other power.

Nor could intelligent power make matter a self-active cause, capable of beginning to move, of directing its movements, and so conforming them to varying circumstances and conditions as to produce a particular effect at a particular time, by impressing upon or imbuing it with laws for its own government: for to be thus governed by law presupposes *intelligence* on the part of the governed; such government of that which has no intelligence involves a contradiction which power cannot reconcile. All that can properly be implied when we refer an event to "the nature of things," or to the "laws of nature," as its cause, is that the intelligence which causes these events acts uniformly. In investigating the *laws of nature* we but seek to learn the uniform modes of God's action.

§ 5. A very popular notion of cause, adopted by many eminent philosophers, is that all events or successive phenomena are connected in a chain of which each successive link is the effect of all that preceded it. These also hold, as an essential adjunct to their theory, that the same causes necessarily produce the same effect, and hence that each of these successive events is necessitated by those which precede it. J. Stuart Mill, one of the able advocates of these views, says:[1]

"The real cause is the whole of these antecedents;" and again, "The cause . . . is the sum total of the conditions positive and negative taken together; the whole of the contingencies, which being realized the consequent invariably follows."

On these and other similar positions of Mill, and the materialistic school generally, I will remark that they do not distinguish between those antecedents which are merely passive conditions to be acted upon and changed and the active agents which act upon and change them; do not distinguish what *produces* from what merely *precedes* change. Life is a prerequisite to death, but cannot properly be regarded as a cause of it.

Again, any cause always acts upon a wholly void and therefore homogeneous future, and if the cause is the *whole of the antecedents*, then, as at each instant the whole of the antecedents is *everywhere* the same, the *effect* would everywhere be the same; and throughout

[1] *System of Logic*, Book 3d, Chap. 5, § 3.

the universe there could be only one and the same effect at the same time.[1]

It is also obvious that on this theory of the "whole antecedents" there can be no possible application of the law of uniformity, that "the same causes produce the same effects;" for the moment the cause — the whole of the antecedents — has once acted, its action and its effect are added to and permanently change it, and the same cause can never act a second time. The advocates of this theory, that "the whole antecedents are the cause," and of the asserted law that "the same causes must produce the same effects," also very generally hold that we get all our knowledge from experience. But it is clear that if the theory is true there can be no experience as to the law, and hence, on their theory, no knowledge to justify them in asserting it.

The foregoing results warrant the assertion that in the present condition of our knowledge the only causative power which we can be said to know, or which we can properly recognize, is that of intelligent being in action, and that all the effects, and especially all the uniform changes in matter, which begin to be, must be attributed to such action, and of course such of them as are not caused by the inferior must be referred to the action of the Supreme Intelligence; that, however difficult the conception, there seems to be no way to avoid the necessity of this constant exercise of creative energy to begin change, and produce uniformity in the results, or to escape the conclusion that every particle that floats in the breeze or undulates in

---

[1] For a fuller statement of this argument see *Letters to Mill on Causation and Freedom in Willing*, p. 43; and the first of these letters as to cause generally.

the wave, every atom that changes its position in the uniform modes of electrical attraction and repulsion or of chemical affinities, is moved, not by the energizing, but by the energetic will of an Omnipresent Intelligence.[1]

§ 6. The question of our freedom in willing has for ages been a prominent subject of philosophical inquiry and discussion, in which much of the diversity in opinions and results seems to have arisen from erroneous notions and defective definitions of will, and of freedom as applicable to willing.

Effort is wholly unique. Through the whole range of our ideas there is nothing resembling it — nothing with which there would seem to be any danger of confounding it, or of mistaking for it. And yet, as to the noun, will, which I regard as merely a name for our faculty to make effort — to try to do — there is much confusion, ambiguity, and error.

In the first place, the will has sometimes been treated as a distinct entity. This finds expression in the phrase, freedom of the will, and opens the way for the argument that if this distinct entity can be controlled by some power extraneous to it, even though by the being of which it is an attribute, then the *will* is not free.

Such reasoning is wholly precluded when we regard the will as simply the faculty or ability of the mind to make effort, and an act of will as simply an effort of the mind to do, and in accord with this view, speak of the freedom of the *mind* in willing, instead of the freedom of the *will*. Edwards, in his celebrated argument for necessity, defines WILL to be "*that by which the mind chooses anything*," and says "*an*

[1] See Note III. p. 337.

act of the will is the same as an act of choosing or choice."[1]

In my view the will is that by which the mind *does* any and every thing that it does at all, or in the accomplishing of which it has any active agency. Limiting its function to the phenomena of choice seems to me peculiarly unfortunate. Our choice is merely the *knowledge* that one of two or more things suits us best; and, as we have just shown, knowledge cannot be determined by will. We may, as in other cases, by effort — by comparing the respective advantages of the several objects of choice — bring about the conditions essential to our knowing which suits us best. The object of the comparative act is to get this knowledge; but the knowledge as to what suits us best — the choice — is itself a fact found, not made or done by us. It is an immediate perception to which the previous efforts, comparative or otherwise, may have been necessary.

Edwards also says, "The obvious meaning of the word FREEDOM, in common speech, *is power or opportunity of doing as one wills.*" But as applied to willing — the *willing* being then the *doing* — this is merely saying that freedom is the power to do as one does, or to will as one wills, or, if the doing (as we will) applies to the realization of the object of our effort, then it makes our freedom in making the effort depend on the subsequent event, which is absurd. It makes our freedom to *try* to do, dependent on our *power* to do. But we may freely make effort — try — to do, what the event proves we have not power to do.

In this popular use of the word freedom, it applies

[1] See Note IV. p. 340.

only to the *doing*, which comes after the *willing*, and is but a synonym for power. Freedom in its more comprehensive sense, and as applied to intelligent being, is simply SELF-CONTROL. Freedom in willing does not imply that the mind's effort is not controlled and directed, but that it is controlled and directed by the being that makes the effort, and is not controlled or coerced by extraneous power.

The consequences of these defective definitions of will and freedom upon the argument are obvious ; *e. g.*, Edwards makes choice and preference identical, and also says, " to *will* and to *choose* are the same thing." It will be generally admitted that our choice as mere preference is not a matter which we can control, that we cannot, *per se*, prefer pain to pleasure, and hence are not free in choosing ; and then on Edwards's assumption that choosing is the same as willing, he logically infers that we are not free in willing.

If we may properly define will as but a faculty to make effort, and an act of will as simply an effort, and discard the assumption that will and choice are the same, these arguments for necessity are eliminated. Leaving for the present the consideration of other arguments for necessity, we will turn to some of the sequences of the foregoing premises.

And first, it is evident that no power can change the past, and that the object of every intelligent effort must be to make the future different from what but for such effort it would be.

This is the only conceivable *motive* to effort. Now, intelligent being, constituted as before stated, has through its feelings an inducement to make efforts to so mould the future as to obtain an increase of those feelings which are pleasurable and avoid or lessen those which are painful; and by means of its knowledge it can distinguish and judge, more or less wisely, between these feelings, and also determine by what efforts it will seek to thus mould the future.

Such a being is in itself self-active, requiring no extrinsic agency to put it in action, or to sustain or direct its activity. How such a being came to be, whether in some inconceivable way it sprang into existence from nothing, or in some manner equally mysterious has been evolved from matter or other preëxisting substance or essence, the genesis of which is no less inscrutable, is not material. A being so constituted has all the elements of self-activity.

Supposing it to have just come into existence, with no other coexisting power in action, it could, on *feeling* some want and *knowing* some mode of effort by which to gratify its want, immediately make the effort; e. g., in the midst of a universal passivity, a being thus constituted could relieve its hunger by plucking and eating the fruit at hand, and such effort, in the absence of all other power, would of necessity be self-controlled and directed, and therefore the free effort or willing of the being that put it forth. In the passive and inert conditions the *intelligent* being perceives a *reason* for acting, and for acting in a particular way; but such acting suggested by and conformed to its *own* perception, which is wholly in itself, is very different from an action coerced by or directed by an extrinsic power, and this difference gives to the former the distinguishing characteristic of freedom, *i. e.*, *self-control*. Intelligent effort, then, and there is no other, thus springs directly from an internal perception of a *reason*. In this reason it has its genesis, and is not dependent on the prior action of any extrinsic power or cause.

But further, if there were other coexisting conative beings or powers, we know of no mode in which the willing of one being can be directly changed by the willing of another or by any other extrinsic power whatever. The willing so controlled would be the willing of this other being or power, and not that of the being in which it is manifested.

But a constrained or coerced willing, a willing which is not free, is not even conceivable. The idea is so incongruous, that any attempt to express it results in the solecism of our *willing* when we are *not willing*.

In conformity with these views we find the fact to be, that whenever we would influence the willing of another, we always try to do it by changing his knowledge. We may seek to do this by simple presentation of existing facts, or by argument upon them; or we may exert ourselves to change the facts, — the conditions upon which he is to act; *e. g.*, we may interpose insuperable obstacles to his intended action, or we may directly produce or change the feelings which prompt his action. But as any such actual change of the conditions is wholly ineffective till it makes a part of his knowledge, these apparently two modes are really only one, and it comes to this, that our only mode of influencing the willing of another is to change the knowledge by which he controls and directs his own willing; and it is evident that this mode is effective only upon the condition that this other does direct and control his own willing and conforms it to his own knowledge.

It would be absurd to suppose that the conforming of the act of will to the knowledge of the being that wills is by an extrinsic power.

It comes, then, to this, that the only conceivable

mode of influencing the will of another is by changing his knowledge, and that this mode is wholly unavailing if this other does not direct his own action by means of his own knowledge, *i. e.*, if he does not will freely.

From these premises it follows, that our willing not only may be, but must be free. From these, too, it follows that every being that wills is a creative first cause, an independent power in the universe, freely exerting its individual energies to make the future different from what it otherwise would be.

The creation of this future, for each successive moment, is the composite result of the efforts of every being that wills. Whatever its grade of intelligence, if it makes successful effort to produce change, it so far acts as an originating creative cause in producing the future.

Again, as every intelligent being will conform its action to the existing conditions to be acted upon, the change in these conditions which is effected even by the lowest order may affect the action of the highest. Each individual acts in reference to his prophetic anticipations of what the future will be without his action, and what the effects of his action upon it will be, including in these effects the consequent changes in the knowledge and action of others.

This *inter*dependence of the action of each upon that of others without interference with the freedom of any may be illustrated by the game of chess, in which each of the players alternately makes new conditions, new combinations, for the *free* action of the other, and this each in turn does with reference to the moves which may follow. They could so play if there were no other power in existence, and each was wholly passive while the other was determining his move, which in such case must be wholly determined and controlled by the party moving, and hence would be his free act.

This equal and perfect freedom of all does not impair the sovereignty of the Supreme Intelligence.

Edwards argues that if the Supreme Intelligence did not foreknow human volitions he would be continually liable to be frustrated in his plans. But Omniscience could at once perceive what action was most wise, or, even if prevision was essential, could search out and be prepared for every possible contingency. It is *conceivable* that a man could do this in the game of chess, and there are games which, though inexplicable to the uninitiated, may practically be so investigated that the best move in every possible contingency will be ascertained, and in which, with the advantage as to the first move, success will be certain to one having this superior knowledge, though he may not foreknow a single move of his opponent.

§ 7. The phenomena of instinct have been very generally deemed exceptional. Our own conscious agency in them is so slight that it escapes ordinary observation.[1]

The well ascertained fact that animals at their birth perform instinctive actions, without previous instruction or experience, furnishes a clue to the solution which brings these phenomena into harmony with all other *voluntary* actions. It indicates, not that the *will*, the voluntary effort, is absent, but that the *knowledge* by which we direct it is *innate*.

In every intelligent conative being the knowledge that by *effort* it can move its muscles must be innate.

[1] See Note V. p. 340.

There is no conceivable way in which the being could itself acquire this knowledge. No movement of its own muscles, without self-effort, could suggest the idea, and it would never discover any connection between the movement of the muscles of another and effort. No such experience or observation of the phenomena of muscular movement has any tendency to elicit or suggest the idea of effort.

But, so far as our observation goes, every animal, man included, is born with this and some additional knowledge which is essential to the preservation of its life. The kid the moment it is born can rise upon its feet and go directly to the source of food which its mother supplies, and it or the human infant would die of hunger before it could empirically learn the complicated muscular movements and the order of their succession which are required to avail itself of its food.

If there is any *self-activity* prior to birth, it still more strongly indicates that the knowledge of some of the modes by which we subsequently act is innate.

In all cases requiring more than one muscular movement we must will such movements in a certain order. It would be in vain to make the muscular movements by which we swallow, before the food was in the mouth. There must be a *plan* of action. If no such *plan* is already a part of our knowledge, we must devise one. Having such plan in our mind, we at once proceed to execute it by the appropriate efforts. In the rational action we ourselves devise the plan. In the instinctive we work by a plan that we found ready formed, innate in the mind.

When we have devised the plan of rational action, and can remember the successive steps, and apply it

MAN A CREATIVE FIRST CAUSE. 283

by rote without reference to the rationale, it becomes a *plan ready formed in the mind*, and the action becomes *habitual*. In such action the process is precisely the same as in the instinctive. The popular consciousness of this similarity finds expression in the common adage, "Habit is second nature."

In both cases we act from a plan ready formed in the mind which we apply without any present labor in devising it; and without the premeditation and deliberation required in this process.

The rational, the instinctive, and the habitual actions, then, all come under one general formula, and are all *efforts of a conative being, incited by its want and directed by its knowledge to the end sought*.

In our rational actions we have obtained the knowledge of the mode or plan of action by our own efforts. In the instinctive, we found it ready made in the mind without effort of our own.

In the habitual, the plan, though we may have originally formed it ourselves, has become so fixed in the memory that for all subsequent action it becomes a plan *ready formed in the mind*, requiring no new effort to reconstruct it.

In all this it is the being directing its effort to the end desired by means of its knowledge.

In the execution of this *plan*, it is obvious that the mode in which we get the knowledge of it can make no difference as to the process by which we execute it; and hence the difference between instinctive and rational actions has been vainly sought in the actions themselves.

There is no difference in the actions, nor in the knowledge itself, nor in the application of the knowledge to direct our efforts, but the distinction is a step farther back, in the *mode* in which we become possessed of the knowledge we thus apply.

As, in the rational actions, the main labor and difficulty, that which tasks our ability, is the forming of the plan of action, the fact that in the instinctive action this plan is ready formed in the mind accounts for the spontaneity, the absence of deliberation, which is one of the most marked features of instinctive actions, and the very little which is left for us to do causes us to overlook our own agency and to refer such actions to an extrinsic power, and hence to regard them as not self-controlled and not free. This mistake in ignoring our own agency also opens the way for the further error that instinctive actions are purely mechanical, which many philosophers of great reputation have asserted. But mechanism is not in itself power; it is only a means by which power is applied.

In regard to those habitual actions which we do by memory of plans of rational actions, if we should forget that the plans for them were originally formed by our own efforts, we should know no difference between them and the instinctive actions.

These views seem to account for all the peculiarities of instinctive actions, and, if they are correct, instinct is not a distinct faculty, property, or quality of being that may be put in the same category and compared with or distinguished from reason, but has relation only to the mode in which we became possessed of the knowledge by which we determine our actions. In regard to the instinctive, this knowledge being innate, we have no occasion to use our reason to obtain it. Hence instinct is often regarded as fulfilling the function of reason.

Whether the innate knowledge of modes and plans

MAN A CREATIVE FIRST CAUSE. 285

is by transmission or otherwise does not affect our theory. The fact that they are thus ready formed in the being without effort of its own seems to be assured by actual observation, and to be sufficient to explain all the peculiar phenomena of instinctive action.

The genesis of our action must be instinctive, founded on innate knowledge, there being no possible way in which, through experience or reflection, we could ever learn by effort to put either our muscular or mental powers in action.

The instinctive actions are of the same character in all grades of being; and in regard to rational actions I see no distinction in kind, but only in degree, between those of man and the lower animals. Descending in the scale of intelligence we will probably reach a grade of beings which do not seek to add to their innate knowledge, nor invent or form new plans to meet new occasions for effort.

The actions of such must be wholly instinctive; but I have seen dogs and horses draw inferences and work out ingenious plans of action adapted to conditions so unnatural and improbable to them as to preclude the assumption that they had been specially provided by nature, through hereditary transmission or otherwise, with the knowledge of the plan they adopted for such exigency.[1]

In regard to habit I would further state that it is but a substitution of former results of investigation and experience for present examination and trial. Through it memory performs the same office for action that it does for knowledge, retaining the acquisitions of the past for permanent use.

If on every occasion for their application we had to

[1] See Note VI. p. 341.

re-learn the letters of the alphabet, there could be very little progress in general knowledge, and so if on every occasion for action we had to devise or examine and decide as to the best plan, we should make very little progress in acquiring modes of action or facility in their application. By these conserving agencies the mind garners what is matured, and is ready for new acquisitions.

The agency of habit in retaining previously considered modes of action, right or wrong, and making them permanent accretions to the moral character, is its most important function.

Having now shown that these apparently exceptional cases of instinctive and habitual actions are really embraced in one general formula, that all our actions are efforts, self-directed by means of our knowledge to the gratification of a want, and consequently are free, I will note some of the conflicting views of the advocates of necessity.

I have already alluded to the fallacies which grow out of regarding the will as a distinct entity, and from the erroneous definitions of it, and of freedom, and also from identifying the latter with choice.

§ 8. But the argument from cause and effect seems to be most relied upon by necessitarians.

I adopt a statement of this argument which has the assent of one of its most distinguished advocates, viz. : If all the circumstances in a thousand cases are alike, and the conditions of the mind also the same, then the willing will be the same, and this uniformity indicates necessity.

This assumes as the basis of the argument that the same causes must produce the same effects.

In the first place I would remark that an intelligent

self-active cause is under no necessity upon a recurrence of the same circumstances to repeat its action, but having in the first case increased its knowledge, it may act differently in the second.

It may with reason be said that with this increase of knowledge the conditions of the mind are different, but if this difference is not tacitly accepted, the hypothesis of a thousand like cases is inconceivable, inasmuch as there could not even be two such.

But giving the argument all that is intended by those who urge it, and granting their assumption that the same causes do of necessity produce the same effects, let us suppose the circumstances in one thousand cases to be alike, and the conditions of the mind at each recurrence of them to be the same, and that one of these conditions of the mind is that of *necessity*, then the same causes of necessity producing the same effects, *the same action follows.*

Again, suppose the circumstances in another thousand cases to be alike, and the conditions of the mind again the same in each case, but that in these, one of the conditions of the mind, instead of being *necessity*, is *freedom*, then the same causes of necessity producing the same effects, *the same action follows.*

Now, as the result is in both cases the same, it cannot possibly indicate whether it is necessity or freedom that is among the conditions, and it proves nothing.

One phase of this argument from cause and effect is that all the present events, including volitions, are necessary consequences of their antecedents. I have already treated of this asserted dependence of the present on the past, and will now only add that intelligent action is always wholly upon the present conditions, and has reference solely to an effect in the future, and it is not material to such action how or when either the active being, as he is, or the conditions for him to act upon, came to be, or how connected with the past, nor whether they had any past. If, however, by the force of past events themselves, or by any causes whatever, there is established a certain flow of events having a tendency to extend into the future, such flow in its effect upon our freedom in willing does not differ from that flow which is the composite result of conative efforts, which I have already considered. Our individual action is always to interrupt or modify such flow. We decide as to our own actions by our preconceptions, our prescience — more or less reliable — of what the future will be with, and what without, our own efforts.

§ 9. The influence of present external conditions is also much relied upon by the advocates of necessity, but I trust it is already obvious that we may vary our free action with the circumstances, that we act as freely upon one set of them as upon any other, and that such action being self-conformed is perfectly free.

The influence of internal phenomena, as the moral character, knowledge, disposition, inclination, desires, wants, habits, etc., which make up the attributes and conditions of the mind that wills, is also much relied upon, and necessarians have been at much pains to show that the willing is always in conformity to these. But in view of the fact that freedom, in the act of willing, consists in the action being self-controlled and directed, it would have served the purposes of their argument much better to have proved that the action was counter to or diverse from the character. They seem to have been especially unfortunate in making successful efforts to prove that our actions are always in agreement with our prevailing choice, or, which with them is very nearly the same thing, with our strongest motive. The moral character of the being is indicated and represented by its efforts, but this manifestation through the efforts does not affect its freedom in making them. A demon is as free as an angel.

Nor is it material to the question of freedom how the being came to be as he is; whether his own character has been the result of his own efforts or of other power or circumstances; or whether his own knowledge, by which he directs his actions, has been acquired with or without extrinsic aid. The fact that his willing will vary with and conform to his character — his disposition and his knowledge — indicates that he controls his action. If he does not, then there is no reason to expect that his action will so conform.

§ 10. The advocates of necessity often ask if a man could will the contrary of what he does will. I would say that he could if he so decided; but it would be a contradictory and absurd idea of freedom, which for its realization would require that one might try to do what he had determined not to try to do. In short, all these arguments of the necessarians, that our acts of will are not free because they must conform to our own character, our own views and decisions, virtually assert that one is not free because he must be free; or, in other words, being of necessity free, he is *constrained* to be free, and hence is not free.

§ 11. Edwards and other theologians agreeing with him have regarded the argument from prescience of volitions, which they hold to be perfect in deity, as very conclusive. They assume not only that a volition which is infallibly foreknown must of necessity happen, but that it must happen by restraint or coercion of the willing agent. This is not a logical inference. Whether a free volition ever can be infallibly foreknown may be doubted. I think I have already shown that such foreknowledge is not requisite to the supreme sovereignty of the universe. But some philosophers, who in their inquiries exclude theology and revelation, also argue that the imperfect prescience, which must be an element in the decision of all our efforts to influence the future, also indicates necessity. Both hold that the possibility of prediction involves necessity as to the volition. But if, as I hope to demonstrate, a free act is as easily foreknown and predicted as one that is not free, this argument is wholly unavailing. If some being by its power *controls* a future event, it of course can foreknow and predict it; but such control of the volition of another, for reasons already stated, I hold to be impossible, involving a contradiction which power cannot reconcile. Aside from this conclusion, the difference between a volition which is free and one which is not free is, that the former is controlled and directed by the being in which it is manifested, and the latter by some extrinsic power. Our principal means of foreknowing what the self-directed, the free, act of an intelligent being will be is its conformity to the known character, habits, etc., of the actor; and if it is admitted that the external power which controls and directs the action which is not self-directed always conforms the act to the character of the being in which the action is manifested, then the probabilities of forming a correct judgment of what the action or effort will be are in this respect exactly equal. But the admission that this conforming of the action to the character of the actor is by an extrinsic power, and not by the actor himself, is an unwarrantable, I might perhaps say an absurd, assumption. In stating it one can hardly avoid a solecism, for the character which is thus presented to us by the actions is not that of the being apparently acting, but of the power or powers which determine the actions. The actions in such case might represent a consistent character, for to the outside observer the actions make the character; but it would be the character, not of the being apparently acting, which we perceive or know, but of the being or power extrinsic to it which we may not know. All our knowledge of beings as individuals, and even of species, would thus be annihilated. The hypothesis of such extrinsic agency in conforming the action to the character of the actor is in various aspects of it a gratuitous and inadmissible assumption.

If it still be urged that the act may be controlled by an extrinsic power that does not conform the action to the character of the apparent actor, then if we do not know this extrinsic power we wholly lose our principal means of predicting what the action will be; and if we do know it, and know it without any effort, we still have to meet the same difficulties, somewhat more complicated by this extrinsic agency, to ascertain what this extrinsic power would determine this unfree act of another to be, as we would to solve the question as to what the more direct and simple, self-determined free act of this other would be; so that on any admissible hypothesis the free act of will is (to all except an intelligent controlling power) more easily foreknown and predicted than one that is not free; and if this argument from the susceptibility to prediction has any weight, it is in favor of freedom and not of necessity.[1]

§ 12. I will now recur to the position before reached, that every being endowed with the faculty of will, a capacity for knowledge and a susceptibility to feeling, has within itself all the essentials of a self-active being, and can begin action, and, so far as it has *knowledge* of a mode, can make effort to produce any effects, and so far as it has *power* can actually produce them, without any extrinsic aid. Every such being is thus a creative first cause, an independent power in the universe, in a sphere commensurate with its knowledge, freely putting forth its efforts to change existing conditions

The power and knowledge of such a being may be very limited; but within the limits of these attributes its action is as *free* as if it were omniscient and omnipotent. Its effort must always be to make the future different from what but for such effort it would be. Such being is thus a co-worker with God, and with all other conative beings, in creating the future, which is always the composite result of the action of all such beings.

If we suppose an oyster with no other efficient *power* than that of moving its shell, and with knowledge of only one mode of doing this, and this instinctive, still, when by its own effort, directed by its own knowledge, it effects this moving, it so far makes the future different from what it would have been, and so far performs a part in the creation of that future.

But I shall deal mainly with our own more intelligent order of beings, which not only knows, but devises modes of actions suited to the varying oc-

[1] See Note VII. p. 344.

MAN A CREATIVE FIRST CAUSE. 293

casions of life, and in which the *creative* powers of effort, incited by feeling and directed by knowledge, are more abundantly manifested.

For the exercise of these creative powers we have two distinct spheres of effort, the one without and the other within us; that without us embracing all material phenomena, and so much of the spiritual as we attribute to other intelligent beings. All this sphere is known to us through our sensations and as an inference from them. Of the phenomena of our own spiritual nature we are directly conscious. The phenomena without us are conveniently called objective, and those within us subjective. Our efforts to effect change in either sphere are always subjective. In efforts for objective change we always begin by a movement of our own muscles. We thus directly change the material status without us, and, as already shown, we may by such change in the external material conditions to be acted upon indirectly influence the free action of others. We can thus by our own efforts make objective phenomena, including the mental action and volitions of others, different from what they otherwise would be.

§ 13. I have already alluded to the two different hypotheses, the one regarding material phenomena as forms of a distinct entity, called matter; the other regarding it as but the thought and imagery of the mind of God immediately impressed upon and made palpable to our finite minds, without any intermediate vehicle in the process.

In neither case the sensations, by which alone we know, or which perhaps are all there is, of the phenomena, are equally real, and are in fact identically the same on the one hypothesis as upon the other. If as a result or corollary of our arguments in regard to cause, or otherwise, the material universe is regarded as the work of an intelligent Creator, working with design to produce a certain effect, then, upon either of these hypotheses, it is the presentation and expression of a conception existing as thought and imagery in his mind before he gave it palpable tangible existence in ours, and the only question as between the two hypotheses is, whether, in making it palpable to us, he transfers this thought and imagery *directly* to our minds, or does this by painting, carving, or moulding, in a distinct material substance.

I have already intimated my leaning to the ideal hypothesis as being more simple and equally competent to embrace and explain all material phenomena.

I will here remark that the adopting of one or the other of these two hypotheses has very little, if any, bearing upon the views which I am presenting: whether the Supreme Intelligence found the matter, in which he expresses and makes his thoughts permanent and tangible, ready made, or made it himself, either as a distinct entity, or as mere imagery of his mind, has in most respects no more significance than the question whether Milton and Shakespeare and Bacon found existing materials for expressing and making their thoughts palpable and permanent, or contrived and made the pen, ink, and paper, which they used for this purpose. In either case we get the thoughts of the author, and can use the same means to express our own, including even in some measure the visible creations in which the Author of all has communicated his thoughts.

Another consideration in favor of the ideal hypothesis is, that by means of it, creating becomes more conceivable to us : we can any of us conceive or imagine a landscape and vary its features at will; this is an incipient creation, which by effort we may make more or less perfect.

Such creations of our own we for the time being locate outside of ourselves, and while we are wholly absorbed in contemplating them, they are to us perfect external material creations.

To make them such to *others* requires that we should in some way impress our conceptions upon their minds, and make the imagery of our own palpable to theirs. Though our faculty of doing this, as compared with that of creating the imagery, seems to be very limited, we are none of us wholly devoid of it. Landscape gardeners, architects, sculptors, painters, and more especially poets, have it in marked degree. In all these it is effected by slow, tentative processes, though in the latter it often appears as a genuine spontaneity, a fiat of creative genius.

We then already have and habitually exercise all the faculties essential to material creation, and with the requisite increase in that of impressing others we could design and give palpable persistent existence to a universe varying to any extent from that which now environs us, which would be objectively as real and material to the vision, even, of others, as the heavens and the earth they now look out upon.

Though these creations of our own are mostly evanescent, and the persistent reality which with great labor and pains we give to some of them is very limited, and the presentation even of these very imperfect, still they show that we have within us the rudiments of all the faculties which on the ideal hypothesis are essential to creating. This hypothesis is further commended to us by the consideration that man having in a finite degree all the other powers usually attributed to the Supreme Intelligence, lacks under the material theory that of creating matter. Corresponding to the Divine omnipotence, omniscience, and omnipresence, man has finite power and finite knowledge, and can make all the ideas and objects of his knowledge palpably present, which is equivalent to, and under the ideal hypothesis is identical with, a finite presence, limited like our other attributes to the sphere of our knowledge. The ideal hypothesis then rounds out our ideas of creative intelligence, relieving us of the anomaly of the creation of matter as a distinct entity, for which we have in ourselves no conscious rudiment of power, and of which we cannot conceive, and we find little if any relief in the alternative that matter has always existed without having been created.

A legitimate inference from the foregoing premises seems to be, that if from any cause one's own incipient creation of objective phenomena should become so fixed in his mind that *he could not change it at will*, it would become to him a permanent external reality. This inference is empirically confirmed by the fact that this sometimes happens in abnormal conditions of the mind.

However conscious we may be of our own agency in the formative process, as to the formations themselves, their subjection to our own will seems to be the only element by which we distinguish our own ideal creations from objective phenomena.

This strongly suggests that the difference between the creative powers of man and those of the Supreme Intelligence is mainly if not wholly in degree and not in kind, and that even in this the disparity, vast as it is, is still not incomprehensible as has been generally supposed. This gives warrant to the logic in which by short steps we attribute all creations and all changes, which we regard as beyond our own power and beyond that of other embodied intelligences known to us, to a superior intelligence with the same powers which we possess and use to create and change, increased, we need not say infinitely, but to a degree corresponding to the effects which we cognize and ascribe to them.

1 will further remark that so long as these creations even of the objective are purely subjective, there is no limit to the extent or the variety of our combinations. We are not confined to any experience of the actual nor constrained by any notion of propriety or harmony, but can make roses bloom in regions of perpetual snow, or locate a sun in the zenith of a nocturnal sky. Nor can we any more conceive of a limit to the extension of these incipient creations than we can of a limit to space. In such formations, and even as to those which we locate in the external, our creative fiat is absolute as to their accomplishment and unlimited as to their extension. But when we seek to make these creations permanent to ourselves and palpable to others, we find our ability to do this is in striking contrast with the power by which we produce them. The paltry changes on a few feet of canvas, or a few roods of earth, or a few descriptive pages, is all that remains of the most magnificent ideal constructions of the most gifted. In this external sphere, the common domain of all, there can be no appreciable monopoly by any.

DISCOURSE II.

MAN IN THE SPHERE OF HIS OWN MORAL NATURE A SUPREME CREATIVE FIRST CAUSE.

IN my former discourse I argued that man is a self-active and self-directed agent, with creative powers which he freely and successfully exerts to change the existing conditions and mould the future. Having, then, treated of the exercise of this creative power in the external, which is the common arena of all intelligent activity, I propose now to speak more especially of its manifestations in the internal, in which each individual has his own special sphere of creative effort, bounded only by his knowledge.

§ 14. I have already argued that some of our knowledge must be innate, and that some of what we acquire is obtained without our seeking, — without our effort.[1] External phenomena come into the mind unbidden, and cannot always be excluded. So, too, the facts and ideas which are already stored in the memory often come into view, and with them the perception of new relations, without any preliminary effort, and these cannot be discarded by any direct effort. This independence of the will gives to these intuitions the distinguishing characteristic of the phenomena of a *sense*, and, with the observed facts, indicates the existence of a *cognitive sense*.

As before stated, our acquisitions of knowledge are always by *simple immediate perception*, and hence in the final assimilation these are all the subjects of the cognitive sense; but some of our cognitions do, and

[1] See page 267.

others do not, require preliminary effort to bring them within the range of this immediate mental vision.

In this there is no difference, *per se*, as to our perceptions of external and internal objects. In the external we may have to remove obstacles to our seeing or hearing, and though our internal cognitions are the mind's more direct perception of what is already within itself, we still often need, by effort, to change the combination or arrangement of the ideas before the resulting relation or truth becomes manifest. In both cases the intuitive perceptions of the sense are distinguished from the results of the rational faculty by the effort required for the latter.

The phenomena of the external are brought within range of our immediate mental perceptions by means of the external organs of sense. For the internal cognitive spontaneity, the main, if not the only, immediate instrumentalities seem to be the operations of memory and association, singly and in combination; but its genesis is often, perhaps always, by suggestion from the bodily organs, through the senses, or the appetites, which much resemble and are closely allied to the senses. The sound of a cannon may call up our knowledge of the battle of Waterloo. The continual flow of ideas through the mind, singly or in trains or groups, is to it an exhaustless source of knowledge. If the mind ever became wholly inactive and oblivious, it could only be aroused and rescued from annihilation by some extrinsic agency. Our spontaneous cognitions of external objects and contemporaneous changes may be presented by the bodily organs of sense in any possible order or combination, and the internal phenomena may come into notice in a like manner, though in the latter the combinations and the order of succession seem to be more subordinated to the associations of experience.

The cognitive sense seems then to be, as it were, the common terminus of the arrangement, organism, or means by which both objective and subjective phenomena are immediately presented to the mind. These presentations become the subjects of our judgments, which may also be with or without preliminary effort: *e. g.*, we perceive at once the difference in the size of a pea and an orange, but do not thus perceive the equality of the sum of the angles of a triangle to two right angles.

To illustrate these processes, suppose the four letters *f, t, i, a*, are put to me to form into a word. It may so happen that I shall see them at first glance in the order *fiat*, and the thing is done, or I may have to proceed tentatively through few or many of the combinations which the letters admit of. So, too, the internal may accidentally come into view in such order that some new relation is immediately apparent, and seems like a sudden flash illuminating the mind from without, without any agency of its own. The circumstances and the perception may thus come under our observation without even an effort to direct attention to them.

We distinguish the various perceptions of the one cognitive sense, first as objective and subjective, and then classify the former as sensations of seeing, hearing, etc.; and, in regard to the latter, we speak of the sense of beauty, of order, of justice, honor, shame, etc. When the subject of these cognitions, and of the judgments upon them, spontaneous or otherwise, is that of moral right and wrong, they constitute the genetic elements of the *moral sense*. But the mere perception or judgment as to right and wrong has of itself no more effect upon the sensibilities than has the cognition that twice five are ten. It is not till we regard it as practically applied in action that it produces any emotion. Such action in others, when it is right, elicits our approval or admiration, and when wrong, our censure or indignation; and in ourselves the triumph of the right inspires us with the pleasurable and elevating emotion of victory, while the yielding to the temptation to wrong brings with it the painful feelings of debility, self-debasement, and dishonor. It is in these emotions of glory and of shame thus excited that we find the manifestation or development of conscience, which is properly the *moral sense*, to the sensations of which the cognition of right and wrong is only a prerequisite. Nor is it material to the quality of our action whether these cognitions are true or false, for the moral virtue of our actions all lies in our conforming them to our *convictions* of duty; and hence, though false convictions may cause our actions to be unwise, they do not affect their morality.

In regard to our action in the objective, I have argued that an innate knowledge that the movement of the muscles is effected by effort is a necessity, but, in view of the foregoing premises, there seems to be no analogous necessity that we should have any such knowledge of absolute right and wrong, or even any faculty or sense by which we can, intuitively or otherwise, acquire such knowledge.

The design of conscience seems primarily not to punish transgression, but to warn us against doing what is injurious to our moral nature. The monition comes in the contemplation of the act, and prior to its consummation, as in case one thrusts his hand into the fire, he feels the pain before he is seriously injured;

and as by frequent repetition the tissues become callous, and less sensitive to the pain, so, too, the more frequent and the more flagrant a man's iniquities, the less the pain which conscience inflicts upon him. This is the reverse of what it should be if punishment were the object. With this warning knowledge of the effect, we are left to our own self-control, our own freedom in action.

§ 15. Our efforts for change in the sphere within us, excepting, perhaps, those for moral construction, are always to increase our knowledge.

The knowledge sought may be of either sphere. Its immediate object often, perhaps oftenest, is to enable us to decide more wisely as to our action in reference to the actual current events of life ; or it may be for the pleasure we derive from the mental activity in the process, and the success which is almost certain to reward our search for truth. We can hardly fail to learn something, if not what we sought. A higher object may be to permanently increase the intellectual power, or, yet higher, to improve our moral nature.

§ 16. For the acquisition of knowledge by effort, mind has two distinct modes, — observation and reflection. By the former, we note the phenomena which are cognized by the senses, and by the latter we trace out the relations among the ideas — the knowledge — we already have in store, and thus obtain new perceptions, new ideas. A large portion of our perceptions, however acquired, are primarily but imagery of the mind, — pictures, as it were, of what we have perceived or imagined. In this form we will, for convenience, designate them as *primitive perceptions or ideals*. By these terms I especially seek to distinguish these perceptions from those which we have associated with words or other signs or representatives of things and ideas.

There is a somewhat prevalent notion that we can think only in words; but it is obvious that we can cognize things for which we have no name, and can also perceive their relations before we have found any words to describe them; and in fact such knowledge or perception generally precedes our attempts to describe them.[1]

These primitive perceptions, or *ideals*, are thus independent of the words which we use to represent them, and to which they may have a separate and prior existence. Even when in a strictly logical verbal process we reach a result in words, it is not fully available till, by a reflex action, we get a mental perception of that which those words signify or stand in place of.

Much of our acquired knowledge is of the relations in and between our primitive perceptions.

In the pursuit of truth by reflective effort we also have two modes. In the first place, we may through our immediate primitive perceptions of things which are present, or the mental imagery of things remembered, directly note the existing relations among them or their parts without the use of words in the process; or, we may substitute words as signs or definitions of these primitive perceptions, and then investigate the relations among the words so substituted.

In the difference of these two modes we find the fundamental distinction between poetry and prose, the former being the ideal or poetic, and the latter the logical or prosaic, method. The poet uses words to present his thoughts, but his charm lies in so using

[1] See Note VIII. p. 344.

them that the primitive perceptions — the imagery of his mind — shall be so transferred and pictured in that of the recipient as to absorb his attention to the exclusion of the verbal medium. We see the painting without thinking of the pigments and the shading by which it is impressed upon us. Every reader may experimentally test this distinction. If it is well founded, he will find that when any portion of a poem, instead of thus picturing the thought on his mind, requires him to get at it by means of the *relations of the terms* in which it is presented, there is a cessation or revulsion of all poetic emotion.

The material universe, which, upon either the ideal or materialistic hypothesis, is the thought and imagery of the mind of God directly impressed on our minds, is the perfect, and perhaps the only perfect type of the poetic mode.

Poetry, thus depending on this prominence of the primitive perceptions, is the nearest possible approach which language can make to the reality which it represents. Assuming that simple observation is common to both, these two modes of investigation — the one carried on by means of a direct examination of the realities themselves, or mental images of them, the other by means of words or other signs substituted for them — also present the fundamental and most important, if not the only, distinction in our methods of philosophic research and discovery.

Each has its peculiar advantages, and both are essential to our progress in knowledge. Like the external senses of sight and feeling, they mutually confirm or correct each other.

The prosaic has the advantage of condensing and generalizing, but is applicable only in a very contracted sphere, extending little, if any, beyond that in which a scientific language has been constructed; while the poetic, dealing directly with the things or their images, is coextensive with thought, perception, and imagination.

The prosaic can do little more than aid us to find and condense what is, and this only in the limited domain in which a language has already been constructed ; while the poetic is prophetic and creative in a sphere as boundless as its fancy.

Syllogistic reasoning furnishes good examples of the prosaic mode, but the purest form of it is manifested in our dealings with algebraic equations. In these we use letters, as signs of quantities (known and unknown), and other signs to express their relations to each other, and then by an examination of these signs and their defined relations, without any reference to any actual quantities, we logically deduce general formulas applicable to all quantities.[1]

All general propositions must be *expressed* in the prosaic mode, and the progress of knowledge usually being from particulars to generals, little advancement can be made without it. The particulars become too numerous and cumbersome for the mind to deal with separately.

But the poetic mode dealing directly with the things as observed, recollected, or imagined, we are by it enabled to advance beyond the limits of language and of the senses. It has a telescopic reach by which it penetrates the future and perceives the earliest dawn of truth.

It is thus the most efficient truth-discovering power, and at the same time furnishes the means of communi-

[1] See Note IX. p. 346.

cating the discoveries it makes in advance of the logical processes.

The greater facility and rapidity of the poetic over the logical process is illustrated by the ease and quickness with which we *perceive* the equality of two figures when one is applied directly to the other, as compared with our ascertaining this equality by means of a geometrical demonstration.

This greater reach and quickness makes the poetic power the essential attribute of genius in all its varieties. But this poetic power, this power of dealing directly with things, or our immediate perceptions of them, though prominent in the more gifted, is not restricted to them, but pervades the whole domain of our intellectual activity.

In its least ethereal and most common form, it is the basis of that common sense which, looking directly at things, events, and their relations, enables us spontaneously to form just opinions, or probable conjectures, of immediate consequences, and to determine as to the appropriate action. From this low estate, when aided by elevated moral sentiments, combined with intellectual power, and invigorated with warm feelings, pure passion, and fervid enthusiasm, it rises to the dignity of inspiration and the sublimity of prophecy.

The facility of application to the current affairs of life which pertains to the ideal processes makes the poetic attribute the main element of practical business ability. The current events of life are too complicated, variable, and heterogeneous for the application of verbal logic. In the mistakes to which even careful and skilful logicians are liable from too hasty generalizations, faulty definitions, and fallacious inferences, we see the danger which would arise if the uninitiated, who are immersed in business, and whose decisions must often be hasty, should rely upon processes of reasoning in which an error in the signification, or in the application, of a term might vitiate their conclusions and lead to disastrous action.

To such the processes of ideality are much safer. In these, without the intervention of words, the mind, at a glance, takes in the actual conditions, and reaches its conclusions in incomparably less time than would be required to substitute the terms, test their precision, examine their relations, and arrange them in the requisite logical order.

The greater quickness with which we examine *particular* cases by the poetic process to some extent compensates for the greater number of instances, which may be embraced in one *generalization* of the prosaic.

Persons who adopt the quicker mode are often notably discreet, wise, and able in the actual conduct of affairs, but from the exclusion of words in the process, and its flash-like quickness, they cannot state the grounds of their conclusions, nor assign a reason for their consequent action.

The poetic processes are also the characteristic feature of what has been termed a woman's reason, which is thus contradistinguished from verbal logic. And the practical application of these processes is illustrated in the quick and clear perception of the circumstances, and sound judgment upon them, with which woman is properly accredited. This feature also leads us intuitively to regard woman as of finer mould, and to expect from her æsthetically and morally more than from the sterner sex. And it is to her command of these more direct and more ethereal modes of thought and expression that we must attribute her superior influence in softening the asperities of our nature, and refining and elevating the sentiments of our race. Hence, too, it is that while the finest and strongest reasoning of philosophy has in this respect accomplished so little, woman has accomplished so much. The refined subtleties of an Aristotle, or the glowing sublimities of a Plato, though presented to us with all the fascinations of a high-toned morality, with all the accessories of graceful diction and persuasive eloquence, are dim and powerless to that effluence of soul which with a glance unlocks the portals to our tenderness, which chides our error with a tear, or winning us to virtue with the omnipotence of a charm, irradiates the path of duty with the beaming eye, and cheers it with the approving smile of loveliness. As compared with such influences, the results of logic or any prosaic form of words are weak.

It is, then, through the poetic processes that we mainly get the perceptions, the knowledge, by which we direct our actions in the varying events and multifarious combinations of every-day life.

Though it is in a subdued form that the poetic power is thus practically available, it still seems a desecration to put such high endowments to such common uses; but we have tamed the lightning and made it run on our errands and drudge in our workshops.

§ 17. I have already touched upon the exercise of our creative power in the sphere without us, in which we act with all other conative beings. But it is in the isolated sphere within us, in the seclusion of our own spiritual nature, that we should expect to find this power most potent, and our efforts, always mental, most successful. And it is in a better knowledge of the character, the relations, and the modes of the poetic and the logical processes with a more general cultivation of the former, and by a more systematic and intelligent selection from these two cardinal modes of investigation of that which is best suited to the subject in hand, or oftener by a judicious application of both to the same subject, so that each may supplement and supply the deficiencies, or correct the errors, of the other, that I look for increased efficiency, reach, and accuracy in the mind's intellectual ability.

The discovery of improved modes for such cultivation, selection, and single or combined application of these two cardinal methods of seeking truth, and the means of making these discoveries accessible and available to the popular mind, are both within the province of the metaphysician, and they open to him an elevated sphere of utility.

The benefits which may be anticipated from exploring this field are not merely those which metaphysical studies confer as a strengthening exercise to the mental powers. They also include the making of the same strength more effective by the invention or discovery of improved modes in their application.

It is true that both these modes of thought must always have been in practical use, but with little or no conscious attention as to the selection or application of them, singly or combined. The neglect or unconsciousness of any such aids is manifested in the not uncommon belief that we always think in words — a belief which is shared even by men of deep philosophic thought.

§ 18. But it is in the sphere of our moral nature that I look for beneficial results far more important than even the increase of intellectual power, and in this more especially through the agency of the poetic element. It is in this realm that we would naturally look for the most congenial sphere of action for our most ethereal attribute. Conformably to these anticipations, I hope to show that, in the formation of character, this power of creating imaginary constructions, and of contemplating and perfecting them, exerts an influence of the highest importance, which, by cultivation, may be enhanced without conceivable limit. This is the mode in which our conceptions of mental or material phenomena most nearly supply the place of actual experience, and in some respects with decided advantages. The occasions for actual experience, too, are casual and uncertain, while the ideal processes are always available. From these supposable events, which are constantly flowing through the mind, we form rules of conduct, or receive impressions, which govern us in the concerns of real life. It is in meditating on these that we nurture the innate feelings, sentiments, and passions, which not only give impulse to transitory action, but become the main elements of the fixed character. He who accustoms himself to this discipline, who, withdrawn from the bustle of the world, tranquilly contemplates imaginary cases, and determines how he ought to act under them, frames for himself a system of government with less liability to error than is possible in the tumultuous scenes of active life. He is not swayed by those interests and passions which so often distort or confuse our vision when we act from the impulses of immediate and pressing circumstances.

The ideal formations may not be accurately fitted to the occasions which actually arise, but the contingency can hardly occur in which some of the vast number of them that may be constructed, even by those most engrossed with the realities of life, will not in some degree be applicable. They will at least furnish suggestive analogies, and in the processes lead to habits of *disinterested* thought, which are so essential to the successful pursuit of truths, and especially of moral truths, which often conflict with the desires of the active moment.

We cannot directly will a change in our mental affections any more than in what are termed bodily sensations. We cannot *directly* will the emotions of hope or fear, or to be pure and noble, or even to want to become pure and noble, any more than we can directly will to be hungry, or to want to be hungry. If we want to take food we are already hungry, and if we want to perform pure and noble actions, and to avoid the impure and ignoble, while this want or disposition prevails we are already intrinsically pure and noble. If we want to be hungry, *i. e.* want to want food, and know that by exercise, or by the use of certain stimulants, or by other means, we may become hungry, we may by effort induce this, in such case, a cultivated want; and if we want to want to be pure and noble and know the means, we may, in like manner, by effort gratify the existing want, and induce the want, the cultivated want, to become pure and noble.

If, from seeing the pleasure which admiring a beautiful flower affords to others, or from any other cause, we want to admire it, we will readily perceive that some additional knowledge is essential to that end; and that the first step is to find, by examination, what in it is admirable. To examine then becomes a secondary want, and we will to examine. The result of this examination may be that its before unknown beauties excite our admiration, and make it, or the gazing upon it, an object of want; so we may also will to examine what is pure and noble till its developed loveliness excites in us, or increases, the want to be pure and noble, and induces a correlative aversion to what is gross and base.

The occurrence and recurrence of our spiritual wants are as certain as those of hunger. We are continually reminded of them by our own thoughts and acts, by comparison with those of others, and by the external manifestations of God's thought and action; and he has placed within us the moral sense, as a sentinel, with its intuitions awakening the conscience, and warning us of what, in wants or means, is noxious to our moral nature with more certainty than the senses of taste and smell tell us of what is injurious to our physical well-being.[1]

It thus appears that want, constitutional, acquired, or cultivated, is the source of effort for internal as well as external change.

The desire to effect some change in the existing or anticipated conditions is the only conceivable motive for the action of any rational being.

As a man cannot do any moral wrong in doing what he believes to be right, his knowledge, though finite, is infallible as to what it is morally right for him to do; and his fallibility in morals must consist in his liability to act at variance with his knowledge or conviction of right, and never in deficiency of knowledge, or even in belief. In this view his knowledge in the sphere of his moral nature is infallible, and were he infinitely wise or certain to act in conformity to his knowledge of the right, he would be infallible in his morals.

It is also evident that the mind must direct its

[1] See pages 300 and 301.

MAN A CREATIVE FIRST CAUSE. 313

efforts for internal change by means of its knowledge, including its preconceptions of the character it would therein build up.

Now such preconceptions are imaginary constructions, incipient creations, in the future.

In its constructions in the external, the mind does not of necessity even consider or recognize the already existing external circumstances. In "castle-building," it often voluntarily discards them, and forms a construction entirely from its own internal resources. Retaining its knowledge of the past, and having the power of abstraction, it could just as well conceive an external creation if all external existences, facts, and circumstances were annihilated. A man thus isolated might imagine a material universe in which all is in his view beautiful and good. He may not make, nor even intend to make, the additional effort to actualize these combinations and make them palpable to others, or permanent within himself.

He has merely exercised himself in constructive effort. So, too, if moved by the aspirations of his spiritual being, he may conceive a moral character, pure and noble, resisting all temptation to evil, and conforming with energetic and persevering effort to all virtuous impulses and suggestions. Though he may make no effort, and not even intend to make any, to realize such ideal conceptions, they are not without their influence. The constructions thus sportively made add to our knowledge of the materials of character, and to our skill in combining them. Poetry, and fiction in other forms, present us with such constructions ready formed by others.

The making of such constructions as harmonize with our conceptions of moral excellence is in itself improving; a determination in advance by persevering effort to conform our conduct to them is a greater step, and the persistent effort to actualize them when the occasion for their practical application has arisen, is, so far as the moral nature is concerned, really their final consummation; for whether the proximate object of the effort is or is not attained makes no difference to its moral quality. The intent or motive is not affected by the success or failure of the effort. The external effect is but the tangible evidence to others of the internal effort which, with the intent, is the real manifestation of the moral element. If a man wills to do an act which is good and noble, it does not concern his virtue whether his effort be successful or otherwise, the effort is itself the triumph in him of the good and noble over the bad and base, and the persevering effort to be good and noble is itself being good and noble.

It follows from these positions that, as regards the moral nature, there can be no failure except the failure to will, or to make the proper effort. The human mind with its want, knowledge, and faculty of effort, having the power within and from itself to form its creative preconceptions, and to will their actual realization independently of any other cause or power, up to the *point of willing* is, in its own sphere, an independent creative first cause. Exterior to itself it may not have the power to execute what it wills, it may be frustrated by other external forces. Hence, in the *external* the ideal incipient creation may not be consummated by finite effort. But as in our *moral nature* the willing, the persevering, effort is itself the consummation, there can in it be no such failure; and the mind in it is therefore not only a creative, but a SUPREME CREATIVE FIRST CAUSE.

We have, then, between effort in the sphere of the moral nature and in that sphere which is external to it this marked difference: while in the external there must be something beyond the effort, *i. e.*, there must be that subsequent change which is the object of the effort before the creation is consummated, in the sphere of the moral nature the effort for the time being is itself the consummation ; and this, if by repetition, ideal or actual, made *habitual*, becomes a permanent constituent of the character, which, through habitual *action*, will be obvious to others — will be a *permanent palpable* creation.

In his internal sphere, then, man has to the fullest extent the powers in which he is so deficient in the external. In it he can make his incipient creations palpable and permanent constituents of his own moral character.

§ 19. In this permanent incorporation of them with his moral nature habit has a very important agency. This may be cultivated and its efficiency increased by intelligent attention, and through it the ideals, the scenic representations which are continually being acted in the theatre within us, may be made available in advance of actual experience, for which, as already suggested, they serve as a substitute, and with some decided advantages in their favor.

In the *sphere of its own moral nature*, then, whatever the finite mind really wills is as immediately and as certainly executed as is the will of Omnipotence in its sphere of action, for the willing in such case is itself the final accomplishment, the terminal effect, of the creative effort.

We must here be careful to distinguish between that mere abstract judgment, or knowledge of what is *desirable* in our moral nature, and the want and the effort to attain it. A man may know that it is best for him to be pure and noble, and yet, in view of some expected or habitual gratification, not only not want to be *now* pure and noble, but be absolutely opposed to being made so, even if some external power could and would effect it for him. We may, however, remark that, as the moral quality of the action lies wholly in the will, and no other being can will for him, to be morally good without his own effort is an impossibility; all that any other being can do for him in this respect is to increase his knowledge and excite his wants, and thus induce him to put forth his own efforts. Even Omnipotence can do no more than this, for to make a man virtuous without his own voluntary coöperation involves a contradiction. The increase of virtuous efforts indicates an improvement in the character of the cultivated wants and an increase of the knowledge by which right action is incited and directed. The influence of such knowledge and wants, becoming persistent and fixed by habit, forms, as it were, the substance of virtuous character.

In the sphere of the internal as well as in the external, the last we know of our agency in producing change is our effort. But in our moral nature the effort is itself the consummation. The effort of a man to be pure and noble is actually being pure and noble. The virtue in the time of that effort all lies in, or in and within, the effort and the intent, and not in its *success or failure.* It is for the time being just as perfect if no external or no permanent results follow the effort. If the good efforts are transitory, the moral goodness will be equally so, and may be as mere flashes of light upon the gloom of a settled moral depravity.

§ 20. Nor does the nature of the actual resulting effect make any difference to the moral quality of the effort. A man's intentions may be most virtuous, and yet the actual consequences of his efforts be most pernicious. On the other hand, a man may be as selfish in doing acts in themselves beneficent — may do good to others with as narrow calculations of personal benefit — as in doing those acts which he knows will be most injurious to his fellow-men; and doing such good for selfish ends manifests no virtue, whether that end be making money or reaching heaven, and brings with it neither the self-approval nor the elevating influences of generous self-forgetting or self-sacrificing action.

A man who is honest only because it is the more gainful would be dishonest if the gains thereby were sufficiently increased. Such honesty may indicate that he is intelligent and discreet, but virtue is not reached till he acts, not from sordid and selfish calculations, but from a sense of right and duty. And virtue is not consummated and established in him till he feels the wrong-doing as a wound, leaving a blemish on the beauty and a stain on the purity of the moral character, the preservation and improvement of which has become his high absorbing interest, and the construction and ideal contemplation of which he has come to appreciate and to value above all other possessions and all possible acquisitions.

The consequences of a volition may prove that it was unwise, but cannot affect its moral status. If at the time of the effort one neither did nor omitted to do anything in violation of his own perceptions or sense of duty, he did no moral wrong, and any subsequent consequences cannot change the moral nature of the past action. No blame or wrong can be imputed to one who did the best he knew.

Again, no moral wrong can pertain to a man for any event in which he has had and could have no agency, which he could neither promote nor obstruct. Until he has put forth effort against his knowledge of duty, or omitted to put it forth in conformity with this knowledge, there can be no moral wrong. There is no present moral wrong, either in the knowledge now in his mind or in the exciting want which he now feels. There may have been moral wrong in the acquisition of any knowledge, or in the omission to acquire any, which required an effort. Such acquisition or omission may have then been counter to his conviction of right.

There can be no moral wrong in the acquisition of that knowledge which he *unintentionally acquires. That a man involuntarily knows that the sun shines, or that a drum is beating, cannot be morally wrong in itself. So, likewise, that any knowledge now actually has place in his mind, can, of itself, involve no present moral wrong-doing, though the fact that it is there may be evidence of a previous moral wrong committed in its acquisition. This he cannot *now* prevent. Such knowledge may have so polluted his moral nature, that it will require an effort to purify it. The polluting arose from the previous effort to acquire, or, negatively, from not making the effort to prevent acquiring, and not from the mere fact of possessing the knowledge, which is now beyond his control, and does not, of itself, alter the moral condition from that state in which the wrong of acquisition left it, though every wrong application of it may do so.

So, also, in regard to the natural *wants*. There is no moral wrong in the mere fact of their recurrence. There may be moral wrong in our willing to gratify a want which should not be gratified, or in entertaining or cultivating one which should be discarded or eradicated, or in the time or in the mode of the gratification. That such want exists at all, or that it should recur at such time, may be proof of a previous wrong effort in cultivating the want, or of an omission to control or eradicate it, or to cultivate some conflicting want; but if its present recurrence is not by our own effort, such recurrence, of itself, can involve no present moral wrong, and merely furnishes the occasion for virtuous effort to resist what is wrong, or to foster and strengthen what is right. The want may indicate the present condition of the moral nature, while it also supplies the opportunities which make both improvement and degeneracy possible. Though that condition may be comparatively low in the scale, yet an effort to advance from it may be as truly and purely virtuous as a like effort at any higher point.

In the *present moment*, then, the knowledge and the want, which exist prior to effort, involve no present moral right and wrong; and as we have already shown that the sequence of the effort does not, it follows that the *moral right and wrong are all concentrated in the effort, or act of will, which is our own free act.*

This and some preceding results are perhaps sufficiently attested by the consideration that the goodness or badness in which one has no agency, or of which he is not the cause, is not his goodness or badness, and he can have such agency or be such cause only by his act of will.

Efforts to be pure and noble, and for corresponding external action, may become habitual, and hence comparatively easy. Through habit, memory performs the same office for our acquirements in *acting* that it does for our acquisitions of knowledge, *retaining or holding fast what is acquired*, and thus leaving the mind at liberty to employ itself in new acquisitions, new progress in knowledge, including modes of action.

We may further observe, in this connection, that our moral wants are more under the control of the mind's acts of will than the physical conditions of bodily wants; and though we cannot directly will not to think of a thing, yet, by willing to think of something else, we may displace and banish other thought; so, too, though we cannot directly will the removal of a want, yet we can put it away by directing our attention to something else, or by inducing another want in its place. And though this is especially true of the moral wants, it partially applies also to the physical. We know, for instance, that by exercise and fasting we can induce hunger; and we may find means of inducing any moral want, and by the use of these means, some of which I have already suggested, may give one moral want a preponderance over another, which, by repetition becoming habitual, will go far to eradicate it and to modify the influence even of a physical want. In such a case the want will then offer no inducement, no temptation; but after the primary want is eradicated there may arise another want from association of former acts of will with enjoyment, which still is a want, the gratification of which is tempting. Habit also may have its influence after the want ceases.

If entirely eradicated, there can be no corresponding volition, and a man habitually holy, who has eradicated the conflicting wants, has annihilated the conditions requisite to his willing what is unholy; and as he cannot be unholy except by his own voluntary act, he has then no power to be unholy. This is, perhaps, a condition to which a finite moral being may forever approximate but never actually reach, never attain that condition in which it is absolutely unable to will what is impure and ignoble.

But by these creative efforts fresh elements of moral character have been produced, which by the assimilating and solidifying forces of *habit* may become permanent accretions to the moral nature, a second nature, not less secure against the ordinary vicissitudes and temptations of life than the innate or earlier acquired principles or modes of action.

Through the knowledge of the means of giving to some of our internal wants a predominance over others, we are enabled by effort to influence our moral characteristics at their very source. Even under circumstances least favorable to the recognition of our spiritual condition, amid the engrossments of sense, the excitements of passion, or the turmoil of absorbing business, external events will often suggest our moral wants, while in calm and thoughtful moments they present themselves as spontaneously as thirst in a summer's day.

§ 21. Having now shown that we can cultivate our wants, and give one or the other of conflicting wants the ascendency, and promote one to the at least partial exclusion of others ; that the knowledge of each individual as to what is morally right for him is infallible ; that the mind can form an ideal construction or preconception within itself without reference to any external existence ; that it can freely make efforts to realize such construction ; and that nothing *beyond the effort* has any influence upon the moral quality of the effort, or of the agent making it, we may more confidently than before deduce the conclusion, that the mind in the sphere of its own moral nature, applying an infallible knowledge which it possesses to material purely its own, may conceive an ideal moral creation, and then realize this ideal in an actual creation by and in its own act of will; and hence, when willing in the sphere of his own moral nature, man is not only a creative first cause, but a *supreme* creative first cause; and, as his moral nature can be affected only by his own act of will, and no other power can will or produce his own act of will, he is also, in the sphere of his moral nature, a *sole* creative first cause, though still a finite cause. Other intelligences may aid him by imparting knowledge; may by word or action instruct him in the architecture; but the application of this knowledge, the actual building, must be by himself alone. Though finite, his efficiency as cause, in this sphere, is limited only by that limit of all creative power, the incompatible, or contradictory; and by his conceptions of change in his moral nature, which are dependent upon the *extent* of his knowledge; and, in this view, the will itself having no bounds of its own, may be regarded as infinite, though the range for its action is finite; or in other words, within the sphere of its moral nature, the finite mind can will any *possible* change of which it can conceive, or of which it can form a preconception; and as the willing it is the consummation of this preconception, there is no change in our moral being, which we can conceive of, that we have not the ability to consummate by effort; and as, so far as we know, our power to conceive of new progress — to form new conceptions of change — enlarges with every consummation of a previous conception, there is no reason to suppose that there is any *absolute* limit to our moral sphere of effort; but that it is only relatively and temporarily circumscribed by our finite perceptions, which, having a finite rate of increase, may forever continue to expand in it without pressing on its outermost bound; and, if all these positions are true, every intelligent moral being capable of conceiving of higher ethical conditions than he has yet attained, has in his own moral nature, for the exercise of his creative powers, an infinite sphere, within which, with knowledge there infallible, he is the supreme disposer; and in which, without his free will, nothing is made, but all the creations in it are as singly and solely his as if no other power or cause existed; and for which he is, of course, as singly and solely responsible as God is for the creations in that sphere in which he manifests his creative power, though, as a finite created being, man, even in this his own allotted realm, may still be properly accountable for the use of his creative powers to him who gave them.

§ 22. The gratification of some of our physical wants being essential to our present existence, they are most imperative and have precedence, but they are in their nature limited and temporary, and, when gratified, cease to demand our effort. In this their function seems to be to train the mind to habits of persevering effort, and thus fit it for the exercise of its powers in the gratification of the nobler wants of its moral being.

In contrast with our physical, our spiritual wants are boundless and insatiable. In our want for progress — for something better than we have yet attained — our activity finds an illimitable sphere, and in our *want* for activity, exhaustless sources of gratification.

§ 23. The examination of past experience and of supposed cases may in some sort be performed in the prosaic mode of verbal representation or logical reasoning; but, from the time required, it is impossible that this method should be generally resorted to, and when it is, though it may establish general principles, it is less moving and has a less direct influence on the conduct than those *scenic representations* which are so faithfully acted upon the secluded theatre within us. *Ideality is in this respect the nearest approach to reality.*

§ 24. There is peculiar consolation and encouragement in the fact that mind possesses in these ideal processes an inherent power of modifying material and other extrinsic influences; that it has an incentive which is as potent in our spiritual nature as sensation is in our physical.

Fortunately, too, the occasions of life which have a tendency to warp the disposition, though frequent, are transient, have their intervals, and in some degree neutralize each other. The ideal conceptions may always be brought to mind, and if we habitually encourage the presence of those only which are pure and elevated, we shall as a consequence become more and more refined and ennobled.

Without this countervailing element our moral nature would seem to be largely the sport of chance, liable to be driven from its proper course by every current of feeling and every storm of passion. Character would then chiefly depend on accidental extrinsic circumstances.

These ideal processes early give a pleasurable exercise to the mind, and, like other sports of youth, are a preparation for sterner work, when from the inflexible material of permanent principles we would construct an enduring moral character. We enact these scenic representations as an alluring gratification, and naturally find pleasure in perfecting our ideal creations.

Our first creative efforts are probably in the material. The child early forms ideal constructions, and seeks with clay or blocks to give them a tangible objective existence. It thus makes its first essays in creative effort. Its efforts, however, are early transferred to the spiritual, and ideas of moral beauty and grandeur, and of glory, honor, and renown, as the results of lofty character and noble action, find place in the young imagination, and furnish the materials and the incentive to such ideal constructions. These may be evanescent, but in vanishing they will still leave visions of grace, beauty, and purity.

We are thus at an early period of life introduced into the domain of constructive moral effort, and the quickening influence which the soul receives in this direction, when the first revelations of unselfish and romantic passion fill it with ideals of loveliness, grace, and elevation, and inspire it with pure and lofty sentiment and energetic virtue, attests the beneficent provision for our early moral culture.

But these benign endowments, so potent for good, are liable to be perverted to evil. We have alluded to our physical wants as the more imperative, but as temporary, leaving us much intervening time to attend to the spiritual. The influence of these temporal wants is, however, made less inconstant by the secondary want of acquisition ; the want to provide in advance the means of gratifying the primary wants when they recur. To this acquisitiveness, even when gratification of the physical wants is its sole object, there seems to be no limit, and this may permanently become the habitual object of effort to the exclusion of the spiritual.

To restrain the influence of the processes of ideality within such narrow limits is unnatural. By doing so the individual voluntarily foregoes the pleasures which arise from the generous emotions, cuts off their connection with the springs of action, and substitutes narrow prudential calculations, low cunning, and artifice, which cramp and degrade the moral nature, and exclude its finer feeling and nobler aspirations.

The power which through ideality we exert over our moral nature, though less nobly exhibited, is as strongly attested in its degrading as in its elevating influences; in the aggravation of selfishness, for instance, no less than in the development of the generous virtues. In the latter case, it seems to advance freely, allured by the delights which attend its progress. In the former it is forced back against the current of its affections and the repulsion of conscious self-debasement.

It seems strange that a labor thus painful in its performance and baneful in its results should ever be accomplished. It is probably in most cases hastily done, in view of some immediate gratification, without considering its permanent pernicious influence, and finally effected and confirmed by magnifying the advantages of selfishness, or the sacrifices of immediate personal interests, which a yielding to generous impulses may have occasioned. The avaricious miser looks upon a liberal man as one too weak to subdue the liberal impulses or resist the pleasure of yielding to them. He knows the pain and labor which his own prudence has cost him, and congratulates himself on his exemption from such benevolent frailties.

§ 25. The elevating influences of ideality are needed to counteract the tendencies of a social system based largely on selfishness, and to neutralize the utilitarian, materialistic, comfort-seeking proclivities of this mechanical and commercial age.

But ideal constructions have been discouraged and repressed as a waste of time, stigmatized as mere spray, or vapors, idle imaginings leading to groundless hopes and illusive views of life. Relieving these processes from obstruction and perversion, and leaving them to their natural course in forming the moral character, would be a very important gain on present conditions.

And this might be affirmatively supplemented by systematic education in this mode of moral culture, making the ideal constructions a subject of study, as an artist now studies his models and pencil sketches with a view to their reproduction in more perfect and permanent forms.

There is at once confirmation of our theory and encouragement as to its practical application in the fact that woman, to whose guiding care the infant intelligence is naturally confided, is by her special endowment of poetic modes of thought and expression so fully equipped for this important work.

I deem it but a reasonable anticipation that whenever this means of moral culture shall begin to be appreciated, and even moderately developed, the effects upon the advancement, upon the elevation and happiness, of mankind will be such as not only to relieve metaphysics from the reproach of being unfruitful, but to show that as it embraces the largest and grandest realm of human thought, it is productive of the most important and elevated utility, a utility far transcending all that has been realized in the domain of the material.

When philosophy shall have fairly entered upon this higher sphere of mental effort for mental progress, it may again disdain its application to any less elevated or less elevating pursuit. But still, when from their celestial heights its votaries look down upon the enduring and beneficent achievement of their predecessors, upon the solid foundation in physical science upon which they are themselves building their more ethereal superstructure, we may trust that they will at least concede to them the merit of having faithfully, intelligently, and vigorously performed their part in the more humble sphere of physical research, and will accord something even of grandeur and of glory to an age which from the chaotic sense-perceptions evolved a material universe of order and beauty, and, taming the wild forces of nature, made them subservient to the enjoyment and progress of man; enabling him without excessive labor to make that ample provision for his physical comforts which was, perhaps, a prerequisite condition to effort for a higher spiritual culture.

§ 26. In metaphysics the progress from abstract speculation to practical utility has not differed from that of the other sciences. All appear to have been at first pursued from a natural love of truth, an inherent curiosity stimulated by opposing mysteries without reference to ulterior benefit. Is this pursuit but the manifestation in us of an instinct nobler in its nature and ministering to higher purposes than those which are essential to our physical existence? Or may not it and the love of approbation and the desire for fame be properly regarded as blind appetites of an elevated character?

The Greek geometricians when patiently investigating the conic sections had no thought of the use which a Newton would make of their discoveries, and when Huyghens discovered the polarity of light he had no idea that the sugar refiner would eventually use it to test the value, for his purpose, of a cargo of molasses.

So, too, metaphysics has been wrought upon for ages for no other reason than that it furnished a pleasurable and invigorating exercise to the intellect, a utility no higher or more direct than might be derived from whist or chess.

§ 27. It will be observed, too, that the solutions of the three problems which, with a very dim vision of their consequences, I have investigated, and to which I have in this paper invited attention, were, if not essential prerequisites, very important aids in reaching the particular practical utility I have herein suggested.

The first of these was the analysis of the fundamental distinction between poetry and prose, and the finding that this distinction is the same as that between the two cardinal modes by which we seek for truth.

The second was our investigation as to man's freedom in willing and the fixing his status as an independent creative power in the universe; the exercise of these powers in the external being very limited and liable to be frustrated by other independent powers, while in the sphere of his own internal being he is supreme, and can there at will consummate his ideal constructions and make them palpable and persistent while he so wills.

The third was the inquiry as to the difference between instinctive and rational actions, and in this incidentally determining the nature and functions of *habit* by which these subjective constructions may be made permanent formations of the moral character and incorporated into our being as a *second nature*.

The first was essential to the discovery and comprehension of the creative powers which inhere in the poetic element, and to the appreciation of its capabilities in its especially appropriate realm of the spiritual, and its important agency in there forming and elevating the moral character.

The second presents the proof of man's free agency, without which, if he could be said to have a moral nature, he could have no agency in its formation or improvement, and no responsibility for its character. If he could be said to have any virtue, he could have no means or opportunity to manifest it in action. There could be no exhibition of it in beneficent action touching himself or others, and he could not use his creative powers for self-improvement or for any other purpose.

And, third, without the agency of habit, our acquisitions in moral action would all be evanescent, and there could no more be progress in moral character than there could be in knowledge without memory. But by this conservative function of habit all of these acquisitions which we *sanction* by repetition in action, or by harboring in thought, are incorporated into and become permanent accretions to our moral character, and veritable exponents of it. That our own action is thus required in the formation of habits brings them in their incipiency within our own control; but from the greater ease with which we perform actions for which we have the plan ready formed, it requires energy and vigilance to prevent falling into habits which our judgment does not approve. To eradicate them at a later period requires much more labor and increased vigilance.

§ 28. We have now endeavored to show: that the only efficient cause of which we have any real knowledge is mind in action, and that there cannot be any unintelligent cause whatever.

That every being endowed with knowledge, feeling, and volition is, in virtue of these attributes, a self-active independent power, and in a sphere which is commensurate with its knowledge a creative first cause therein, freely exerting its powers to modify the future and make it different from what it otherwise would be; and that the future is always the composite result of the action of all such intelligent creative beings.

That in this process of creating the future every such conative being, from the highest to the lowest, acts with equal and perfect freedom, though each one, by its power to change the conditions to be acted upon, or rather, by such change of the conditions, or otherwise, to change the *knowledge* of all others, may influence the free action of any or all of them, and thus cause such free action of others to be different from what but for his own action it would have been.

That every such being has *innately* the ability to will, *i. e.* make effort, which is self-activity ; and also the knowledge that by effort it can put in action the powers by which it produces changes within or without itself.

That the only conceivable inducement or *motive* of such being to effort is a desire — a want — to modify the future, for the gratification of which it directs its effort by means of its knowledge.

That when such being so directs its effort by means of its *innate* knowledge, it is what is called an *instinc-*

tive effort, but is still a self-directed, and consequently a *free*, effort.

That when the mode or plan of action is devised by itself, by its own preliminary effort, it is a *rational* action.[1]

That when, instead of devising a plan for the occasion, we through memory adopt one which we have previously formed, we have the distinguishing characteristic of *habitual* action.

In the instinctive and habitual we act promptly from a plan ready formed in the mind, requiring no premeditation as to the mode or plan of action.

But in all cases our effort is incited by our want, and directed by means of our knowledge, to the desired end, which, whatever the particular exciting want, is always to in some way affect the future. In our efforts to do this in the sphere external to us, which is the common arena of all intelligent activity, we are liable to be more or less counteracted or frustrated by the efforts of others. In it man is a co-worker with God and with all other conative beings, and in it can influence the actual flow of events only in a degree somewhat proportioned to his limited power and knowledge.

But that in the sphere of man's own moral nature the effort is itself the consummation of his creative conceptions, and hence in this sphere man is a *supreme* creative first cause, limited in the effects he may then produce only by that *limit* of his knowledge by which his creative preconceptions are circumscribed.

And further; that as a man directs his act by means of his knowledge, and can morally err only by *knowingly willing* what is wrong, his *knowledge* as to this is infallible; and as his *willing* is his own free act, an

[1] See Note X. p. 347.

act which no other being or power can do for him, he is in the sphere of his moral nature a sole creative cause solely responsible for his action in it.

His only possible moral wrong is in his freely willing counter to his knowledge of right. He must have known the wrong at the time he willed, or it would not be a moral wrong. Hence the knowledge by which he directs his acts of will is here as infallible as that of omniscience, and his power to will within the limits of his knowledge being unlimited, he cannot excuse himself on the ground of his own fallible nature, but is fully and solely responsible for all the wrong he intended, or which he foresaw and might by right action have prevented. Conversely, a rightful action indicates no virtue beyond the knowledge and intent of the actor. The failure to make an effort demanded by the convictions of right is in itself a wrong. That in the domain of his own moral nature man is thus supreme indicates it as his especial sphere of activity. Ages of successful effort in the material has been the preparation for its successful occupation, and we may reasonably expect that the advance into the more ethereal realm of the spiritual will be marked by the sublimest efforts of pure and lofty thought, and that the results in it will be the crowning glory of all utility.

§ 29. In favor of these conclusions and against the doctrines of necessity and of sole material causation, I would here suggest an additional argument from final causes.

I cannot demonstrate, but I have a confiding faith that all progress in truth will increase the happiness and conduce to the elevation of man, and also in the converse of this, that whatever tends to diminish our happiness and degrade our position will be found to be erroneous.

It is clear that, by adopting the materialistic views, we should be deprived of all the dignity of conscious power, and with it of all the cheering and elevating influences of the performance of duty, for that which has no power can have no duties. Instead of a companionship with a superior intelligence, communicating his thoughts to us in the grandeur and beauty of the material universe, — the poetic imagery, the poetic language, of which it is the pure and perfect type, — and in his yet higher and more immediate manifestations in the soul, we should be doomed to an inglorious fellowship with insensate matter, and subjected to its blind forces. That sublime power, that grandeur of effort, by which the gifted logician, with resistless demonstration, permeates and subdues realms which it tasks the imagination to traverse, and that yet more God-like power by which the poet commands light to be, and light breaks through chaos upon his beautiful creations, would no more awaken our admiration or incite us to lofty effort. We should be degraded from the high and responsible position of independent powers in the universe, co-workers with God in creating the future, to a condition of mere machines and instruments operated by " stimuli " and " molecules " ; and though still with knowledge and sensibility to know and feel our degraded position, — " so abject, yet alive," — with no power to apply our knowledge in effort to extricate and to elevate ourselves. We might still have the knowledge of good and evil ; but having no power to foster the one, or to resist the other, this knowledge, with all its inestimable consequences, all the aspirations which it awakens, and all the incentives to noble deeds which it in combination with effort alone makes possible, would be lost. And this dreary debasement would be unrelieved by that last hope which now mitigates our worst despair, — the hope that death will bring relief. For all mutation now being but changes in the indestructible atoms of matter, by means of its motion which is also indestructible and eternal, there would be little left to die, as there would again be little left for which to live. For all this I see no compensation in the materialistic doctrines now so predominant.

§ 30. We have observed that all our efforts are incited by our wants; that in our physical nature there is an innate constitutional provision by which they recur without any agency of our own; and there seems to be good reason to believe that through a moral sense, or other constitutional provision, the wants of our spiritual nature also recur without our bidding. And we can hardly fail to see a portion of this provision in our constantly recurring aspirations for something higher and better than we have yet attained; and in all our æsthetic tastes, the delicate sensibilities of which are continually touched by the significant and suggestive beauty, harmony, and grandeur of God's visible creations, with their ever varying expression appealing directly to the soul in that poetic language of imagery and analogy which is comprehended by all, and exerts on all a persuasive and elevating influence. We are thus continually reminded of the wants and the capacities of our spiritual being, for no one capable of reflection can look upon the exquisite models, the vast, the grand, the beautiful, the perfect, thus presented to us, and not see that to all this there is a counterpart; that there is something which perceives and appreciates, as well as something which is perceived and appreciated; that within his own being there is an inchoate universe, to him as boundless, and which is his especial sphere of creative action. Here is opened to his efforts an infinity of space in which, as already shown, he is a supreme creative power, a sphere already canopied with twinkling thoughts, dimly revealing the chaotic elements requiring his efforts to reduce to order and cultivate into beauty, and making visible a darkness which continually demands from him the fiat, "*Let there be light.*" Constructing this universe within is the great object of existence, the principal if not the sole end of life.

Happy he who, faithfully working in the seclusion of this his own allotted space, so constructs this internal universe, that when from the genetic void it breaks upon the gaze of superior intelligences, all the sons of God will shout for joy, and the great Architect shall himself pronounce it GOOD.

NOTES

NOTE I.

The phrase " First Cause " is used not in relation to time, but to indicate an *independent, originating cause.*

NOTE II.

I have elsewhere defined cause to be " that which produces change." Cause always implies the *exercise of power*, with which it is often very nearly identical. When this exercise of power is wholly insufficient and produces no effect, it will perhaps be most convenient not to regard it as cause, and it is excluded by the definition, " that which produces change."

But when one power in action is directly counteracted by another, so that neither produces any change, but only prevents the change which the other alone would produce, each of the powers is still *effective*, and perhaps should be regarded as cause, — the cause of things *remaining unchanged,* — and a better definition of cause may be, *that which makes the future different from what it otherwise would be.*

NOTE III.

I have argued, from the admitted qualities and properties of mind and matter, that mind — intelligence — in action is the only real cause, and especially that this alone can begin change. That in virtue of its distinguishing characteristics of feeling, knowledge, and volition, it is within itself a self-acting cause, capable of acting without being first acted upon, and being thus endowed at its birth, its earliest actions — the instinctive — are, like all its subsequent ones, voluntary efforts suggested by its feelings and directed by its knowledge to the change desired. That the knowledge essential to such direction of the effort is innate, or exists from the moment of birth, is a legitimate inference, because the most simple that the observed facts admit of, and at the same time most in harmony with all our subsequent observation and experience. These genetic instinctive actions are thus found to be subject to the same conditions as our subsequent rational actions, all being *voluntary* actions, suggested by feeling and directed by knowledge to the end wanted.

The advocates of materialistic causation in the outset, as might have been anticipated, encounter serious difficulty as to the genesis of action or change. For the inauguration of change, a self-active power, or cause, is essential. We do not differ materially as to the problem presented for solution. Bain, one of the most able and thorough expounders of the materialistic doctrine, says, " *The link between action and feeling* for the end of promoting the pleasure of exercise is the precise link that *must exist* from the *commencement* ; the pleasure results from the *movement*, and responds by sustaining and increasing it. The *delight thus feeds itself.*" [1] Passing over some of the many assumptions of this statement, I would inquire how began, or whence came, this "*commencement*" of this "*movement*," from which *results* the *pleasure of exercise* which *responds by sustaining and increasing it, and thus feeds itself?* In the same paragraph, in connection with such muscular *exercise,* he speaks of " spontaneous movements being commenced," and after it says, " We must suppose the rise of an *accidental* movement," and again of " the *random tentatives* arising through spontaneity." From all this the legitimate inference seems to be, that he regards these movements as commencing without any cause or reason whatever. The materialistic theory could reach no further than this, and here stops far short of the generalization by which I have identified these genetic instinctive movements with our subsequent voluntary, rational actions, with no generic difference in the actions themselves, which are only distinguished by the different manner in which we become possessed of the knowledge by means of which we direct our efforts to produce such movements.

The advocates of material causation rely much upon physiology to support their views, and think they find empirical confirmation of them in the phenomena of the nervous system — its material structure of brain, spinal column, ganglions, and nerve centres, with its connecting and permeating nerve fibres, with

[1] *The Emotions and the Will.* Will, chap. ii. p 315.

nerve currents, similar to the electric, flowing through them. This is a very interesting and a very useful branch of physiological research, but I fail to see its bearing upon the question as to what is the efficient cause, and what its nature and properties.

Suppose a man is looking at the machinery in a mill, the propelling power of which is, as is common, in a separate room. The observer, in tracing the source of motion, finds first the main shaft or axis coming through the division wall which limits his sight, and upon it a very large main or driving wheel, or pulley. This main shaft extending through a large portion of the room, and having upon it other lesser pulleys, from which other motion is communicated by belts to other shafts on either side, and from these, and in some cases directly from the main shaft, the motion is communicated by smaller belts to the various machines, and in some of these by small cords to each portion of them. In this arrangement, with its large driving wheel at the head of the main shaft with other pulleys on the same, with the belts leading from them and putting other shafts on each side in motion, and the smaller belts and cords giving motion to each separate machine, and finally, in some, to each minute individual part — each particular spindle, — we have an apparatus very analogous to that of the brain, spinal axis, ganglia, or nervous centres, and connecting and permeating fibres of the nervous system ; but no one, by any examination of the phenomena, would, in this application and distribution of the power to the machinery, learn anything as to the *nature* or kind of power in the adjoining room. He could only learn what it could *do*. He could not even tell whether it was a steam-engine or a water-wheel. In view of the results of physical science its votaries would not hesitate to assert that, be it what it may, the *solar heat* is one of the intermediate agencies of its efficacy, and, if my views are correct, it is at least equally certain that in regard to both the mill and the nervous system the genesis of the power is *intelligence in action.*

Many of Bain's statements as to the spinal axis, the ganglia, the nerves with their nerve currents and counter currents passing to and fro in the transmission and distribution of power, would require very little change in the phraseology to make them pertinent to the shafts, pulleys, and belts which constitute the motor apparatus of the mill.

He says, "When the mind is in exercise of its functions, the physical accompaniment is the passing and repassing of innumerable streams of nervous influence," and as an inference from this, says, "*It seems as if we might say, No currents, no mind.*"[1]

So, too, when the steam-engine, or other motive power, of the mill is performing its functions, there is a constant passing and repassing of the belts through which its power or influence is distributed and communicated to the machinery ; but the logical inference in both cases seems to be, not that in the absence of these movements there would be no power or cause, but simply that when there is no *action of the power or cause there is no effect*. If the apparatus ceased to move, we could not thence conclude that the *unseen power* had ceased to exist. It might be merely detached, and with undiminished vigor still be performing its functions, and even with its activity increased, by being rid of the attachments which had encumbered and retarded it.

The conclusion of Bain assumes that the "passing and repassing" — the movement — is itself the genetic cause to which there is no antecedent cause. He thus consistently puts it in the same category with those "accidental movements" and "random tentatives" of which he has before spoken.

Note IV.

By this definition Edwards makes the *will* an *instrument* of the *mind*, and then speaks of the *freedom* of the *will*. Under such a definition one might as well speak of the freedom of the hammer which he is using to drive a nail, as of the "freedom of the will." The definition virtually begs the question.

An *instrument* must be controlled and directed by that which uses it, and hence, if I have rightly defined freedom, cannot be free ; but the intelligent power, the *mind*, that controls and directs it, may be.

Note V.

If we call the *knowledge* by which we direct our instinctive actions *innate*, and all that we subsequently acquire without effort *intuitive*, the only application of the term instinctive will be to actions ; or to ideas, or knowledge *born* in us, after our own birth, without our agency. Of this there are some indications in our subsequent experience.

[1] *The Senses and the Intellect*, 2d edition, § 25, p. 66.

NOTE VI.

In my father's house we had a large black Newfoundland dog, named Gelert, with which my youngest sister and two other little girls had much amusement. They had a little carriage in which they harnessed him, he seeming to take a lively interest in all their sports, and a full share of the enjoyment. He was a favorite of all our large household. At one time, by his absence at night, he subjected himself to suspicion, and it was resolved to restrain his nocturnal wanderings, but for several successive evenings thereafter he succeeded, by watching his opportunity, in slipping out as some one entered the back door. Increased vigilance at last prevented this, and after all the household were in, Gelert found a bone, he had himself probably left in an outer room, which he took into the kitchen and there began to gnaw it. The cook did not usually permit this, but on this occasion refrained from driving him out, and he, against all law and precedent, with the bone in his mouth, made his way into the parlor, and there went round holding it up to each person in turn. Gelert had evidently devised a plan similar to that which Walter Scott, in his "Quentin Durward," ascribes to the Bohemian Hayraddin, who by persistent indecorous conduct contrived to get himself turned out of the convent of Namur.

My sisters had a vigorous and very intelligent horse that they drove for many years. He was much petted and allowed, in their rambles, to largely exercise his own discretion. If he saw one of his favorite thistles by the roadside he would turn aside to crop it. He was usually very discreet, but after he got into his dotage and was retired from service on his rations, he became somewhat *coltish* and mischievous. In good weather he was generally at large, and on several occasions tried to entice the factory team to run away, by going near them as they stood in harness and turning and running in a frolicsome way in front of them. In this he was not wholly unsuccessful.

He would untie his halter. I do not think he comprehended the intricacies of the knot, but that he dealt with it as a man does with a tangled skein, the convolutions of which he cannot trace ; *i. e.*, he shook it, and pulled at it in divers ways, till he found a part that would yield and draw out. Tom would thus often get out of the stable, and when some one attempted to teach him, he would playfully let him get near and then spring away and repeat the operation. On one occasion he was near being caught, in consequence of treading an his loose halter, but he presently seized the farther end of it in his teeth, threw up his head with a triumphant air, and trotted off.

I had a horse (Charlie) of the Morgan breed, which is noted for intelligence. I very frequently drove him to one of my mills, about twelve miles from my home, generally going over a long and very steep hill, but sometimes going around it. On one occasion I had, as was my custom, got out of the carriage at the foot of the hill to walk up it, but lingered behind to pluck some wild grapes. Charlie had got some distance ahead, when he came to the fork where the road around the hill diverged. I saw he hesitated a moment, and then with a very decided step took the road around. I called out Charlie! and he immediately turned and went through the intervening bushes to the direct road, though in doing so he had now to go up a very steep ascent, with no path, and up which he had never before been. He not only rationally interpreted my calling to him, but correctly estimated the relative positions of the two roads, and the mode of getting from one to the other, in which he had no experience, and neither this nor the significance of my calling are in the province of instinct.

On another occasion, in driving Charlie, I took an apple from my pocket, bit it, and not finding it to my taste, cast it aside. Just then Charlie came to a hill, slackened his pace and stopped, as he often did, to see if I would get out and walk up it. The ascent was so gradual that I deemed his suggestion unreasonable, and said "Go on, Charlie," when he turned his face toward me, and made such an unmistakable movement of his lips, that I got out and went back a few steps to get the apple for him.

My youngest brother, Joseph, had a short-haired Newfoundland dog, named Argus, which he trained with care, and it became an excellent retriever. I sometimes got him to take the bridle in his mouth and lead a saddle-horse from the mill to my father's house, nearly a mile distant.

In the course of his training, my brother, walking by a brook, directed the dog to bring a speckled turtle that he saw in the grass. This was so repulsive that my brother was obliged to place it in the dog's mouth, but he soon dropped it, and this process was repeated with similar result, until Argus swam across the stream and dropped the turtle on the other side, out of my brother's reach.

On one occasion my brother dropped his knife in a large pasture, and after walking on about a quarter of a mile, sent Argus back to find it. He soon returned, but brought nothing, and was again sent back with the same result. In a third effort he was gone a long time; but at last returning in high glee, my brother felt sure he had been successful, and was much surprised when the dog laid a mass of earth at his feet, in which was a cigar stump my brother had cast aside on the way. The dog had enveloped the cigar stump with earth, and so protected brought it in his mouth.

In these cases, and especially in the cases of Gelert with his bone, and of Argus with the tobacco, there was a marked devising of a plan of action adapted to new conditions, to meet new exigencies, and this, if my analysis is correct, is the especial characteristic of rational, as distinguished from instinctive action.

I have spoken of the impossibility of our learning to move our muscles by effort; and actions which we readily perform instinctively might bother or puzzle us to do by the logical or ideal processes.

A fast trotting horse, if he attempted to move his four feet by premeditation of the successive movements of them, would probably move very slowly and only walk, or be confused and stumble. The difficulty would increase with the number of feet.

> "The centipede was happy quite,
> Until a toad, in fun,
> Said, pray which leg must follow which?
> That work'd her mind to such a pitch,
> She lay distracted in a ditch,
> Consid'ring how to run."

Most men, I think, if they attempted to make some of the muscular movements, *e. g.* of the eye, by rational investigation of the mode, would find themselves in a similar predicament.

The same thing occurs in regard to our *habitual* actions, and especially as to those for which we have acquired the mode by mere memory, without the aid of the reasoning faculties. We can, *e. g.*, often write a word offhand correctly, when, if we deliberate, we are bothered, and some other way of spelling it seems just as reasonable and as likely to be right.

Note VII.

There are cases in which, knowing the circumstances, we may be morally certain what a man's volition will be. A starving man will eat if he can. A man will *try* to escape from a burning house in which he is about to be enveloped in the flames. It is said that horses will not do this, but, when in danger of being burned, persistently resist being taken from their stalls, and will even run back to them after having been gotten out of danger.

An incident of my childhood may illustrate this action of the horse, which cannot be classed with the instinctive.

Before I was five years old I had crossed the street from my father's house with a cousin, a little girl of my own age, and seeing a horse and carriage coming very rapidly towards us, I impulsively ran back towards our house, and called to my cousin to do so. The result was that I got over safely, but my cousin was knocked down by the horse, and that she escaped instant death and without even serious injury, was deemed miraculous. The incident made a deep impression upon me, and I have always remembered that I thus acted because I thought we would be safe only on the side of the street on which we lived. On former similar occasions I had found that I was there in no danger, but had no experience as to the other side. The horse, probably by association, feels safest in his stall.

Note VIII.

That in a strictly logical process we do not always perceive a result in advance of the expression for it, is illustrated by an incident of my boyhood, and which, at the time (spring of 1819), I had no idea had any metaphysical significance. I knew that the top of a carriage-wheel moved faster than the bottom, and it occurred to me to ascertain the ratio. My thoughts almost immediately took this form. Suppose the carriage is going at the rate of ten miles per hour, then the velocity of the periphery of the wheel round its axis is ten miles per hour, and the bottom point, moving in the direction of the tangent, is (by this motion round its axis) moving backward at the rate of ten miles an hour, while at the same time, by the moving of the whole carriage, it is carried forward ten miles per hour. Here are two motions equal and opposite, and of course there is no motion at all. I was astonished. There was obviously no mistake in the reasoning, and yet the result seemed as obviously false. My confidence in such reasoning was not less than in the stability of the law of gravitation, and if I had seen the rocks about me suddenly move upward, I could not have been more confounded. The relations among the terms had forced me to a conclusion, which I not only had not perceived in advance, but did not believe when I reached it. A little further investigation, however, satisfied me that the conclusion was correct, and enabled me to prove and illustrate it in various ways. I have had much amusement in discussing this problem, having very generally found other persons as much astonished at the result as I had been.

It is a curious fact that people equally confident that the bottom point does move, differ as to whether it moves backward or forward. One evening an acquaintance of mine, then recently converted, got into a warm discussion with some passengers in a Southwestern steamer. They all asserted that the bottom point did move, and some of them, in terms more forcible than urbane, expressed the opinion that only a fool would think it did not. I was within hearing, and being called upon by my friend went to his aid, and said to his excited opponents, "You say the bottom does move?" They promptly answered yes, but some of them added, "or how could it go round on the axle?" while others said, "or how could it keep up with the carriage?" This indicated diversity in their views. I then said, "Pray tell me which way it moves, backward or forward?" This divided them into two very nearly equal parties, each finally insisting that the others were bigger fools than those who said it did not move at all. My friend and myself soon left them, but the next morning we found some of them still wrangling, and that they had several times during the night examined some of the wheels of the engine, the movement of which, each party claimed, practically sustained their position. Though not germane to the present inquiry, I will add that the simple fact is, that the *whole* wheel is revolving about its bottom point as a centre. The velocity of each point and its direction are easily ascertained. The centre or axis of the wheel, of course, goes forward just as fast as the carriage ; the bottom not moving at all, the top of the wheel moves just twice as fast as the carriage. Every point in the ascending side of the periphery moves directly towards what at the instant is the top of the wheel, and every point on the descending side directly from it. The first tendency to motion of the bottom point is directly up, *i. e.*, its direction at its start from the bottom point is perpendicular; though like every other point its velocity and direction are not the same for any time, still the first infinitesimal motion of the bottom point is infinitesimally near to the perpendicular.

NOTE IX.

The important function of language as the instrument of logic indicates the importance of a thorough knowledge and mastery of all its resources to enable one nicely to discriminate and adapt it as nearly as possible to the finer distinctions and shades of thought which exist in the primitive perceptions of things and ideas, and the delicately varied relations among them, for which, in the logical processes, verbal symbols are substituted.

This consideration gives additional significance to the much mooted question as to the value of linguistic studies, and contributes an additional argument in their favor. In regard to a composite language, formed as ours has been, it seems obvious that without a liberal acquaintance with those languages from which it has been largely derived and in which it has its roots, the knowledge of our own tongue must be very imperfect. Such acquaintance with the sources of our language must have its advantages not only in the all-important respects of greater accuracy in the meaning of the terms, and nicer precision, discrimination, and clearness in their use, upon which the soundness of our logical conclusions is so dependent, but also in the greater facility and celerity in the mental processes by the aid thus afforded to the memory, the knowledge of a single root or trunk immediately suggesting the numerous branches which spring from it.

The want of such knowledge is perhaps even more felt in stating the results of the logical processes than in their acquisition. In thinking, if at a loss for the proper word, we can for the moment use the mental perception instead; and if in writing we adopted the analogous plan, we should insert a picture of the thing instead of the name of it, as is often done in children's books.

The writer is unable to supplement these *a priori* conclusions with any affirmative experience, and can only say that in using language as an instrument of thought, or for expressing its results, he has felt that he was under disadvantages both as to precision and facility which a fuller knowledge of languages, and especially of their genetic elements, would have obviated.

I have spoken of the resolution of algebraic equations as furnishing the purest type of verbal reasoning. For these a special language has been devised, so flexible that it can be readily and accurately fitted to each particular case.

But the relative advantages of different systems of language, or of other symbols for ideas, is more conspicuous in the greater ease with which we deal even with simple arithmetical problems by means of the Arabic system of notation as compared with the Roman. More extended and intricate calculations, easily accomplished with the former, seem almost impracticable with the latter.

Those who insist most strongly on the supremacy of the logical processes seem most prone to question the utility of the linguistic studies which, in the views I have presented, appear to be most important aids to these same processes.

NOTE X.

There is, then, in the attributes of instinct and reason, no *generic* difference between man and brutes. They are common to both, varying only in *degree*. The ratio of the instinctive to the rational is so much greater in brutes, that it is generally regarded as surpassing that of man. The three fundamental elements of mind, knowledge, feeling, and volition, are also common to both. Brutes have less knowledge, and hence the sphere of their voluntary action is more limited; but I see no reason to suppose that within this sphere there is any limit in the will itself — any bound to their volitional ability to make effort. The limit in them, as in the higher orders of intelligent being, is always in the *knowledge* of a mode of action to reach the end desired, and not in the *will*. Nor is there any reason to suppose that the bodily senses are not the same in kind in man and brutes, and, in fact, each of these may be found more acute and perfect in some one or more of the latter. The reverse seems to be generally true of the mental emotions. To this, fear seems a notable exception, and perhaps surprise, though it is less marked. But brutes also evince affection, hatred, revenge; they are elated by successful achievement, and depressed by failure ; they have emulation, and manifest pride in victory and shame in defeat. There is warrant for asserting that they contemplate beauty and deformity with different emotions ; but this is in a very limited sphere, and it is doubtful if they recognize the antithesis, or even the difference, between the sublime and the ridiculous. If this is the limit of their most elevated thought, we may reasonably assume that they never rise to the contemplation or the conception of the grandeur of action from an internal personal conviction of *duty*, and that it is the addition of the *moral sense* that makes the generic distinction, and elevates man above the rest of the animal creation.

ANALYSIS OF CONTENTS.

CAUSATION AND FREEDOM IN WILLING.

LETTER I. — CAUSATION.

Mr. Mill's positions and arguments. — Imply that change may take place without power. — If "invariability of sequence" is the only relation, philosophy is reduced to the observation and memory of the order of succession 1–4

Origin of our notion of Cause. — Sir William Hamilton's answer to the doctrine that we get it from our acts of Will. — His argument does not touch that theory; much less does it disturb my positions. — The notion cannot be acquired by outward observation or internal experience. — Prior to this the knowledge of the mode of effort must exist, and also the "prophetic anticipation" of effect, which Mill, Hamilton, and Mansel agree in rejecting. — The notion must be innate. — This confirmed by the phenomena of instinct. — Not essential to our notion of Cause to know all the intermediate steps from its first action to its final effect. — Possible that we have been conscious of the intermediate effects between effort and muscular movement 4–11

What is our notion of Cause? Ability to do something — power to do — to change what is to what, as yet, is not. — Not essential to the idea to know that we can extend the effects of effort beyond our muscles, or beyond the moment. — This may be added by experience. — The notion does not reach the *essence* of Power or Cause, but still is useful in the study of phenomena, and in finding what has power, and under what conditions it is manifested. — Comte ignores causal power, but admits that it was originally predicated of spirit power 11–12

What is Cause? Has the notion we derive from conscious efforts and anticipated effects been properly superseded? Sir William Hamilton, unexpectedly against me as to the origin, and as to the idea itself, has not found the battlefield. — His

theory merely asserts that he cannot conceive that Cause has made something out of nothing. — Cause that which produces change. — Mr. Mill speaks of effects which certain causes are fitted to produce. — Why is one thing better fitted than another to *invariably precede* any event ? — Cause always the correlative to effect, and is power in successful action. — Our notion both of Power and Cause derived from an innate knowledge of effort and its anticipated effect; but we can only know our ability to cause any specific effect by experiment 12–16
Cause implies effect, and effect implies change. — To say that for every effect there must be a cause, is to say that for every change there must be motion or activity. — If that which changes is self-active, we do not look beyond it for the Cause; but otherwise we seek to connect it with a self-active Cause.— Intelligent being the only self-active Cause known to us. — Experience leads us (properly or not) to regard matter in motion as a Cause, but not a self-active Cause. — If the motion of matter had a beginning, it must be referred to the action of intelligent being, and is thus rather an instrument by which such being extends its effects in time and space. - Uniformity in the action of matter, and also of spirit, enabling us to anticipate the future. — Our knowledge of power by effort more conclusive than of that by matter in motion. — Effort is itself the act of power. — All effort is either to gain knowledge or move our muscles. — Only to mind in action, and to matter in motion, we attribute Causative power. — Matter has no power of selection. — Matter cannot begin change. — Matter not necessary to extend the effects of intelligent effort 16–25
The effect must be simultaneous with the action of its cause. — Must wholly result from causes in action at the time it occurs. — Reasons why the notion that Cause must precede its effect has obtained 25–29
Mr. Mill's views and definitions of Cause, viz., "The real cause is the whole of the antecedents," or the assemblage of phenomena which invariably precedes the effect. — These formulas indicate a mode of finding what are causes, but do not define them. — They do not distinguish causes from mere passive conditions. — Under them darkness must be a Cause in the change from darkness to light. — That people differ as to which of the antecedents is the Cause, is no ground for inferring that all of them are causes. — Inexpedient to confound in the one word Cause the passive conditions which resist change with the active agency which changes them. — All the cases of Causation stated by Mr. Mill properly referable, either to mind in action or matter in motion 29–36

ANALYSIS OF CONTENTS. 351

Substitutes for our notion of Cause as derived from intelligent effort. — 1. Generalized Phenomena, as Gravitation. - 2. The phenomena themselves fixed or flowing. — 3. Uniform succession, or Uniformity itself. — Under first head causal power sometimes assumed to be in the name, sometimes in the facts named, and sometimes attributed to a mere hypothetical power indicated by or embodied in them. — No Causal power in the mere names. — To predicate it of the generalized facts would make them collectively the cause of themselves individually, involving the existence of the collection prior to that of the individuals of which it is composed. — The hypothesis of an unknown power has its types in the ancient mythology, and in the rude notion of our Indian tribes. — Science has its manitous. — Mere hypothesis cannot properly supersede our innate knowledge of power by effort, or even of our empirical knowledge of power by matter in motion. — The ancient Divinities and the Indian Manitous were spirit causes, the manitous of science are often material; have these their primitive type in Fetichism ? 36-39
Second substitute. — The phenomena themselves. - Mr. Mill regards these as more properly causes, and includes as "permanent causes" both "objects" and "events." — Also holds that "the real cause is the whole antecedents." We agree that the law of uniformity applies to all unintelligent Cause. — The *whole* antecedents are the same at every point of space, and hence the effects should be the same. — The whole past being everywhere the same, and acting upon a void and therefore homogeneous future, the effect should everywhere be the same. — If the whole past, as a causal power, produces an effect, then this effect is added to the aggregate cause, and the same causes can never act again. — If it is insufficient, and produces no effect, then, there being no change, it can, under the rule of uniformity, only repeat its insufficient action, and there would be an end of change. — Failure of effect cannot be such a new event as of itself to add a new element and make the insufficient Cause a different and sufficient Cause, unless the Cause is intelligent. — The "whole prior state" never can occur again, and no case of the uniformity of Causation can arise. — The hypothesis that the "order of succession" is in separate fibres avoids some, but not all of the difficulties. — It also necessitates a plurality of causes from the origin of existence. — This violates the law of Parsimony 39-48
Fixed existences cannot be the cause of any subsequent change. — If Cause in virtue of mere existence, they would change themselves at the instant of coming into existence, and never could

become fixed. — The Cause cannot be completed by some new phenomenon. — Fixed or stable events being excluded, Cause can only be mind in action and matter in motion. — Permanent material existences cannot act in conformity to law . . . 48-51
Third substitute, first division of it. — No Causal power, etc. — This idea a result of physical science. — Attributing Causal power to observed uniformity common to every stage of empirical knowledge. — If no Causal *power*, all events would spring into existence spontaneously and contingently, without order or adaptation. — Nothing to conform things to order by a beneficent design. — Material effects and their uniformity depend on some power of matter in motion. — There must be some power to produce the observed uniformity. — To meet this necessity it is asserted that the power or cause inheres to the uniformity itself. — But the things to be accounted for are the events and the uniformity of their succession. — Under this hypothesis a thing is said to succeed another because it *always does so*. — This phrase now superseding the *generic names* of phenomena. — Both traceable to uniformity, and both making the collective events the causes of themselves individually 51-54
The ideas of Cause and of uniformity are essentially distinct and different. — Nor is succession a necessary element of our idea of Cause. — It is complete without the knowledge of its effect. — The succession comes after the Cause, and makes no part of it. — It is only the evidence that Cause *has* existed. Succession is the effect, and to make it Cause is to make it the Cause of itself. — All theories of Causation must bring us to something already active, or that has the ability to become so. — In my view, spirit Cause cannot be dispensed with — must always have existed. — Lapse even of infinite time does not preclude our speculating on the primordial conditions of existence. — Our interest in the study of the succession of events not lessened by its being distinct from Causation. Our knowledge of the uniformity of succession important only because we have *power* to act upon the future. — Except in regard to instinctive action, it is because of the uniformity in the effects of effort that we can know how to influence the future; this uniformity may be an occult necessity, but this does not affect our freedom in making the effort 54-59

APPENDIX TO LETTER I.

Correspondence with Professor Rood on the common belief that the sun cannot be seen till about 8' after it is on the visible horizon 60-62

LETTER II. — FREEDOM IN WILLING.

Subject stated 63
Definitions of Freedom and of Will restated 63
Necessity. — Its various meanings. — Associated with compulsion as its antecedent, and with invariability as its consequent. — Free action may be as invariable as coerced action. — Only when Necessity implies compulsion that it is opposed to Freedom 64–67
Intelligent effort a beginning of the exercise of power, and not an effect of some previously exerted power. — The being that wills is a power, and not merely an instrument through which power is transmitted. — Interdependence arising from each varying the conditions for others, and also changing their knowledge and wants. — This does not interfere with their freedom. — Positions in support of these views stated . . . 67–72
The issue as to the control of volition by previous conditions. — Illustrations from matter in motion all fail at the point of *effort*, to which there is no known similitude 72–76
Mr. Mill's arguments embraced under the following heads: —
  1. The argument from cause and effect, or that volition is a necessary effect of its antecedents.
  2. The influence of present external conditions.
  3. The influence of internal phenomena, including the character, knowledge, habits, and wants of the being that wills.
  4. The argument from prescience, or possibility of prediction. Motive is embraced in both the second and third categories 76–77
The arguments should rest upon the phenomena of voluntary action, some of which are here stated. — All effort is made to vary the future. — The agent must have a conception of what the future will be without his effort, and also what with his effort. — The former a *primary*, the latter a *secondary* expectation. — Freedom not dependent on the success of the effort. — Actor considered as a sole agent of change, and also as acting in conjunction with other causes. — Universal passivity. — Difficulty of conceiving absolute commencement of action. — Note on Sir Wm. Hamilton's idea of Causation. — The want of variety or of activity may be a ground for beginning action. — Apparent similarity of the conditions of the beginning of material movement and of mental action. — Differences in the actual phenomena. — Intelligence free to begin action whenever

it perceives a reason for it. — Hypothesis of universal passivity foreign to experience. — The more practical questions are, Can intelligent conative being. passive among changing events, of itself begin action ? Is his effort determined by the current of events, or by himself ? Freedom in willing does not involve power to do what we will 77–86
Examination of the first of the four arguments or categories. — The question as to the mind's ability to begin action covers the same ground. The necessitarian argument that mind before it can act must be first acted upon by some causative agency in the past, is applied to all these categories. — Some positions bearing on them all. — Our knowledge of the past has no more Causative power than that of the future. — The only conceivable modes in which causative powers of the past can reach the present, are by means of matter in motion or of intelligent action. — These really present active powers. — Conceivable that the past may influence present action of these causes by changes it has wrought in the conditions to be acted upon, or in the characteristics of the power that acts upon them. — Argument from cause and effect. — Object of volition is to interfere with and change its uniformity. — Uniformity suggests necessity, but in fact aids us to vary the future. — The argument only proves that the *Will* is unfree, not that the *mind* is. — Necessitarians enforce and illustrate this argument from cause and effect by the phenomena of matter in motion; as well illustrate the phenomena of material motion by that of mental effort. — They resemble each other not in themselves, but only in this, they both produce effects. — Mind alone makes effort. — In its effort it has two distinct objects, external change, and increase of its own knowledge. — To produce external change, including that in the knowledge or action of others, we always begin by moving our own muscles. — To increase our knowledge, we often begin and end with mental effort. — Phrases "muscular effort" and "mental effort" do not imply difference in the actor, but in the subject or object of his action. — Further analogies and differences between matter in motion and mind in effort 86–97
All the arguments against freedom under the first three heads assert or assume that to act, mind must be first acted upon. — Experience against this. — Our ability to start from a universal passivity at least doubtful 97–99
The more practical question is, Can the individual, himself passive, in the midst of changing conditions, of himself begin action ? Action, whether upon fixed or flowing conditions, based

upon expectation; and any change in this is a change in our
knowledge. — Change from a passive to an active state attested
by experience and observation. — Beginning of effort as marked
as beginning of sensation. — Necessitarian argument from cause
and effect asserts that volitions do begin to be. — Same argument makes the whole destiny of the being depend upon the
time and place at which it was dropped into the current of
events. — These questions ultimately rest on consciousness. —
Its dicta cannot be urged as proof even that we make effort,
much less as proof that effort is free or unfree. — Mr. Mill's
objections to such proof by Sir Wm. Hamilton too broadly
stated. — In willing we have a prophetic anticipation of the
effect, and the knowledge of the mode of moving the muscles
must be innate 99–103
Does freedom require that we should be able to will the contrary? The case supposed by Mr. Mill "to murder" or "not
to murder," raises the question, not of freedom, but of character. — The notion that ability to do the contrary is essential
to freedom reached through a logical error. — Such ability
would indicate the reverse of freedom. — What is meant by
ability to will the contrary? — The position reducible to the
absurdity that one is not free because he cannot be otherwise
than free 103–106
Returns to the question of our ability to begin action. — Hypothesis of action by one suddenly transferred to an unknown
forest. — No difficulty in conceiving a beginning of action in
each individual, nor of the beginning of each particular action.
— In this misled by the analogies of material phenomena 106–107
Effort of a conative intelligence requires no prior application of
power. — It is isolated from the past. — No consequence when
the conditions commenced, nor whether they ever had any commencement. — Experience in the supposed cases of action at
the instant of the creation of the active being, or of the conditions. — On every occasion for action there is some change,
making as an entirety a new creation commencing at the instant. — No power in the quiescent phenomena, nor in our
perception of them. — Advocates of Causative power in the
past cannot object to the hypothesis of non-action of such
causes 107–111
Instinctive action the same as if all the elements were created
at the instant. — Volition does not require that the active being,
or the conditions, should have had a past existence. — Nor
does it matter by what power or cause the conditions are
brought about. — Influence of our knowledge of past causes

considered. — The whole past, so far as it relates to action, has culminated in this knowledge. — Not material to the active agent what other, or whether any other causes are producing change. — Power to begin action the peculiar attribute of conative intelligence. — Note on Sir Wm. Hamilton's not recognizing a power to begin action 112–116
This beginning of action by the mind the thing now to be accounted for. — Unfortunate use of the word Cause to designate *compulsory power*, and also the perception of future results, which is a *reason* for effort. — It is through matter in motion that we seek to connect change, in that which cannot change itself, with a self-active power. — Having done this, we look no farther for the power, but may still inquire how it came to exist, and under what conditions it exists and produces effects. — The past can only indirectly affect the mind's action by having changed the mind itself, or the conditions upon which it acts 116–120
In the conditions (internal and external) you find the power or influence which determines the mind to determine. — This word *influence* produces confusion and underlies much fallacy. — Like cause, it is applied to power, and also to the perceptions of a reason. — Perception of a reason, being a form of knowledge, belongs to our third category, leaving us in the second to consider only the power of external conditions 120–121
Second category, or influence of the external conditions. — Difficulty of conceiving of any mode in which these can act the will, or control the mind in its acting. — The argument must be general, and assert that the mere existence of conditions of any kind excludes freedom, and these conditions being always prerequisites of effort, effort is always controlled by them. — More reasonable to attribute volition to the active being than to the passive conditions. — Otherwise the power to act upon and change is attributed to the passive subject which is to be acted upon and changed. — That the being wants change in the conditions does not imply that these conditions have any power to change themselves mediately through his action, any more than that they can directly act upon and change themselves without his agency. — From confounding reason with cause, and the conditions with the *perceptions* of them, the conditions come to be regarded as the causes instead of the subjects of effort. — The conditions are necessary to effort as passive subjects, but not as the active agents. — External conditions do not act the will. — This would imply that the Will is a distinct entity to be acted upon 121–124

ANALYSIS OF CONTENTS. 357

To suppose that volition in one mind is produced by the action of another, involves all the difficulties of self-originated action, and some others in addition. — We always seek to vary effort in another, indirectly, by changing his knowledge. — This we always do by changing the external conditions; but these conditions or changes, and the mind's perception of them, are two entirely distinct and different things. — Causative powers in the past may have made the present conditions. — But the nature of these conditions, or any differences in them, do not effect freedom. — The conative intelligence, whether acting as sole cause or in connection with others, acts upon its expectations of the future. — It makes no difference whether the uniformity in material phenomena arises from the necessary action of blind forces, or from the free action of a supremely wise intelligence which does not vary from the wisest mode. — Argument for control by the conditions is founded on the assumption that the volition varies with, and conforms to, the conditions. — If true, control could not be properly inferred from this assumption. — But effort is in fact conformed, not to the conditions, but to the mind's perception of a mode of acting upon them . . . 124–129
(Third Category.) Necessitarians affirm that the volitions must be in accordance with the "dispositions, desires, aversions, and habits, combined with outward circumstances." — That they follow "moral antecedents as certainly as physical effects follow their physical causes," and hence argue that they are not free. — It is our knowledge or view of the outward circumstances which affects our determinations — The moral antecedents are merely characteristics which make the being what it is, and distinguish it from what it is not, and any influence of the character is that of the being thus constituted. — Character made in the past. — Doctrine of freedom does not assert that the mind makes the conditions (external or internal), but only that in view of them it determines its own effort — If he has before changed his own character, he may do it now, and so far change and determine the action which conforms to it. — The process by which we determine effort is the same as that by which we change our characters, and hence the two may be simultaneous. — The instantaneous exercise of a new power breaking the chain of past causation is the peculiar attribute of conative intelligent being. — But if his character never changed, or even if changed every instant, and by some extrinsic power, he might still act freely. — To change the action of others, we seek to change either their knowledge or the conditions to be acted upon. — Types of these two modes. — But we agree that

we can change our own characters. — My positions give a broader significance to your statements on this point. — But to answer the Owenites requires the admission that we can act without being first acted upon. — Otherwise we are placed in a current of events in which we have no control of our destiny. — We do not float, but swim. — Does the current cause the swimming? — Relation of punishment to freedom and necessity 129-137
The hypothesis of necessary succession involves the doctrine of election and reprobation. — Means of changing our own characters. — The doctrine of necessary succession also involves that of a multiplicity of causes in the commencement and through the whole series. — This applies to the formation of character. — But having the attributes of self-activity, it is not material to freedom what the other characteristics are, nor how acquired. — A demon is as free as an angel 137-141
That the act of a virtuous person is virtuous, indicates freedom; if it were vicious, this would indicate the absence of self-control. — The necessitarian argument is general, asserting that as volition must conform to the character, it is controlled by it. — This assumes that the character is distinct from, and extrinsic to, the willing being. — Even admitting this, the inference of necessity is not legitimate. — Conformity of acts to character indicates freedom. — Taking intention into account, there can be no discrepancy between them. — Proving the necessary conformity only affirms the truism that the thing is of necessity equal to and like itself, and that the action of the being will be a manifestation of its own character, and not that of another. — Such conformity indicates self-control or freedom . . 141-144
The influence of the particular elements of character, as dispositions, habits, etc., examined in detail. — " Disposition " sometimes means present inclination, and sometimes a fixed general character. -- Character may change at the instant of action, and, hence, though action always conforms to the character at the instant, there is not always a general or habitual disposition to which it conforms. — Dispositions, inclinations, desires, etc., but modifications of want. — They often suggest the objects of effort, from which we select by a preliminary examination. — This examination is always an effort to increase our knowledge, and find what, under the existing conditions, will suit us best. — The particular inclination or disposition of the occasion more obviously liable to be changed, in this process, than the general character. — The object of the examination often is to test the expediency of such change. — Conflicting inclinations, desires, etc., among which we must choose. — Not

till they have culminated in choice to try to do, that they are related to action; and this choice, being the knowledge that one effort suits us better than others, is a relation of knowledge to action. — By knowledge the questions as to effort and non-effort, and as to what efforts, are decided. — That the present action is as the present inclination, not only indicates freedom, but is essential to its manifestation. — Necessitarians assert, that as the volition must conform to the disposition, etc., the willing being is controlled by this necessity, and hence not free. — This conformity to choice is the especial characteristic of freedom, and some logical entanglement is required before there can be any difficulty to explain. — The argument asserts that freedom is not free because it is constrained to be free 144-148

Term *habit* always applied to the general or formed character — In habitual actions we adopt modes previously discovered, saving the labor of the preliminary examination. — Habit not a mysterious power compelling action, but only a name for a particular phase of the general relation of knowledge to action. — As well attribute such compulsion to "customary" or "imitative" actions. — The reasons against making other characteristics distinct entities controlling volition, apply also to habit, and, in addition, habit is a product of repeated action; and, hence, such action cannot primarily be produced by habit. — Conformity of action to disposition, desire, etc., is but conformity to the being's own view, and the position of Necessitarians is here against themselves 148-151

Influence of Motive. — Vicious circle. — Sir Wm. Hamilton's reply to Reid, suggesting that the cause of the act be called motive. — He seeks what is self-contradictory, a being acting freely, and yet not controlling its action. — Mind does not act contingently, but always on the perception of an inducement. — No objection to calling this inducement a motive, but important to examine this motive before deciding that it conflicts with freedom. — Mr. Mill calls moral antecedents motives, and makes "desires and aversions" prominent. — These are not entities having power, but states of the mind in which it still controls its own action. — Desire or want does not produce action, but is one of the passive conditions to which the mind adapts its action — Motive is always the mind's *expectation* of future effect, and this is *knowledge* 151-154

All the relations of the conditions (intrinsic and extrinsic) to action are now shown to be concentrated in want and knowledge, bringing us to Mr. Mill's statement, as quoted in "Causation" (1st page). That statement of my positions, in the main, I accept. — The invariable conformity of volition to want and knowledge, here admitted, does not favor necessity, nor militate against freedom. — I also assent to the essential facts there asserted. — Thus agreeing in facts so nearly ultimate, there seems little room to differ, except as to the name of the result. — Reasons why I call it freedom. — It would be a queer sort of freedom in which a man would or could do, or try to do, what he did not want to do, or try to do. — The invariability in the case is only that of the being's effort to his own notion of the means of attaining the end — a necessity that free actions must be free 154–156

The act must be so conformed by some cause or power. — The only essential elements in the case are the intelligent being with his knowledge, the effort he makes, and the conditions to be changed. — The question as to control by the conditions has already been disposed of. — Effort not an entity with power or knowledge. — Want and knowledge cannot want or know, or direct action. — To suppose the conformity is produced by an extrinsic intelligence, involves all the difficulties of self-action, and others still greater. — Such extrinsic agent must know the views of the actor, and also some mode of controlling his volition. — No direct mode of doing this known or conceivable. — Can only be done by changing his knowledge, which, in the very process of conforming, changes that to which the act is to be conformed. — As we never attempt to make the act of another conform to his knowledge, this difficulty never practically arises. — What we do attempt is to change the knowledge of another, so that his conforming act will be different. — The hypothesis of extrinsic control still involves the necessity of intrinsic, which it was intended to discard. — The conformity by intrinsic control is consummated by the *effort to do*; but by the extrinsic only when the effort is successful. — If these views do not prove the extrinsic hypothesis impossible, they show that it would be absurd to adopt it in preference to the intrinsic 156–160

It is the being that determines in view of its want and knowledge; and even if want and knowledge are extrinsic to the willing being, they are still but extrinsic conditions of action, and not powers that act. — Want influential only as known, and in the last analysis volition depends only upon knowledge. — Knowledge induces effort only when it embraces some desirable change to be effected, and some mode of action to effect it. — No power in this prophetic knowledge to make an effort, or determine its direction 160–161

ANALYSIS OF CONTENTS. 361

It cannot be the past events which conform our acts to themselves, or to anything else, for when our recollection differs from the event, our actions are conformed to the recollections, and not to the events. — It may still be said that our knowledge or belief, right or wrong, is the product of the past. — Knowledge being a characteristic, the same reasoning which has been applied to the position that the character generally is formed in the past, will apply to it also. — It is not the past facts, nor the memory of them, but the ability which the being now has to direct its effort to a future result, that influences its action. — But the being is continually acting upon an *aggregate* of knowledge created at the instant, and which, as *entireties*, had *no past*. — All the distinguishing characteristics of intelligent being are essential elements of its freedom. — The illusion seems to be in attributing control to some portion of the being, then reasoning as though this portion were extrinsic to it, or as though control by the being, of its own action, were incompatible with its freedom. — It is not any of these characteristics or states of the being, but the conative being of which they are characteristics or states, that feels, knows, and acts 161-163
Not material to the question what theory we adopt as to the substratum of matter or of spirit. — My argument is apparently strongest on the hypothesis that the being is constituted of its characteristics with no substratum. — But a substratum which was only a nucleus, adding no other characteristics to the combination, would, in reality, make no difference. — If the substratum is a characteristic, then the being or thing is still but a combination of its characteristics, and exists only as such, in either case equally sustaining my position that control by the characteristics is control by the being. — Can a substratum be anything more than a characteristic of many individuals otherwise distinguished from each other ? — No argument can go back of the properties. — In some respects *extension* of matter most nearly conforms to our notion of a substratum . . 164-165
From this point of difference, as to the relations of the characteristics to the being they characterize, our views diverge, and lead to very different conclusions. — Note in regard to Mr. Mill's classing knowledge among the *external* motives . 166-167
My object when replying to Edwards. — Questions then reserved, and now considered. — Our actions usually predicated upon our anticipation of what other causative agents will do. — In this we agree. — Does it conflict with my position that volition is causal action ? — Law of cause and effect at most only asserts that effects. not causes, are necessitated. — Or if volition is an

effect, then the question which concerns the freedom of the *being* is, does he cause the volition? — The analogy of any mechanical causes and their effects might prove that volition, as a distinct entity or a mere effect, is not free, but not that its cause is not free. — We rely upon the uniformity of material phenomena. — When we see two solid bodies approaching each other, we know that some change must occur. — But no particular change of necessity, or which we could know *a priori*. — Various results equally conceivable and possible. — We still want some directing power, blind or percipient, to determine among these possibles. — Note on argument from design. — The ground of prediction is uniformity, not necessity. — Cause of the uniformity is not essential to foreknowledge, nor do we usually seek it for this object. — Uniformity in material changes may be but uniformity in the action of an intelligent cause of them. — Omniscience not liable to vary its plan, and if It directs Its own action we have additional means of predicting it. — The uniformity of material phenomena, or of cause and effect, indicates freedom. — Our volitions may be additions to God's knowledge, and reasons for varying His action. — All these variations may be embraced in a more extended uniformity. — In seeking the law of material uniformity we only seek the uniform modes of God's action. — A large material domain in which God acts as a Sole First Cause unvaried by change in His knowledge. — No reliable uniformity of human actions to external conditions. — More reliable as the ability to acquire knowledge lessens. — Wisdom does not aid one in predicting what the unwise will do. — Omniscience in this respect has no advantage. — We may foreknow such events as we can produce, but *volition* in others cannot be thus foreknown 167–175

"Possibility of Prediction." — Meaning of this Phrase.

A being acting as sole cause might predict what he has power to produce. — But this case can never occur in regard to volition. — Mr. Mill's argument rests not on the degree of ease or of difficulty of prediction, but on the " possibility of prediction." — An argument founded on such possibility as cogent as if founded upon actual prediction, but then is in a vicious circle. — My position requires prescience of the volitions of others, but not infallible prescience. — We often err by mistaking what others will do. — Mr. Mill virtually asserts that we can attain certainty when we know the antecedents. — This may be true if we know all the antecedents, including the being's last deter-

minations. — We then know it because the being does itself determine its volitions, and is free 175–179
Future volition cannot be known as an isolated fact, as an existing thing may. — If it could, this would destroy the presumption of necessary connection with its antecedents, and apply to free volitions as well as to unfree. — Such prescience would not indicate that the volition was not produced by the willing being, nor even that it did not produce itself. — The only "possibility of prediction" rests on the mind's control of its own volition. — If predicted without knowing the mind's final determination, the connection with the prior antecedents is broken, and the prediction does not prove any connection of that which is predicted with these antecedents. — Argument for necessity must then recede a step, and show that, by the antecedents, the mind is "determined to determine." — Doubt as to whether such determination can be predicted. — There may be two or more modes which will suit the actor equally well. — By arbitrary decision among these, the chain of cause and effect is broken 179–181
The mind's determination cannot be dependent on things and events extrinsic to it, for when its view differs from these, the determination conforms to the view. — Hence only as these things and events affect our knowledge that they affect our determination. — Can we so know the knowledge of the agent as to predict his determination ? — Volition always a new power thrown in, breaking the order which would otherwise obtain, and also that it may be a beginning of action, having no past, indicate that there is no necessary connection with past antecedents, or means of predicting from them. — The peculiar difficulty is, that the knowledge on which the determination depends is liable to be changed in the very process of determining. — In instinctive, habitual, and customary actions, we do not seek new knowledge, and in these prediction is most reliable. — In all other cases we seek more knowledge for the purpose of determining, and thus, in the very act of determining, change the knowledge upon which the prediction of the determination is based. — The possible changes in such cases are infinite. — The data in such cases are insufficient, and prediction impossible. — To suppose that we can foreknow the result of the preliminary effort to determine begs the question, and also assumes the success of that effort, which is another very uncertain element. — This illustrated : A seeks to foreknow the determination of B. — Every attempt to do this must be through the knowledge of B, and assumes that B will conform his acts

to his knowledge, whether freely or not makes no difference to the "possibility of prediction." — The chain of connection of a future volition with present known conditions as easily foreknown if it is free as if necessitated 181–186
Prediction only indicates uniformity, not necessity. — Hence necessity cannot be inferred from prediction. — Freedom is an element of our expectation. — The difficulty of prediction least at the extremes of intelligence, because in these the liability to change of knowledge is least. — In all, some steadfastness in knowledge on which we rely. — Our power to influence another also a ground of prediction. — Illustrated by a move in chess, or otherwise changing the knowledge. — Faith in the future act of another is faith that he will perceive a reason for such act, and freely conform his action to it 186–190
Admitting that that which can certainly be predicted must of necessity come to pass, the question arises, is a Volition which is controlled by the willing agent less "possible of prediction" than one which is controlled by extrinsic power, or than one which he controls in another being? — It cannot be urged that the volition is controlled by some power or force more uniform in its action than the being in which it is manifested. — Such discrepancy would prove that it was not by such extrinsic power. — The possibility of prediction proves freedom rather than the contrary 190–192
Necessitarians test their views by "statistical results," which, having a certain degree of uniformity, admit of like degree of certainty of prediction. — Our primary wants being similar, and all drawing knowledge from the same reservoir of truth, and acting upon similar conditions, it requires some element of diversity to account for the individual variations. — Having shown that uniformity in the actions of individuals does not conflict with freedom, it seems needless to argue that uniformity in the aggregate of these actions does not. — If the variations on the one side "neutralize" those on the other, the estimated aggregate variations may be very much reduced. — The uniformity of aggregates is a uniformity of a second order — a *Uniformity of Diversity.* — Without diversity there could be no *average species* of uniformity 192–195
Perhaps nothing but finite volitions of finite free agents can produce the variety which is the basis of the average uniformity of aggregates. — Illustrated by a machine for shuffling cards. — Only intelligent cause can produce the variation in the particulars which makes room or occasion for the calculations of changes or averages. — That each selects his act from all pos-

ANALYSIS OF CONTENTS. 365

sible acts accounts for the observed diversities which are the subjects of these averages. — These have no bearing upon the question at issue 195-196
Reasons why attempts to solve the question of our freedom in willing have so often been unsuccessful 196-200

APPENDIX TO LETTER II.

Existence of Matter 201-219
Our Notion of Infinite Space 219-226

MAN A CREATIVE FIRST CAUSE.

DISCOURSE I. — MAN A CREATIVE FIRST CAUSE.

§ 1. GENERAL INDIFFERENCE TO THE SUBJECT.

Utility of Metaphysics. It may add to intellectual power, and thus improve that which invents or makes all other utility, but its special sphere of utility will be found in our moral nature . 264

§ 2. CHARACTERISTICS OF MIND.

Knowledge, feeling, and volition. Mind knows, feels, and wills. The will is its only real faculty. An act of will is simply an effort. All intelligent beings are thus constituted, and to these attributes there is no conceivable limit 265

§ 3. RELATIONS AND FUNCTIONS OF MENTAL CHARACTERISTICS.

It is conceivable that we might have knowledge only, but we could not have feeling without knowing it. We might have knowledge and feeling without will, but will without these would be dormant and merely potential. An unintelligent being cannot be *self-active*. Our sensations are not dependent on the will, nor is our knowledge. The truth is often apparent without effort. The additions to our knowledge are always *simple immediate mental perceptions*. Feeling (sensation and emotion) incites to action, but is not itself active. Knowledge enables us to direct our efforts, but is itself passive. By will we produce change and thus act as cause. Our own will is the only cause of which we are directly conscious. Means by which we come to know ourselves, our fellow-beings, and God as *causes* 266-268

§ 4. Existence of Matter and its Relations to Cause.

We know matter only as an inference, from the sensations which we impute to its agency, and these are not conclusive us to any such external existence. The phenomena are all as fully accounted for on the hypothesis that they are the thoughts and imagery of God's mind *directly* impressed upon our own. In either case it is the expression of his thought, and to us equally real. Matter and spirit are still contradistinguished. The ideal hypothesis is the more simple and more nearly in accord with powers we ourselves exert. We can ourselves create such imagery, and to some extent make it durable, and palpable to others. But we find no rudiment of power in these creations of our own, and no reason to suppose that any increase of power in the creator of them could imbue them with any. If matter exists, being inert, it can have no power to change itself, and even if endowed with power to move, being unintelligent, it could have no tendency to move in one direction rather than another. Such power of self-movement would be a nullity, and matter can only be an instrument which intelligence uses to aid its efforts. Against these arguments it may be said that matter has always existed and was always in motion, as intelligence, with *its* activity, is presumed to have had no beginning. To assume the existence of both when one is sufficient is unphilosophical, and the spiritual should have precedence. It is inconceivable that matter, which does not know, should create spirit, which does know; while it is quite conceivable that spirit should create all we know of matter. But whether matter, even if in motion, can be a cause or power, depends upon this question: If left to itself and the moving power withdrawn, would it stop or continue to move? If its tendency is to stop, it could not even be an instrument for conserving or extending the effects of other power. Power could not make matter self-active, or the subject of government by law. Quiescent it could only be acted upon 268–273

§ 5. Of Past Events as Cause.

The theory that of every successive event, "the real cause is the whole of the antecedents," does not distinguish between the passive conditions acted upon and changed, and the active agencies which act upon and change them. And further, the necessary adjunct and corollary to this theory of succession is, *that the same causes must produce the same effects.* But all cause acts upon a wholly void and therefore homogeneous future;

ANALYSIS OF CONTENTS. 367

and as at every instant the whole past is everywhere the same, the successive effects must at each instant be everywhere one and the same. On this theory of the whole antecedents, the same causes never could act twice, and there could be no proof from experience that the same causes must produce the same effect. The only cause we can logically recognize is that of intelligent effort 273-275

§ 6. FREEDOM IN WILLING.

This has been a prominent question for ages. It has been obscured by erroneous notions and defective definitions of will and freedom. Defects in Edwards's definitions of these terms and the consequent fallacies in his results. Will is the faculty of *effort*. An act of will is an effort, a trying to do. Freedom as applied to willing is *self-control*. The object of every effort must be to make the future different from what it otherwise would be. This is the only conceivable motive. A being with a faculty of effort, want to incite, and knowledge to direct it, is a self-active being; could act if there were no other power or activity. The will cannot be directly controlled by any extrinsic power. The only way it can be influenced is by changing the knowledge by which the being directs its act of will, and this would not avail if the being did not will freely. The notion of a coerced will, and the expression for it, are self-contradictory. It *is willing* when we are *not willing*. The future is always the composite creation of the free efforts of all conative beings acting as independent powers in the universe. The action even by the lowest order may influence the action of the highest. This interdependence of the action of each without interference with the freedom of any is illustrated by the game of chess. This equal and perfect freedom in all does not impair the sovereignty of the Supreme Intelligence . . . 275-281

§ 7. INSTINCT, REASON, AND HABIT.

Instinctive actions have been generally deemed exceptional. We perform them so easily, that our agency in them escapes observation, and hence they have been regarded not only as not self-controlled, but as necessitated and even as purely mechanical. That all animals at birth, without previous instruction or experience, act instinctively, indicates not that the voluntary effort is wanting, but that the knowledge to direct it is *innate*. In all cases requiring more than one movement we must have a plan. In the instinctive actions, the plan is innate, *ready formed in the mind at birth*. In the rational actions, we have to devise the *plan*.

When by repetition *in act or thought*, we come to remember the successive steps of this plan, and apply it by rote, without reference to the *rationale*, it also becomes a *plan ready formed in the mind*, and our action becomes *habitual*. In it the process is the same as in the instinctive, and hence the common adage, *Habit is second nature*. The differences in the three kinds of actions do not lie in the actions themselves, nor in the knowledge, nor in the application of it to direct the actions, but farther back, in the *mode* in which we obtain the knowledge we thus apply. The instinctive and habitual and rational actions are all self-directed by knowledge to the end desired. The genesis of our actions must be instinctive. Through habit, memory performs the same office for action that it does for knowledge, retaining the acquisitions of the past for future use. The agency of habit, in thus conserving previously considered modes of action, and making them permanent accretions to the moral character, is its most important function 281-286

§ 8. NECESSITARIAN ARGUMENT FROM CAUSE AND EFFECT.

Necessitarians assert that if all the circumstances, including mental conditions in a thousand cases, are the same, the action will be the same, and that this uniformity proves necessity. Admitting this, whether one of the conditions in the thousand cases is that of *necessity* or of *freedom* does not vary the uniformity of the result, and hence the result cannot indicate either necessity or freedom 286-288

§ 9. INFLUENCE OF EXTERNAL AND INTERNAL CONDITIONS.

We act as freely on one set of conditions as on any other, and such action, being self-conformed to the external conditions and our internal desires, is free. Necessitarians have been at much pains to prove that our actions are always in conformity to our choice or desire, inclination, disposition, and moral character. This proves self-control, *i. e.*, freedom. Proof that our willing may run counter to our choice, inclination, etc., would have better subserved their purpose. The moral character is manifested in the willing, but our freedom is not affected by it. Nor is it material to the question of freedom, *how the being came to be such a being as it is* 288-289

§ 10. COULD ONE WILL THE CONTRARY?

It is absurd and contradictory to suppose that freedom requires that one might try to do what he had determined not to try to do. The arguments of the necessitarians that our acts of will are not free, because they must conform to our own character, desires, and decisions or judgments, virtually assert that one is not free because he is constrained to be free 289

§ 11. ARGUMENT FROM PRESCIENCE.

Edwards and others hold that prescience of a volition proves necessity. They illogically assume that it must happen by restraint or coercion of the willing agent. If a free act is as easily predicted as one that is not free, the argument wholly fails. In the known character and habits of the actor we have a means of foreseeing what he will do, *provided he acts freely.* If his action is controlled by extrinsic power, even if we know the power, all the same difficulties exist as to its action in controlling the act of another, with the added difficulty of finding what the effect of this extrinsic power on the apparent actor would be. So that the *free act* is more easily foreknown than a coerced or unfree act 289–292

§ 12. A BEING WITH WILL, KNOWLEDGE, AND FEELING, IS SELF-ACTIVE. SOME CONCLUSIONS RE-STATED.

Within the limits of its power and knowledge, such a being is as *free* as if it were omnipotent and omniscient. An oyster that can only move its shell, in doing this so far creates the future. For the exercise of his creative powers man has two spheres of effort, the external and the internal, conveniently designated as objective and subjective. The former is known to us as an inference from our sensations. Of the latter we are directly conscious. Our efforts for change in either sphere are always subjective. For objective change we always begin by a movement of our muscles 292–293

§ 13. IS MATTER A DISTINCT ENTITY.

Whether we adopt the materialistic or the ideal hypothesis, the sensations by which alone we cognize matter are the same, and on either it is the expression of the thoughts and conceptions of its creator, and the only question is, whether he transfers this thought and imagery directly to our minds, or indirectly, by painting, carving, or moulding them in a distinct substance. The former is the more simple, and equally explains all the phenomena, and has an advantage in making creation more conceivable to us. Any one can conceive a landscape, and vary it at will. This is an incipient creation, which we can very imperfectly, to some extent, represent in durable form and impress on the minds of others, showing that we have within us the rudiments of all the faculties which on the ideal hypothesis are essential to creating. The landscape we imagine we can change at will, and by this alone we distinguish it from that cognized by sensation. If our own incipient creation should become so fixed in our mind that we could not change it at will, it would be to us an external reality. This sometimes occurs. This suggests that the difference between the creative powers in man and the Supreme Intelligence is mainly in degree and not in kind, and that the disparity, vast as it is, is not so incomprehensible as has been generally supposed. To our own incipient creations there is no limit in extent or variety. 293–297

DISCOURSE II. — MAN, IN THE SPHERE OF HIS OWN MORAL NATURE, A SUPREME CREATIVE FIRST CAUSE.

§ 14. A COGNITIVE SENSE INCLUDES A MORAL SENSE.

That the additions to our knowledge are simple immediate perceptions, not dependent on the will, gives them the character of the phenomena of sensation, and indicates the existence of a *cognitive sense*. Some of these increments do not and others do require preliminary effort. In this there is no difference *per se* as to our perceptions of the external and internal. Intuitive perceptions are distinguished from the rational by the preliminary effort for the latter. We distinguish the perceptions of the cognitive sense as objective, seeing, hearing, etc., and subjective as the sense of beauty, justice, shame. And when right or wrong is the subject of it, it is the *moral sense* 298–302

§ 15. OUR EFFORTS FOR INTERNAL CHANGE ARE ALWAYS TO INCREASE OUR KNOWLEDGE.

We may seek knowledge of the external or internal. Its object is oftenest to enable us to direct our actions wisely in the current affairs of life; but may be for the pleasure of the pursuit, or in the possession. A higher object may be to permanently increase the intellectual power, or still higher, to improve the moral nature 302

§ 16. THE TWO MODES OF SEEKING KNOWLEDGE. THE POETIC AND THE PROSAIC.

By observation, we note the phenomena cognized by the senses, and by reflection we trace the relations among the ideas —

the knowledge — we already have in store, and thus obtain new ideas. A large portion of our perceptions are primarily but imagery — pictures — in the mind. In this form we will designate them as primitive *perceptions* or *ideals*, to distinguish them from those which we have associated with words. In this primitive form we can think of, and examine them and their relations; and a not uncommon belief, that we can think only in words, is erroneous. Or we may substitute words for these primitive perceptions, and then investigate the relations among the substituted words. In the difference in these two modes we find the fundamental distinction between poetry and prose, and also in the two cardinal modes of seeking truth: the former being the ideal or poetic; the latter, the logical or prosaic. The material universe, in the imagery of which God has inscribed his thoughts and conceptions, is the pure and perfect type of the poetic; while the prosaic or logical is very accurately represented in the solution of algebraic equations. The poetic mode has the greater reach, and is the most efficient truth-discovering power. It is an essential attribute, but is not limited to men of genius. In its least ethereal forms it is the basis of common sense, and the main element of practical business ability. It is also the characteristic of what has been termed a woman's reason, giving to her quick and clear perceptions 302–308

§ 17. ONE METHOD OF INCREASING THE EFFICIENCY OF THE INTELLECT.

It is in the higher and more general cultivation of the poetic mode, and a more systematic and intelligent selection from the two cardinal modes of that which is best adapted to the subject in hand, or by a judicious combination of both, that we may look for the increase of intellectual ability. The discovery and propagation of such modes is in the province of the metaphysician, and opens to him an elevated sphere of utility 308–309

§ 18. OUR CREATIVE POWER IN THE FORMATION OF CHARACTER, AND THE AGENCY OF HABIT.

It is in our moral nature that our most ethereal attribute naturally finds its most congenial sphere of action. Statement of a mode in which our power of creating and perfecting imaginary constructions may be made practically available in the construction and elevation of moral character. The ideal constructions supply the place of actual experience, and in some respects have the advantage of it. We cannot directly will

change in our mental affections. The recurrence of our spiritual wants is as certain as that of the physical. As a man cannot do moral wrong in doing what he believes to be right, his knowledge though finite is infallible as to what is morally right for him. In castle-building we discard the external, and work from our internal resources, and may conceive a material universe or a pure and noble moral character.
The persistent effort to actualize these ideals is their final consummation. There can be no failure except the failure to will, and mind is here a Supreme Creative First Cause.
In the permanent engrafting of these ideals upon the character, habit performs a very important part. We must distinguish between the mere knowledge of what is desirable and the effort to attain it. A man may know that it is best to be pure and noble, and yet not only make no effort, but be unwilling to become so. To become good without one's own effort is an impossibility 309-315

§ 19. IN THE MORAL NATURE THE EFFORT IS ITSELF THE CONSUMMATION OF ITS OBJECT AND INTENT.

The virtue is all in the effort and the intent, and not in its success or failure. If the efforts are transitory, the moral goodness will be equally so 315-316

§ 20. THE RIGHT OR WRONG OF MORAL ACTION IS ALL CONCENTRATED IN OUR OWN FREE ACT OF WILL.

The nature of the effect makes no difference to the moral quality of the effort. The consequences of one's actions may be really pernicious when his intentions are virtuous, and may be beneficent when his designs were vicious. A man who is honest for gain will be dishonest if the gain thereby is sufficient. Virtue is not reached till he acts from a sense of right and duty, nor established till he values moral beauty and purity above all other possessions and all possible acquisitions. No moral wrong can be charged to a man for an event in which he had and could have no agency. There is no present moral wrong either in the knowledge or in the exciting want now in his mind, nor in the acquisition of that knowledge which he passively acquired. There is no moral wrong in the recurrence of our natural wants, though there may be in our willing to gratify them, or in the time or manner of doing this. Hence the *moral right and wrong* is all concentrated in the act of will — our own free act. A man can be good or bad only by his own agency — his own willing. Through habit memory performs the same office for action that it does for knowledge — retaining what is acquired, and thus leaving the mind at liberty for new acquisitions. We cannot directly will not to think of a thing, but we can discard the thoughts of it by willing to think of something else, and can do the same as to a want. This especially as to *moral* wants. If any one of these is eradicated, there can be no corresponding volition. By thus giving some of our internal wants a predominance we influence our moral characteristics at their source 317-321

§ 21. RECITAL OF SOME OF THE FOREGOING CONCLUSIONS.

From these it follows that man, in the sphere of his own moral nature, is not only a creative, but a *supreme* and also a *sole* creative first cause. In this sphere the finite mind can will any possible change of which it can conceive, and the willing in it, being the consummation of the conception, there is no change in it of which we can conceive that we cannot bring about 321-323

§ 22. OUR PHYSICAL WANTS ARE MORE IMPERATIVE BUT ARE LIMITED AND TEMPORARY, WHILE THE SPIRITUAL ARE BOUNDLESS AND INSATIABLE 323

§ 23. IDEALITY IS THE NEAREST APPROACH TO REALITY, AND FULFILS THE OFFICE OF EXPERIENCE.

The scenic representations acted in the theatre within us are the nearest approach to reality, and have more influence than logical reasoning 324

§ 24. GOOD AND EVIL INFLUENCES OF IDEALITY.

Ideality is as potent in our spiritual nature as sensation is in our physical. Our first creative efforts are in the material, but early transferred to the spiritual, and there quickened by the influence of unselfish and romantic passion on the young imagination. But this beneficent endowment is liable to be perverted to evil, and especially through our physical wants, which are made less inconstant by the want of acquisition. The power of ideality, though less nobly exhibited, is more strongly attested in its degrading than in its elevating influence . . 324-327

§ 25. SYSTEMATIC MORAL TRAINING IN THE FORMATION AND STUDY OF IDEAL CONSTRUCTIONS.

This much needed to counteract a social system based largely on selfishness, and to neutralize the materialistic comfort-seeking proclivities of this mechanical and commercial age. But ideal contructions have been discouraged and stigmatized as idle imaginings, leading to groundless hopes and illusive views of life. Relieving these processes from such obstruction would be an important gain, and might be supplemented by education making ideal constructions a subject of study. For this there is encouragement in the fact that woman, to whose care the infant intelligence is first confided, is by her special endowments so fully equipped for this work 327-328

§ 26. ALL SCIENCES FIRST PURSUED MERELY FOR MENTAL GRATIFICATION.

Metaphysics has been thus pursued to the present time. In it the progress from abstract speculation to practical utility has not differed from that of the other sciences. All have been first pursued from a love of truth, and a curiosity stimulated by opposing mysteries, without reference to ulterior benefit. Metaphysics has thus been wrought upon for ages 328-329

§ 27. SOLUTION OF THREE PROBLEMS ESSENTIAL TO THE PRACTICAL UTILITY OF METAPHYSICS.

First, the analysis of the fundamental distinction between poetry and prose, and in it that of the two cardinal modes of seeking truth. — Second, our freedom in willing and the fixing of man's status as an independent creative power in the universe. — Third, the inquiry as to the difference between instinctive and rational actions, and in this incidentally determining the nature and functions of habit, by which our subjective constructions may be made permanent formations of moral character and incorporated into our being as a *second nature*. The forming of habits is under our control, but requires vigilance . . . 329-331

§ 28. SYNOPSIS OF PRECEDING RESULTS, AND DEDUCTIONS FROM THEM.

Man's supremacy in the domain of his own moral nature indicates it as his especial sphere of action. Ages of successful effort in the material sphere has prepared the way for the occupation of the spiritual, and we may expect that the advance into it will be marked by the sublimest efforts, and that the results will be the crowning glory of all utility 331-333

§ 29. ARGUMENT FROM FINAL CAUSES.

I have faith that all progress in truth will conduce to the happiness and elevation of man, and that whatever tends to diminish our happiness and degrade us will be found to be not true. Influences of the materialistic doctrines for which I see in them no compensation 333-335

§ 30. CONCLUDING REMARKS.

By a constitutional provision our wants, physical and spiritual, recur without preliminary effort. Our æsthetic tastes are continually touched by the beauty and grandeur of God's visible creations. Man is thus reminded that there is within his own being an inchoate universe equally boundless, and which is his especial sphere for the exercise of his creative powers, requiring his effort to reduce it to order and to cultivate it into beauty. Constructing this universe within is the principal if not the sole end of life 335-336

www.ingramcontent.com/pod-product-compliance
Lightning Source LLC
Chambersburg PA
CBHW021336300426
44114CB00012B/978